10. Special equipment
What special equipment is required, and what are its space requirements? Is security a factor?
4, 39, 41–52, 54–59, 155

11. Materials
What materials need to be uniquely considered or rejected?
97, 101, 107–109, 120–21, 160

12. Acoustic control
What special acoustical considerations affect the design?
39, 44, 87–114, 141

13. Lighting design
What special lighting (day and artificial) considerations affect the design?
3, 43–44, 46, 129–38, 142

14. Interiors issues
What special considerations (scale, color, texture, finishes, furnishings, special features) affect the planning of interiors?
38–39, 131, 143, 160

15. Wayfinding
What special factors determine signing systems?
1–2, 72, 76, 115–28, 150, 152

16. Preservation/modernization
What special considerations (historical authenticity, infrastructure retrofit) arise when renovating a facility of this type?
125–26, 139–54

17. International challenges
On international projects, what special considerations influence marketing, design, presentations, document production, and field presence?
25–26, 32

18. Operation and maintenance
How will design decisions influence the operation and maintenance of the completed facility?
137, 160, 163–73

19. Key cost factors
What are the principal determinants of the total construction cost?
4, 158, 170

20. Finances, fees, feasibility
What are the typical techniques for financing this facility?
158, 166–67, 170

BUILDING TYPE BASICS FOR

performing arts facilities

BUILDING TYPE BASICS FOR

performing arts facilities

Stephen A. Kliment, Series Founder and Editor

HUGH HARDY

H³ Hardy Collaboration Architecture LLC

With chapters by AUERBACH POLLOCK FRIEDLANDER,
JOSHUA DACHS, KEITH GERCHAK, CHRISTOPHER JAFFE,
DAWN SCHUETTE *and* LAWRENCE KIRKEGAARD, PAUL MARANTZ,
JACK MARTIN, RICHARD PILBROW, *and* DUNCAN WEBB

WILEY

JOHN WILEY & SONS, INC.

This book is printed on acid-free paper. ∞

Copyright © 2006 by John Wiley & Sons, Inc. All rights reserved

Published by John Wiley & Sons, Inc., Hoboken, New Jersey
Published simultaneously in Canada

For general information on our other products and services or for technical support, please contact
our Customer Care Department within the United States at (800) 762-2974, outside the United
States at (317) 572-3993 or fax (317) 572-4002.

Wiley also publishes its books in a variety of electronic formats. Some content that appears in print
may not be available in electronic books. For more information about Wiley products, visit our web
site at www.wiley.com.

Interior layout and production: Jeff Baker at BookMechanics

Library of Congress Cataloging-in-Publication Data:

Hardy, Hugh, 1932-
  Building type basics for performing arts facilities / Hugh Hardy ; with
chapters by Joshua Dachs ... [et al.].
    p. cm. — (Building type basics series)
  Includes bibliographical references and index.
  ISBN 13: 978-0471-68438-1
  ISBN 10: 0-471-68438-4 (cloth : acid-free paper)
  1. Theater architecture. 2. Theaters—Designs and plans. 3. Centers for
the performing arts—Designs and plans. I. Title. II. Series.
  NA6821.H227 2006
  725'.83—dc22
                            2005010712

Printed in the United States of America.
10 9 8 7 6 5 4 3 2 1

CONTENTS

Preface *Stephen A. Kliment*   vii

Acknowledgments   ix

Foreword *Hugh Hardy*   xi

1 Planning the Theater   1
Hugh Hardy
H³ Hardy Collaboration Architecture

2 A Place Designed for Performance   7
Joshua Dachs
Fisher Dachs Associates

3 An Auditorium and Stage Design Guide   19
Richard Pilbrow
Theatre Projects Consultants

4 Stage Design: Technology and Flexibility   41
Leonard Auerbach, Steve Pollock, Steven Friedlander
Auerbach Pollock Friedlander

5 Backstage Planning   53
Keith Gerchak
Theatre Projects Consultants

6 Incorporating Building Codes   65
Jack Martin
H³ Hardy Collaboration Architecture

7 Principles of Acoustic Design   87
Dawn Schuette and Lawrence Kirkegaard
Kirkegaard Associates

8 Flexibility in Acoustic Design   115
Christopher Jaffe
Jaffe Holden Acoustics

CONTENTS

9 Lighting Public Spaces   129
Paul Marantz
Fisher Marantz Stone

10 Bringing the New to Old Theaters   139
Hugh Hardy
H³ Hardy Collaboration Architecture

11 Organization: Process and Team   155
Hugh Hardy
H³ Hardy Collaboration Architecture

12 The Business and Art of Theater Management   163
Duncan Webb
Webb Management Services, Inc.

Glossary   175

Bibliography   177

Index   183

PREFACE

STEPHEN A. KLIMENT *Series Founder and Editor*

A curious reaction to the great volume of musical and theatrical works available on DVD and other virtual media has been the immense public interest in seeing and hearing the actors, singers, musicians, and lecturers in live performance. While legal and illegal downloading of online entertainment flourishes as never before, the public flocks in ever larger numbers to theaters, where they can observe performers in the flesh. Indeed, according to a 2002 survey of public participation in the arts developed by the National Endowment for the Arts (NEA), 81 million adults attended some sort of live performance in 2002—five million more than in 1992. By comparison, people participating in the arts through broadcast or recorded media showed statistically significant declines—five percentage points when viewing TV, VCR, or DVD; seven percentage points when listening to classical music on the radio; and five points listening to recordings. Other performing arts saw similar declines, according to the NEA survey; but in overall totals, broadcast and recorded media participation still outnumbered attendance at live performances (www.arts.gov/pub/research.html).

This hunger for live performance extends an extraordinary challenge to architects and their acoustical, engineering, and other consultants: they must now design spaces that not only make live performance a rewarding experience but also equal the acoustic quality and physical comfort enjoyed by fans in their own living rooms.

This volume in the Wiley "Building Type Basics" series explores the planning and design of theaters. Its purpose is to help architects and their consultants develop a space program and arrive at design solutions that meet the needs of theatergoers and those who finance, build, and run those theaters.

Hugh Hardy, principal of the architecture firm H^3 Hardy Collaboration Architecture in New York City, has chosen and coordinated the contributions of a cadre of eminent consultants in performance place design, stage technology, acoustic design, and lighting design, and he has himself contributed chapters on theater planning and the project delivery process. He also provides a crucial chapter on the controversial topic of updating, preserving, or restoring historic theaters—a topic that typically pits the nostalgic yearnings of theatergoers against the contemporary needs of theatergoer safety, the Americans with Disabilities Act (ADA), lighting, new materials, and twenty-first-century theater productions.

Places for the performing arts come in many types and configurations, but always critical, as the authors point out, is the ability of the audience to see and hear well and to enjoy the experience. Underlying the design process are financing, feasibility, and the diverse roles of the design and construction team, sponsor, banks, impresario, and manager.

All these factors are treated in this volume of the Wiley "Building Type Basics" series. The book is organized into twelve chapters. The first three address theater planning, performance place, and auditorium design. The next two explore the technology of stage design and back-of-house considerations. The chapters on acoustic design, each with its own vantage point, are followed by chapters on lighting the public spaces, on delivering the theater project from programming through opening night, on building codes, on management and operation, and as noted, on the restoration of historic theaters. Case studies supplement the text.

As Hugh Hardy has noted, "Our purpose is to encourage exploration and to free designers from an overabundance of technical concerns, encouraging them first to explore the principles guiding the disciplines represented in theater design." To highlight the fact that several approaches are possible, Hardy's consultants have varying but valid perspectives on their subjects. The architect's job is to harness the team to create a seamless design that brings enjoyment to audience and performer alike.

Performing Arts Facilities, like the other volumes in the Wiley series, is not a lavish coffee-table book heavy on color photography and weak on usable content. Instead, it contains hands-on information that architects, their consultants, and clients require to carry out their respective roles, especially in the crucial early phases of a project, when the right decisions are far-reaching. Students at schools of architecture, planning, and urban design will also find the volume useful.

Following the series format, and for the convenience of the reader, *Performing Arts Facilities* is indexed for ease of use. The index to the Twenty Questions, on the front and back endpapers, leads to answers to questions most commonly asked about a building type in the early phases of its design. The Twenty Questions cover predesign (programming) guidelines, the project delivery process, design concerns unique to the building type, site planning, codes, ADA matters, energy and environmental challenges, engineering systems, lighting and acoustic pointers, signs and wayfinding, preservation issues, and cost and feasibility factors.

I know you will find this volume helpful, informative, and inspiring.

ACKNOWLEDGMENTS

Stephen Kliment, founder and editor of the "Building Type Basics" series for John Wiley & Sons, Inc., had the idea for this book. Knowing of my affection for theater and experience in the design and restoration of theater buildings, he suggested I put together a volume in the series. After initial hesitancy about finding the time to complete such a demanding assignment, I succumbed to his encouragement, which led me to gather the team of consultants who have joined in this effort. The collaborative nature of theater suggested that a combination of talents would benefit the project, presenting more than one point of view. Therefore, in this volume, some fields of expertise involved in the planning and design of a theater are in some cases represented by more than one consultant. The result is a sterling list of professionals, each addressing a different aspect of theater design.

John Czarnecki, acquisitions editor at Wiley & Sons, has been a stalwart supporter of the contractual and administrative requirements of this endeavor, and I am most grateful for his assistance.

All of the contributors to this volume have been generous with their time, insightful in their commentary, and patient with the difficult process of shaping a welter of material into a practical, useful volume. I extend my thanks and admiration to all of them.

I must also pay tribute to Susan Packard, whose determination to see this book written in clear and concise language has brought editorial discipline to the enterprise. Angela Chen's polite, persistent, and organized assistance in obtaining images and permission to reproduce them was invaluable.

Much of Chapter 5, Backstage Planning, would not have been possible without the contributions of Bryan Landrine and Michael Egan, Equity stage managers. Michele Weathers Smith, company manager of North Carolina Theatre in Raleigh, allowed photography of the load-in for the production of *Fiddler on the Roof.* Paul Marsland, production supervisor of the BTI Center for the Performing Arts at the Raleigh Convention and Conference Center Complex, allowed photography of the backstage facilities, accommodated a tour of the facility, and offered additional insight.

I am especially grateful to Nathaniel Addleman, PE, engineering manager, Rolf Jensen & Associates, Inc., and John Darby, assistant facilities manager, Shubert Organization, for their significant contributions to Chapter 6, "Incorporating Building Codes."

Hugh Hardy

FOREWORD

HUGH HARDY *FAIA*

I began this book in 2003, as a partner with Hardy Holzman Pfeiffer Associates (now dissolved), and many of the projects it contains were realized through the skills and dedication of my partners, Malcolm Holzman and Norman Pfeiffer. Like architecture, theater is a collaborative art. In addition, the contributions of HHPA's principals, associates, and staff made these buildings possible. H³ Hardy Collaboration Architecture is a successor firm to HHPA and is equally dedicated to the realization of buildings for the performing arts.

This book explores the planning and design of theaters. It is intended to assist professionals who are new to the subject and to delineate the choices that must be made during the design process. We cover the myriad variations of theater design, surveying all kinds of halls, identifying their basic elements and describing how they interact. We include essays by professionals in eight firms. The contributors are experts in their fields, and each addresses an aspect of creating a theater: acoustics, code compliance, design, lighting, management, planning, restoration, and technology. The book is but an introduction, meant to encourage continued exploration of the subject. A bibliography at the end lists sources for further study.

There are no formulas for good theater design. The guidelines offered here support theater architecture's main precept, that the immediacy of the performance experience should shape all aspects of a theater project and infuse its architecture with discovery. Bringing audiences together gives theater its strength. We therefore urge designers to consider first how a theater building is to be used—by both audience and performer—before investigating the technology of presentation.

CHAPTER 1

PLANNING THE THEATER

HUGH HARDY *H³ Hardy Collaboration Architecture*

While no two theaters are alike—varying in capacity, use, and character—each brings audience and performer together in different ways. Commercial theaters concentrate on large capacity, spectacle, and audience amenities, while community theaters stress program variety and intimacy. Teaching theaters require technological simplicity, generous support areas for classrooms, and large, open spaces for technical instruction.

PLANNING FROM OUTSIDE TO INSIDE

The architect is the professional responsible for the total theatergoing experience and must remember that it starts when patrons leave their bus, train, or car to approach the theater.

Parking

Parking must be designed so that it does not diminish the pleasure of theatergoing. Perhaps the ideal solution for a summer festival is that for performances by the Glimmerglass Opera, in Cooperstown, New York, where an adjacent, terraced hill is used as a parking lot. Here, the theater site itself is left relatively free of automobiles, and the audience promenades to the opera house around a small pond. The worst situation must be at Lincoln Center, New York City, where opera audiences dressed in their finery must contend with the oil slicks of a dimly lit underground garage before arriving at a suitable entrance to the grandeur above (see Color plates 1 and 2).

It may appear that new, automated parking systems can prevent such indignities and permit patrons to claim their cars while standing in a well-designed environment, separate from the cars themselves. But these systems, in which machines manipulate and stack cars, are not practical for theaters because audiences arrive and depart all at the same time. Although the inclusion of allied activities in the theater, such as retail, food, and beverages, lengthens the amount of time patrons spend in the building, their arrival and departure are concentrated in ways that do not respond to a single point of control.

Signage

Signage performs two functions. It identifies what is playing within a hall, and it contributes to the event of theatergoing. Marquees with flashing lightbulbs are a holdover of the movie-house era, when competing electric displays beckoned to pedestrians along city streets. In suburban locations the prevalence of automobiles generates large parking lots, where conventional marquee lettering, hundreds of feet away, is too small to be read. Instead, large pylons at the entrance to parking lots identify activities taking place in the performance halls. The exterior of a freestanding building, properly lit at night, may itself be an advertisement, creating a sense of excitement, as one approaches.

Wayfinding

The path from the front door of a performance hall to the auditorium should be clear without graphic identification. The way to restrooms, seating, box office, lounges, and concessions should be obvious to patrons without complex signage. At intermission, the audience should not be confused by unclear circulation patterns. Instead, the building's design should allow the audience the pleasures of people-watching and clear access routes to all amenities. Symmetrical plans help in this regard, but if site restrictions place public space on only one side of the auditorium centerline, extra care must be taken to ensure that patrons are not confused by routes to remote seating areas.

Public Space

Arrival in the public spaces should intensify the sense of anticipation. In this age of home entertainment, going out has become increasingly significant, heightening the pleasures of gathering together. Audiences come not only to see a performance but to socialize, drink, snack, schmooze, and see who's who. Therefore, public spaces, both outside and inside, need to be generous. At least ten square feet per person should be allotted for lobby space, and circulation corridors should be eight feet wide at the very least. By contrast, Broadway theaters have no lobbies, and crosstown streets must serve this purpose. The sidewalk jumble of traffic, bars, restaurants, and the partial shelter of marquees make for a lively setting in the city, but these juxtapositions are inconvenient and not an acceptable model for design of contemporary public space.

Food and Beverage

Audiences increasingly expect to find food and beverages in the public spaces of theaters. The logistical pressures of contemporary life do not always permit predinner

theater, and intermission snacks are both welcome and income-producing. Full-service kitchens, however, are not required. Instead, prepared food can be brought in for sale on a daily basis. Depending upon local building codes, it is even possible to create mobile food and beverage areas without running water, greatly simplifying their installation and adding flexibility. However, extra space must be alloted for such socializing areas.

Allied Uses of Public Space

Well-designed public lobby spaces can be used for special events on their own. Weddings, dinners, conference sessions, and presentations provide added income for the theater. The Brooklyn Academy of Music (BAM) increased its public space by converting a former ballroom into a multiuse area that includes a shop selling BAM souvenir items (from T-shirts to books), a lounge, and a full-service restaurant. A vital extension of the formal presentations in the opera and cinema houses next door, the public space is actively programmed for related lectures and other informal offerings, such as jazz concerts, gospel singing, video presentations, and dance.

DESIGN ISSUES

Transparency

Architects currently have a fascination with public spaces that are completely enclosed in glass. This visibility makes for nighttime excitement when viewed from the outside, as audiences arrive and move through these spaces. However, lobbies with glass walls are not transparent by day. Moreover, the pageantry of audience movement patterns takes place only when there is a performance. When the theater is not in use, the glass becomes a blank wall. Views of parking lots or the surrounding city or countryside from inside glass lobbies, furthermore, often fail to contribute to the theatergoing experience. Therefore, glass must be used with a full understanding of its transparent *as well as* reflective qualities, ensuring that people can enjoy seeing each other.

Natural Light

Those who use theater workspaces—offices, rehearsal rooms, and even dressing rooms—gain from the sense of release brought by the incorporation of windows and the resulting changes in natural light. Dance studios, in particular, benefit from natural illumination. The shadowing of natural light makes moving bodies seem more three-dimensional if outside and inside lighting levels are balanced to avoid glare. If needed, black-out shades can be provided for rehearsal rooms used for studio performance.

Multiple Theaters in One Building

It is best, when planning for several theaters in one building, to join their stages, keeping them on one level, if the site permits, so they can share furnishings and equipment. Heavy elements, pianos, and other musical instruments can be moved about most efficiently when the stages are on a constant level and when there are direct (but acoustically separate) entrances to each auditorium. It is also good to join the public areas so that multiple audiences can mix and mingle, taking advantage of the space allotted for all the theaters.

Circulation

All these connections are difficult to achieve when more than two theaters are involved, because audiences are seated at different elevations, especially if stages are not at a common level. This complexity affects not only level linkages with public areas but also compliance with wheelchair-access regulations. Overlapping activities make circulation for the simultaneous use of several halls different from that required for only one. Concession facilities in multiple-theater buildings must be clearly located and sized for both large and small audiences. Their placement requires a thorough understanding of circulation patterns to ensure each has access to all public spaces.

Wheelchair Access

Elevators and circulation paths should be clearly identified to guarantee ease of use by patrons in wheelchairs. Ideally, contemporary theaters have complete wheelchair access to each seating bank. However, it is not possible to create positions at every seating level. Instead, it is legitimate to give access to each price range. Note, too, that wheelchairs position patrons higher (19–21 in. from floor to seat for persons taller than 5 ft 4 in.) than conventional theater seats (17–18 in. from the floor). Therefore, wheelchairs cannot be placed in front of fixed theater seats if sight lines are to be acceptable. Floor levels must be adjusted and easy access from the aisles provided. A second space, next to the wheelchair, must also be made for a disabled person's companion or seeing-eye dog. The best solution is to provide flexible locations that allow removal of conventional seats to make open platforms for wheelchairs. Current standards mandate elevators and ramps for balcony access (see Chapter 6).

Context

The performing arts have proven to be a catalyst for downtown renewal, encouraging the growth of nearby restaurants and retail shops as well as other cultural entities. Lincoln Center has transformed the upper west side of Manhattan. In an urban setting it is therefore important to recognize that intended uses of adjacent properties can influence the long-term success of performing arts projects. Audiences are more likely to attend nighttime performance in a lively area of town than in a place isolated from other activities. Suburban locations also offer opportunities for development on adjacent properties. Therefore, site planning in these areas should consider long-term land use of adjacent properties.

PROJECT COSTS

The full range of costs must be addressed at the onset of programming. "Soft" costs, such as permits, fees, furniture, equipment, graphics, fund-raising, site costs, landscaping, and night lighting, are 20–30 percent of the construction cost. The usable, or "net," square feet of the project must be increased to identify the "gross" square feet, which include wall thicknesses, utility spaces, and mechanical rooms. In theaters, this "gross" figure is often an additional 65 percent of the square footage.

Any large-scale project (more than 20,000 sq ft) requires the assistance of a cost consultant. Square-foot costs alone cannot be used for budgeting theaters because of the large volume of performance and rough finishes in support areas. Square-foot costing is appropriate in back-of-house and administrative areas, but auditorium and stage-house costs must be based upon recently constructed examples. To be accurate, figures for mechanical and electrical systems must be separated from general construction and specifically assigned to the auditorium. Despite these concerns, square-foot costs for budgeting new theaters are often used, and as performance places become more complex and the building codes more demanding a theater's overall cost can reach more than $1,000 per sq ft.

POOR PLANNING

Poor planning at the outset can lead to cost overruns after the building is designed and the project is sent out for bid. Compensating for such excess late in the process can severely curtail equipment, finishes, and materials, yet these are the very elements that define public experience in a theater. A perfect structural or mechanical system is wasted if the public spaces are banal. Other mistakes include mismatching a theater's capacity and its use. This kind of miscalculation can lead to rooms that are too large or too small for their functions, congested circulation in the public areas, or inadequate support space. Such setbacks can be avoided by retaining a theater consultant at the beginning of planning.

THEATER CONSULTANTS

The theater consultant's role is to interpret and define requirements for performers, public, and staff and then identify the spaces that best serve the theater's intended uses. The consultant can then accurately determine what support areas are needed (dressing rooms, scene studios, or costume shops) and the size of rehearsal facilities and administration space. Their adjacencies and circulation requirements can then be defined. The theater consultant helps identify appropriate technology and advises on the crucial decision of a performing space's capacity.

COLLABORATION

Planning for theaters requires the coordination of many professional disciplines together with a clear set of priorities. The distinctions among performance types must be understood so that each building meets the needs of both audience and performer. The architect's role is to provide a balance among conflicting points of view, establishing priorities based upon a clear understanding of program needs.

CHAPTER 2
A PLACE DESIGNED FOR PERFORMANCE

JOSHUA DACHS *Fisher Dachs Associates*

From play to play, artist to artist, city to city, culture to culture, and decade to decade, "theater" means something different. And yet, at its core, it does not change. It is all theater—convention, imagination, illusion, realism, and montage. Over time the pendulum of theater fashion swings along several axes. New forms are explored, old forms revived, experiments conducted, old truths rediscovered. Old and new coexist in the theater, sometimes even on the same stage at the same time.

There will always be a wide variety of theater artists working in a variety of ways. Some may embrace technology, some may be Luddites. It is all storytelling. Visual artists, such as Bill Viola, who create video installation pieces in museums, have not killed painting, and the show *Beatlemania,* which made extensive use of film and video projection on Broadway in the late 1970s, did not end traditional productions of Shakespeare.

START WITH THE ART
Different kinds of storytelling want different kinds of spaces. The job of the theater architect is to support the storytelling. If theater architecture is not conceived of from that point of view, it fails.

You face hundreds of issues when designing a theater. Some have to do with specific challenges, such as code compliance and a variety of ADA (Americans with Disabilities Act) regulations that are peculiar to theater buildings. Some have to do with creating a clear and efficient backstage layout. Others have to do with

character, establishing a look and feel for a building that is appropriate to the specific company or institution it will house. These are all important, but the central challenge, the one that has defeated the majority of architects in the past hundred years, is to make a space that supports the storytelling it is meant to contain. It sounds much easier than it is.

Start with the artists who will use the space. Their attitude toward their work, toward formality, and toward flexibility will fundamentally shape the architecture. Their point of view has an impact on the program and on the materials, colors, technology, and geometry of the performance space.

Some theaters are built for a single use or purpose; others need to do many jobs.

DEFINITIONS
Putting aside movie theaters, there are many different kinds of theaters.

Commercial Rental Houses
These theaters, built as investments and intended to turn a profit through rental income, are rare outside of New York City and a handful of major American cities. The majority of theaters operating today with commercial rental as a business plan were built in the 1920s, generally in major urban markets. Large-scale musicals and occasionally straight plays generally fill the bill. They typically range in capacity from 950 to 1,600 seats, although a few built since the 1960s seat 1,800 or more. If there is no show on, the place is padlocked.

Apart from the stage and seating area, few spaces are provided beyond the basics needed to support a performance (some dressing rooms, public restrooms, a lobby, perhaps a concession stand—that is about it). Other than a basic rigging system on stage, no technology is provided. The show itself is expected to provide the stage lighting, audio systems, and production communications systems, which the show's producer leases from rental companies for the entire run. The show also builds and installs all the scenery, effects, and whatever specialized machinery it needs at its own cost. Consequently, these venues are sometimes called "four-walls houses," because all you get when you rent them are the four bare walls.

Dedicated Commercial Venues

Las Vegas, Nevada, and other major entertainment destinations (Atlantic City, New Jersey; Orlando, Florida; and Branson, Missouri) have developed another venue form, one that is tailor-made to the specific requirements of a particular show. Perhaps the best example is the theater that was built for Cirque du Soleil's production *O*. This venue, which seats 1,800, was designed to accommodate the deep pools, custom-designed underwater stage lifts, and overhead trapeze machinery required for this extraordinary water-based show. In fact, there are a number of Cirque shows running in Las Vegas and Orlando in theaters that were built specifically to accommodate them. Each show is expected to run for many years, justifying the enormous design and construction investment.

Theaters have been purpose-built for a variety of shows and entertainers. These facilities are often extravagantly equipped to support the highest level of theatrical spectacle. The auditoriums are generally plain boxes (except in the case of the recent Cirque shows), and the dressing rooms and support areas are tailored to the minimum needs of the show. Often there is no dedicated lobby or public restroom, and the venue opens directly into an existing casino floor or hotel corridor.

Performing Arts Centers

These theaters are generally built by public entities or nonprofit organizations. Consisting of one or more performance spaces, they typically house several local resident companies as well as a wide range of touring productions. These facilities are built to serve the public good, like museums, and are operated to fulfill a cultural mission. Often this means accommodating performances by local resident companies at below-cost rents, presenting a carefully curated season of national and international touring artists and entertainment, and filling in with

selected rentals to outside promoters or corporate users. They operate at a loss, generally earning 50–80 percent of their actual running costs, and must supplement earned revenue with annual fund-raising or endowment income. Often built to foster urban revitalization and economic development as much as for cultural needs, these buildings are expected to be open and active as much as possible, even when there is no show on.

These theaters are generically known as "presenting houses," because they do not create the work that appears on stage but present work produced by others. They are the retailers, not the manufacturers, of the theater trade. Most performing arts-center theaters accommodate a range of performance types, like Broadway, ballet, modern dance, opera, and sometimes symphonic music. When unamplified symphonic music is a part of the mix, the hall is generally known as a multipurpose house. In truth, all theaters—and even dedicated concert halls—are multipurpose buildings and are used in a variety of ways.

Performing arts centers have a wide range of spaces. They may include one or more theaters, most typically a large, multipurpose theater of 2,000–2,700 seats, a smaller theater of 350–750 seats, and sometimes a flexible studio theater seating 75–250. This allows a variety of performance types, touring shows, and local arts groups to be accommodated.

To support such a wide range of users, performing arts centers are fully equipped. They have complete rigging, stage lighting, audio, and production communications systems that can be used by incoming productions (sometimes for a fee). Local user groups rely on having this equipment available to them when

◀◀ The 1,500-seat Shubert Theater, in New York City, is a typical commercial-theater operation. It is owned by the Shubert Organization and rented to independent producers for open-ended runs of commercial productions. The producer-tenant shoulders all the risk. A complicated lease agreement ensures the theater owner a guaranteed rental fee, income from bar and concession operations, and other revenue streams. All labor and maintenance costs are charged to the tenant. When there is no show, the theater may be dark for months at a time. Henry B. Herts, architect. Photo by Len Allington.

▶ *At Arena Stage, Washington, D.C., the 816-seat in-the-round Fichlander Stage will be reduced to 650 seats, retaining the arena form. Acoustics for the spoken word will be improved. The 514-seat Kreeger Theater, a modified thrust stage, will be updated with current technology and amenities. A new space, dubbed "The Cradle," will provide a 200-seat intimate theater in which to nurture American plays and playwrights. It will offer artists a versatile, technically sophisticated space without the pressure and financial expectations that burden the larger venues. Central to the design is a common lobby linking all three spaces. Rounding out the 250,000-GSF program are new spaces for rehearsals, classes, physical production, administration, a small parking garage, apartments to house out-of-town cast members, and modern audience amenities. Harry Weese, architect; Bing Thom Architects, architect. Fisher Dachs Associates, theater consultant, and the Talaske Group (acoustics), designers. Image courtesy of Bing Thom Architects. Digital rendering by E. V. Radvenis, Inc.*

they rent the venue to present their work. Touring shows often travel with their own stage lighting or audio systems tailored to their specific needs but tie into the venue's own "house equipment" as needed. Where symphony orchestras must be accommodated, an orchestra shell is provided that can be removed or shifted out of the way when not in use. One or more motorized orchestra-pit lifts may be provided to accommodate large opera orchestras and much smaller Broadway-musical pit orchestras (Color plate 1).

Professional Producing Theaters

These are generally built by nonprofit theater companies to produce seasons of plays or musicals mainly for a subscription audience. These companies may be driven by the unique vision and leadership of a particular artistic director or be organized around a more generic cultural mission and run by an artistic director reporting to a nonartistic, all-volunteer board. Companies vary widely in size and artistic outlook, and their facilities may include one or more theaters. Spaces may seat fewer than a 100 to more than 1,000. Like performing arts centers, these theaters require some form of subsidy. Because these spaces must reflect the personality of an artistic organization rather than simply serve as a receptacle for a variety of programs, these projects offer the meatiest material for the interested architect.

While generally smaller than performing arts centers, these facilities are the most comprehensive in program and equipment. Theaters like the Guthrie, in Minneapolis, Minnesota, or the Arena Stage, in Washington, D.C., consist of as many as three venues and a variety of seating capacities, generally falling into large (750–1,200), medium (300–500), and small (75–200). Because they are actually producing shows, they may include complete facilities for construction and

◀ Holcombe T. Green, Jr.,
Theater and the School
of Art, Yale University,
New Haven, Connecticut.
Deborah Berke & Partners
Architects. Photo by
Catherine Tie.

painting of scenery (including metal, plastics, and woodworking capabilities), costume construction and wardrobe storage, prop and furniture construction and storage, soft-goods (stage draperies) construction and storage, rehearsal spaces, and offices for a large artistic, administrative, marketing, and fund-raising staff. Each performance space is as fully equipped as possible, with sufficient stage lighting, rigging, audio, and production-communications systems to minimize outside rental expenses.

University Theaters

University-affiliated theaters come in three sizes. Small theaters, in the 100–400-seat range, are built to train young actors and technicians. Medium-sized theaters, in the 400–1,000-seat range, are designed to accommodate more fully realized performances that may be designed and directed by faculty members and may feature graduate act-

ing-program students. Large theaters are used to fulfill a university's role as a leading cultural provider to both campus and off-campus communities, and may be as large as some performing arts centers' main spaces, in the 1,500–2,500-seat range. The first two types are generally operated by a drama department, and the last is usually operated along the lines of a performing arts center, but subsidized by the university.

Like professional theaters, university facilities are equipped with everything they need to rehearse and produce their own shows. In addition to providing performance opportunities, most university theater departments provide their students hands-on experience in scenic and costume construction, lighting, and the stage-design disciplines, and they may require their students to "crew" the university shows. Examples are the McCarter and Berlind theaters at Princeton University and the student theater at Yale University.

Community Theaters

School auditoriums and community theaters are generally built to contain amateur adult or student activity. In addition to their own schedule of productions, they sometimes accommodate outside rentals or present touring groups and lectures. Usually they are built as a part of another institution, such as a library or religious center, and occasionally they are built by long-established amateur theatrical organizations. Every organization is different, but many of the larger community theaters have well-equipped scenic-production facilities, store large inventories of stage equipment, and present ambitious, fully realized productions.

PROJECT VARIABLES

Clearly there are many things that differ from project to project, and that is why there is no such thing as an ideal theater. The client's commercial or artistic objectives, the play's subject matter, and the way theater artists choose to express that subject can differ wildly. An architect approaching a theater design commission has to understand and work with a number of variables.

Scale

Different artistic offerings have different scales. Ballet involves corps of dancers and wide-open spaces. Grand opera calls for enormous sets, big voices, and huge casts. Some plays, like the Greek classics or Shakespeare, have an epic scope. Others are intimate kitchen dramas with a handful of characters. Apart from the economics of each genre (which drive seating capacity), they demand different scales of *theatrical space* and imply a different relationship with the audience.

Form

Adding complexity, there are varied formats that artists might choose to work in. Some are typical of a particular genre, such as the opera and the proscenium stage. Each presents its own set of architectural challenges.

Flexibility

Would that a space could satisfy *all* configurations, as needed. That is what the so-called studio theater (or experimental or black-box theater) is meant to accomplish. People have been experimenting with this idea for 50 years and have concluded that:

- The more seats you have the less flexible the theater will be;
- Unless you have unlimited free labor, you will not change things around much, because it is cumbersome and takes a long time;
- Automated systems are expensive;
- Modular systems have limits to their flexibility, because you have to conform to the module;
- Eighty to 150 seats are probably about as many as you ought to have.

Multipurpose theaters must be flexible enough to accommodate the variety of art forms, Broadway to symphony, for example. (See Color plate 4.)

Technology

Do not be seduced by technology. It is just a tool, and it changes constantly, so you should never design a theater around technology. What kind of stage technology should one expect in the future? Virtual reality? Dirt floors and wooden benches? High-tech laser shows and spectacles?

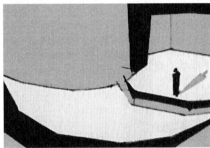

◀ *Diagrams by Ming Cho Lee. At Yale University, the architect Deborah Berke renovated 80,000 sq ft and designed a 30,000-sq-ft addition to a 1950s Jewish community center originally designed in part by Louis Kahn. It is now home to the new Holcombe T. Green, Jr., Hall, which houses the School of Art and the Yale Repertory New Theater. Deborah Berke Architects, Fisher Dachs Associates, Jaffe Holden Acoustics, and the scenic designer and Yale professor emeritus Ming Cho Lee constituted the planning team for this new space, designed for student work at the Yale School of Drama. From* Theater Check List, *drawings by Ming Cho Lee.*

Tricks age quickly. Video projections may be novel in one production, but do you really want to use them in *every* show? How many times a decade will you actually use a turntable? My colleague Joe Mobilia likes to say that "the future arrives in a truck." Touring shows bring their own equipment. We do not know what will come next, except that it will be big and will have to be plugged in. Broadway theaters, which were mostly built in the 1920s, now accommodate the latest robotic, computer-controlled lighting and stage technology (to say nothing of air-conditioning), which was not dreamt of when these buildings were created.

The key to making a theater accommodate change is not mysterious; after all, people have been adapting buildings for hundreds of years. For now it means providing extra electrical power in the stage area to cover unforeseen technologies and making it easy to deploy electrical and data cable throughout the theater without resorting to unsightly tape on carpet and other tripping hazards. Try to provide easily accessed (if it is not easy, it will not be used) and well-concealed cable paths to connect the stage, the orchestra pit, the

▶ The New Jersey Performing Arts Center, in Newark, New Jersey, is a 2,750-seat multipurpose house; it is shown here in stage mode. Barton Myers Associates, architects, with Fisher Dachs Associates, theater consultant, and Artec, acoustics. Photo by Jeff Goldberg/Esto.

sound-mix position in the house, the control booths, and all the stage lighting and speaker locations in the auditorium. In the future, another set of approaches will evolve to adapt buildings to newer technologies.

CONSTANTS

Liveness

In spite of the diversity of types, sizes, seating capacities, and users, some things remain constant. Theater buildings are all designed to accommodate live events—

real-time interactions between human beings. This is the unique selling proposition of live performance. If you cannot *feel* the liveness of it, feel the reactions of the rest of the crowd, feel that you are all sharing a moment, then you may as well stay home and watch TV. Architecture is key to making a space succeed, regardless of the seating capacity, and its tools are form, geometry, color, texture, and scale manipulation, which must be carefully orchestrated with this human experience in mind. There is no one way to bring it about; each project requires thoughtful application of all the architect's skills and instincts.

Seating and Sight Lines

While amplification has improved over the years, and audibility can be provided in the most enormous spaces, human performers come in only one size. There are limits to human vision. You cannot see facial expressions from farther than 60–65 ft, and actors that far away look very, very small. A small, far-away performance does not have a very powerful impact. Making a performer look larger and closer and making the audience feel they are in the same small room as the performer are the ultimate goals of theater architecture.

When the seating capacity is small, these effects are relatively easy to achieve. As the capacity rises beyond 500 people, this intimacy becomes increasingly difficult to achieve, and the architect has to become ever more inventive. Simply put, try hard to get the audience as close to the stage as possible by developing the most compact footprint you can. In a large theater, add one or more balconies to develop a more vertical, less elongated arrangement.

Plain Geometry

Do everything possible to enhance the focus on the stage and help the actor seem large, but decrease the scale of all the other dimensions, surfaces, and elements in the room. Break down wall planes with box seats or lighting positions, use the ceiling plane to help reinforce the plan geometry, and generally do everything possible (even using lighting and color) to manipulate the viewers' scale perception and make them see a big actor in a small room.

This is one of the most challenging and least understood aspects of theater architecture. A great way to learn is to look at historical examples. A hundred years ago architects had a rich architectural language that lent itself to these kinds of efforts. Contemporary designers have to work much harder to achieve a good result, because there is no equivalent vocabulary to employ. The language (architectural detailing) has been stripped bare.

Good Bones

While buildings can adapt to new technologies over time, bad geometry is forever. The job of the theater architect is to build theaters with really good bone structure that will endure and be worth renovating in 40 years. *People* are the constant: their size, the way they naturally tend to gather around something interesting, the limitations of their hearing and vision, and their ability to sense one another's presence and share a feeling, a moment. These things never change.

Remember that the architecture is the *container* for the performance, not the performance itself. You can *enrich* the experience without stealing the spotlight.

THE FUNDAMENTALS

Theater architecture is a rich and complex field in which to work. The design problems it presents have to do with fundamental architectural questions—how do you make a room feel small, how do you give focus to a room, how do you weld a group of individuals into a community of souls that can feel something together, and what is the geometry of sharing? Engage these problems and apply all your skills and you may succeed. Ignore them, and you will fail, regardless of how trendy your facade or how good your publicity.

Theater design is also a technological problem. It requires sound planning in the stage, backstage, and public areas, detailed technical coordination, and skill and experience with seating and sight-line issues.

A final word of caution—leave theatrical innovation to theater artists. Modern architectural history is littered with un-built ideal theater schemes devised by architects and regarded by theater artists as uninteresting curiosities. That is because, in most cases, they are one-trick wonders, built around an idea about projection technology or an abstract geometric concept. Spaces that truly inspire theater artists and audiences do not force you to use them in one particular way. They are layered with possibilities and ambiguous enough to be read and used in many ways, regardless of their form.

CHAPTER 3

AN AUDITORIUM AND STAGE DESIGN GUIDE

RICHARD PILBROW *Theatre Projects Consultants*

A successful theater does not simply have good sight lines and acoustics; it is a space in which performance comes alive. An actor can step onto a stage and immediately sense whether the auditorium has the potential to spring to life.

In a theater the arts of opera, ballet, musicals, drama, dance, and classical or popular music are performed with the active participation of an audience. The stage and backstage are a machine with which to prepare and present the performance; the lobbies are places of social congregation; but the auditorium, the heart of the theater, is a place of communication designed to enhance the vital interaction that creates the theatergoing experience.

ENERGY AND COMMUNICATION

Theater is about communication of ideas, emotions, energy, and spirit. This communication is not merely between player and spectator but among the audience members themselves. An audience must feel a sense of togetherness—of being one, of sharing—participating in the performance. Energy emanates from the performer—like a stone thrown into a still pond. The ripples of energy radiate from the performer and are received by every spectator, magnified by the interaction between them (laughter, applause, a hushed silence, knowing smiles, tears, whispers), and in turn returned to the stage to inspire an even greater performance. To support this process the architect of a good theater clusters the audience in as intimate and dynamic a relationship as possible.

Legacy

The clustered audience is clearly represented in all of the most successful historic theater forms. The theaters of ancient Greece and Rome gathered huge audiences into semicircular amphitheaters. From the times of the Elizabethan courtyard theaters (such as Shakespeare's Globe Theatre) through to the early twentieth century, all theaters brought their audiences into a lively three-dimensional relationship with the stage by employing multiple balconies and surrounding boxes.

Configuration

However, during a large part of the twentieth century, theater artists, directors, and architects overlooked the audience's active role. From the 1920s to the 1970s we were obsessed with rules of sight lines, acoustics, and technology, while the modern movement in architecture stripped theaters of decoration. The result was cold, impersonal fan-shaped spaces with audiences seated in seemingly endless rows (frequently on one level) facing an often-distant stage. Such arrangements thwarted the instinct to gather and worked against the energy and ease of communication that theaters had engendered in previous ages. Only since the late 1970s has theater architecture rediscovered the values of intimacy that were fundamental to the theaters of our ancestors.

In today's rapidly changing society, live performance competes with high-definition video, interactive computers, and every conceivable inducement to make audiences stay at home. But live perfor-

▶▼ *The Hummingbird Centre for the Performing Arts, Toronto, Ontario. Typical 1960s fan-shaped auditorium. Drawings and photo courtesy of Theatre Projects Consultants, Inc.*

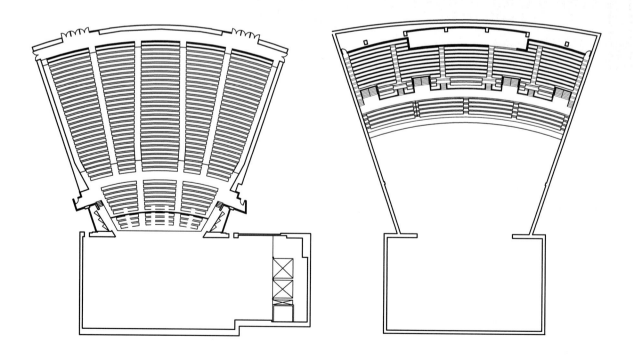

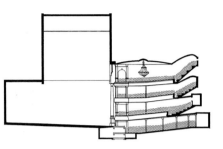

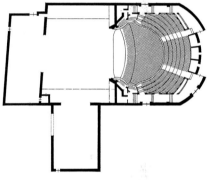

mance has one attribute—a secret weapon—with which the newer media cannot compete: it alone is alive.

Intimacy

Every effort should be made to enhance the life and energy of live performance. The past shows a way ahead. Before electricity and amplification, theaters simply had to be intimate. The opera houses of Europe and the theaters of London's West End and New York City's Broadway were the product of four hundred years of evolution. Theater owners built theaters for audiences, whom they both knew and understood. They knew that

theater sparked to life when an audience was tightly gathered together and close to the actor. This three-dimensional stacking of an audience in a tight embrace of the stage makes for that acceleration of human energy—a sense of participation—that in turn makes every performance a unique event.

PURPOSE AND FORM

A theater may encompass many types of activity: opera, ballet, musicals, drama, dance, and classical or popular music. They all require a place where people congregate, but each has its own needs, both in the auditorium and on the stage.

▸▲ *Theatre Royal, Royal Center, Nottingham, England. Example of nineteenth-century three-dimensional theater. Drawings and photo courtesy of Theatre Projects Consultants, Inc.*

▶ *Four variations of the courtyard theater illustrate basic actor and audience relationships—arena, thrust, end-stage, and traverse stage. Drawings courtesy of Theatre Projects Consultants, Inc.*

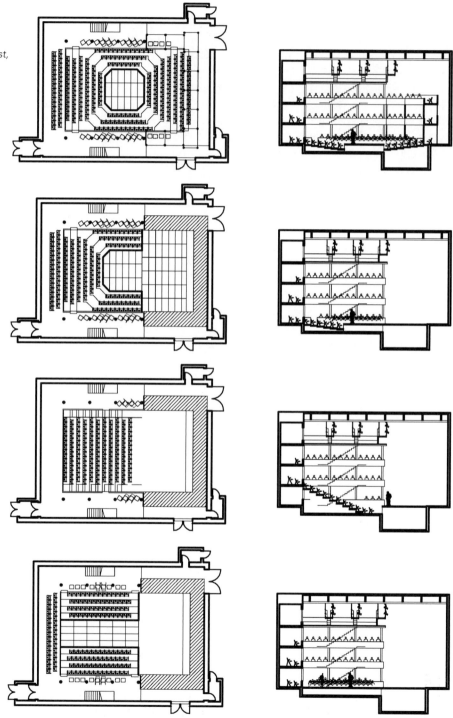

In each theater type there may be various relationships between performer and audience: arena, thrust, courtyard, proscenium, and traverse. Almost every variation of the actor-audience relationship has been explored in the twentieth century, and each has its own value.

By convention and for many practical and economic reasons, some art forms are associated with a particular theater shape. For example, opera and ballet are usually performed in a proscenium theater, with an orchestra pit between stage and audience.

The term "proscenium" is often misunderstood to mean a theater with stage divided from auditorium by a frame separating actor and audience. Only in the last 150 years has this been true. Before that time, the acting area—the proscenium (meaning "before the scene")—was the forestage in front of the proscenium. The performer was in front of the stage and within the audience space. The proscenium was a link between the audience, the actor, and the scenic world, not a barrier. Through the nineteenth century, population growth brought greater audience demand for seats, orchestras grew in size, and scenic and lighting demands changed. The actor was pushed upstage and finally behind a proscenium frame.

In the early years of the twentieth century, in reaction to the ubiquitous proscenium and in an attempt to bring actor and audience into a more vibrant relationship, experiments with thrust, arena, and other forms of "open" stage began. But only in the late 1970s was the realization to occur that all theaters can be improved by seating the audience in a three-dimensional relationship to the actor rather than on a single level.

Theater Forms

The following describes the principal forms of theater and audience configurations and presents examples of recent theater buildings. Dimensions are also included, but they must be taken as indications only. Whatever the form, there is no ideal theater; each is the product of the theater's context and the wishes of the user companies and artistic leadership.

Arena stage

In an arena theater the audience sits on all four sides of the stage. In this form there must be a sufficient playing area in the correct relationship to its encircling audience. Generally the stage is about 20–30 ft across and has access at each corner (vomitorium) for actors, scenery, furniture, and props. Overhead suspension and a trap room below are often required. Lighting the actor on the open stage must be done from all sides and every angle, and a carefully conceived layout of overhead positions is required to provide a coherent angle of light from every direction. Surround sound effects may be elaborate, and provision for multiple loudspeakers may be required.

Surround stage

This is a stage whose apron extends around the front sides of the auditorium. Commonly found in university theaters in the 1960s, it created a very wide playing area that often lacked the necessary concentration of audience attention required in a good theater.

Thrust stage

In a thrust-stage theater the audience surrounds three sides of the stage. Usually raised two or three steps above the front row of the audience, the stage is often

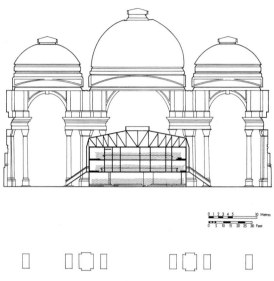

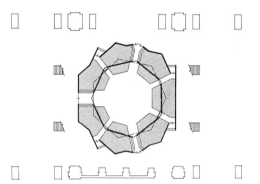

about 20–30 ft wide and is often surrounded by a lower "moat" between stage and audience, with access from two vomitoriums. In addition, behind the thrust, a stage with or without a fly tower offers the director and scene designer the possibility of adding a world of scenic illusion beyond the audience space. The center of the thrust should be at the "crossroads" of the stage, and the path from the vomitoriums should be at a 45-degree angle in plan from the front and from the upstage corners as well as from the main stage behind. Lighting and sound requirements for the thrust are similar to those for the arena.

Courtyard theater

The Elizabethan, Restoration, and Georgian theaters of England (sixteenth through eighteenth centuries) inspired the modern courtyard theater. This is a rectangular auditorium of modest size surrounded by two or three balconies. The central area, with seating and stage, may be completely flexible, to provide end-stage, thrust, arena, multistage, or flat-floor "promenade" capability. The balconies create intimacy; the sight lines afforded by the room's limited width (usually 34–44 ft) allow the acting to take place along the central axis, from one end

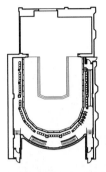
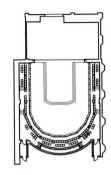
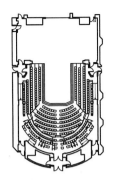
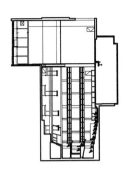

of the room to the other, while preserving the audience's view. Within one space, intimacy combines with flexibility while the balconies provide verticality, allowing the theatrical experience to range from the most intimate to the epic.

Proscenium theater

There is a wide spectrum of modern proscenium theaters. These range from the small drama theater to the largest opera house. They may — or may not — have an orchestra pit or a forestage, often of variable size. The impact upon the audience of an actor passing through the proscenium coming into the auditorium space is powerful.

The width of proscenium drama theaters in the United States varies from about 40–45 ft, while European widths are often 30–36 ft. For opera, ballet, and musicals, prosceniums are generally wider, perhaps 45–55 ft. Proscenium theaters in the Far East, which traditionally place musicians to the side of the acting area, are much wider again, 80–100 ft.

▲◀ *Chicago Shakespeare Theater, on Navy Pier, Chicago, demonstrates the potential of a thrust stage, backed by a full fly tower within a courtyard-style muiltilevel auditorium. VOA Associates, architect. Theatre Projects Consultants, theater consultant. Drawings and photo courtesy of Theatre Projects Consultants, Inc.*

◀◀ *Royal Exchange Theatre, Manchester, England. The Royal Exchange provides an outstanding example of an arena stage. The theater itself is a construction of steel and glass set within an enormous hall: the Victorian Royal Cotton Exchange (1874). Three levels of audience surround a central stage, bringing 740 people within 32 ft of the center of the acting area, creating one of the most intimate theater spaces in the world. Elaborate lighting and sound and an overhead, motorized-winch system provide a sophisticated theater capable of creating an elaborate visual and aural environment. Levitt Bernstein Associates, architect. Theatre Projects Consultants, theater consultant. Drawings courtesy of Theatre Projects Consultants, Inc. Photo courtesy of the Royal Exchange Theatre, Manchester.*

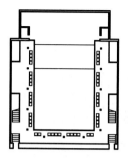
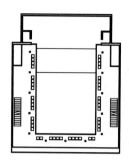
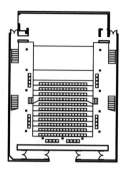
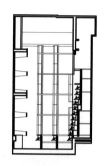

▲▶ Cottesloe Theater in the Royal National Theatre of Great Britain, London. This experimental studio theater has fostered an extraordinary flowering of new and classic drama productions and inspired many similar theaters around the world. Sir Denys Lasdun, architect. Theatre Projects Consultants, theater consultant. Drawings courtesy of Theatre Projects Consultants, Inc. Photo by Mike Smallcombe.

The height of the proscenium depends upon acoustic requirements and the auditorium's proportions, but may vary from 24–32 ft. Opera and musical theaters' are higher, 30–45 ft or more.

Ideally, the width of the stage itself is two or three times the width of the proscenium, to allow scene changes to be prepared offstage. The absolute minimum is 20 ft offstage on either side. An architectural drawing of the stage can be deceptive, because it almost never shows the scenery, lighting, actors, technicians, and paraphernalia that will fill the backstage.

Again, in an ideal world, the stage depth equals the proscenium width, but this proportion is often limited by site or budget restraints. For drama the mini-

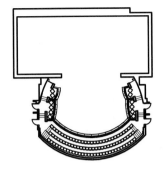

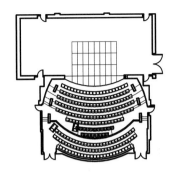

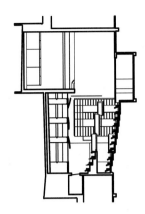

◀▲ South Coast Repertory, Julianne Argyros Stage for the South Coast Repertory Theater, Costa Mesa, California. The Argyros Stage is an exceptionally intimate 336-seat proscenium theater with a small forestage, one balcony, and boxes on the sides that step down toward the stage. These stepping boxes are a miniature version of a uniquely American form of auditorium, inspired by the theaters of early twentieth-century Broadway. Cesar Pelli Associates, architect. Theatre Projects Consultants, theater consultant. Drawings courtesy of Theatre Projects Consultants, Inc. Photo by R. A. Hansen.

mum is 35 ft, for musicals 45 ft, and for opera or ballet 50 ft. An opera house, which has much heavier scenic demands, may have ancillary stages to the rear and at one or both sides capable of containing a complete setting ready to be rolled on-stage for another act or scene or even another opera.

Above the stage in the fly tower is the gridiron, from which most of the scenery and lighting is suspended. It should be three times the height of the proscenium opening (with two-and-a-half times being the minimum). The grid is a working surface, above which should be space (minimum 10 ft) for access and the necessary machinery—loft blocks, winches, and other equipment—that is usually suspended from the underside of the roof. On either side of the fly tower are galleries from which the flying system is operated and to which lighting instruments may be fixed. Some sophisticated theaters employ power flying (motorized and controlled by microprocessor) for suspension.

The auditorium of a proscenium theater contains a large proportion of the theater

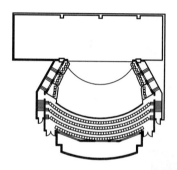 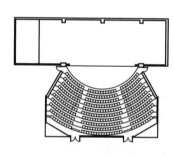 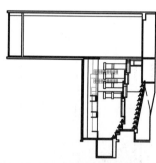

 *▲▶ The 500-seat Steppenwolf Theatre, in Chicago, is derived from a model similar to that of the Argyros Stage, in Costa Mesa, California. But here the urban, gritty nature of the company's work is reflected in the interior, built in concrete and steel, demonstrating how a proscenium theater can offer many kinds of ambiance. James Morris, architect. Theatre Projects Consultants, theater consultant. Drawings and photo courtesy of Theatre Projects Consultants, Inc.*

technology, perhaps as much as a third of the lighting and sound equipment. This must be positioned in multiple locations in the ceiling, around the walls, in the fronts of balconies and boxes, without destroying the essential ambiance and togetherness of the audience.

Opera and ballet should also be seen in as intimate surroundings as possible. But productions, particularly of opera, use large casts, chorus, and orchestra, even animals, with massive scenery and complex lighting. Opera singers, unable to sing on consecutive nights, cause daily changes of production. This scale and fre-

quency of change puts an enormous load on the scenery-handling capacity of the stage and is consequently very expensive.

Across Europe almost all the historic opera houses are smaller than 2,000 seats. Rebuilt to modern standards of comfort, sight lines, and safety, they seat perhaps 40 percent fewer people, but their multi-level, horseshoe plan shape offers an ideal acoustic and visual environment for opera and ballet. (See Color plate 3.)

New theaters in construction in Athens, Greece, Copenhagen, Denmark, and Oslo, Norway, are in the 1,200–1,600-seat range. But in the United States and

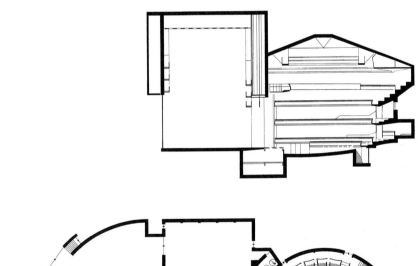

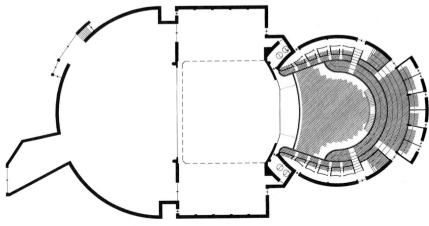

◀ The Glyndebourne Opera House, Sussex, England. The 1,200-seat Opera House is an exquisite reworking of the classic opera house, with fine architecture, acoustics, and theater design. Sir Michael Hopkins & Partners, architect. Theatre Projects Consultants, theater consultant. Drawings courtesy of Theatre Projects Consultants, Inc.

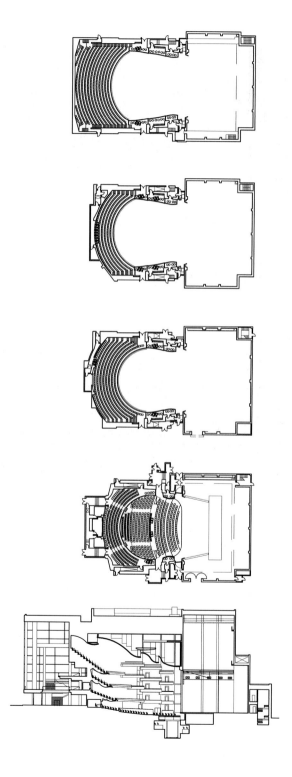

Canada, economics and an entirely different approach to government subsidy dictate a much larger seating capacity. New opera houses planned in Dallas, Texas, Kansas City, Missouri, Miami, Florida, and Toronto, Ontario, will have upward of 2,000 seats, but each draws upon the European horseshoe opera-house tradition.

The multipurpose hall

The multipurpose hall emerged with a poor reputation from the period of fan-shaped theater architecture, yet it has to combine the qualities of both the concert hall and the lyric theater. A good contemporary multipurpose hall is a blend inspired by the traditional opera house and the large theaters of Broadway and London's West End. These latter, after the invention of the iron cantilever in the mid-nineteenth century, allowed balconies to be built that brought audiences closer to the stage, with a greater overhang than in the traditional opera house. Excessive overhangs tend to force acoustic compromise, but today a balance can be struck to create greater intimacy in a large theater, where amplified as well as natural acoustics are the goal.

The multiform theater

The multiform theater can be adapted from one configuration to another: thrust to proscenium, for example. Various experiments in the 1960s, such as the Vivian Beaumont Theater, at Lincoln Center, in New York City, failed to achieve a high-quality auditorium in either of its two layouts. In a small studio theater this variation is quite easily achieved. The courtyard style, with its limited width between balconies, helps to overcome side sight line problems and ensures theatrical quality in a variety of

ways. But on a larger scale this transformation is a challenge: more seats to move requires more technology or labor. But air-pallet technology does enable large sections of architecture and seating to be reconfigured.

Unconventional theater
Theatrical performance can occur almost anywhere: in a converted warehouse, church, storefront, library, garage, or in the open air. Some of the most exciting theatrical experiences seem to happen in these informal surroundings. Is this suc-

cess attributable to their built-in character? Does the previous use of the space make a psychological contribution? In any event, productions in such venues require theatrical lighting and sound technology, and they benefit from an intimate and three-dimensional relationship between performer and audience.

Concert halls
Concert halls are theaters built solely for music, and while the acoustic design determines the shape, proportion, and construction of the room, *(cont. on page 35)*

◄◄ ▲ *Overture Center for the Arts, Madison, Wisconsin. This 2,100-seat multipurpose hall achieves the change from theater to symphony by employing an enormous orchestra shell, weighing 350,000 lb, complete with pipe organ, which moves from rear-stage storage to fill the proscenium opening. Cesar Pelli Associates, architect. Theatre Projects Consultants, theater consultant. Drawings and photo courtesy of Theatre Projects Consultants, Inc.*

◀▶ *The 2,300-seat Mead Theatre, at the Benjamin and Marian Schuster Performing Arts Center, Dayton, Ohio. Here the transformation is obtained by bringing the symphony orchestra forward into the auditorium with a massive reflective canopy overhead, thus creating a one-room space reminiscent of a pure concert hall. Cesar Pelli Associates, architect. Theatre Projects Consultants, theater consultant. Drawings courtesy of Theatre Projects Consultants, Inc. Photo by Len Allington.*

▶▶ *Derngate Theatre, Northampton, England. The Derngate converts from a concert hall seating 1,400 people, with raked orchestra seating, balconies, and boxes around the concert platform, into a lyric opera house–style proscenium theater and then into a flat-floor hall. This latter is used for arena staging of sports, exhibitions, dinners, and social events. Derngate has been successful for more than twenty years (averaging 380 performances per annum), a reminder that to optimize their usage almost all the old opera houses of the eighteenth century could similarly convert from raked seating to a flat floor. Renton Howard Wood Levin Partnership, architect. Theatre Projects Consultants, theater consultant. Drawings courtesy of Theatre Projects Consultants, Inc.*

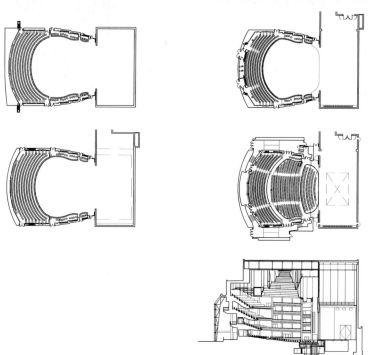

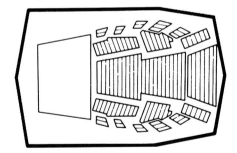

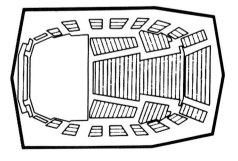

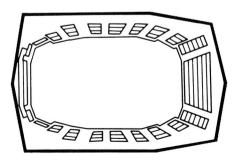

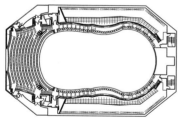
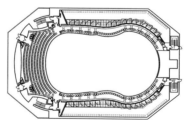
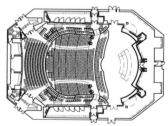

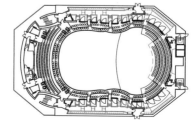
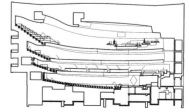

▲ ▶ *Verizon Hall in the Kimmel Center for the Performing Arts, Philadelphia, is home to the Philadelphia Orchestra. Rafael Vinoly Architects. Theatre Projects Consultants, theater consultant. Drawings and photo courtesy of Theatre Projects Consultants, Inc.*

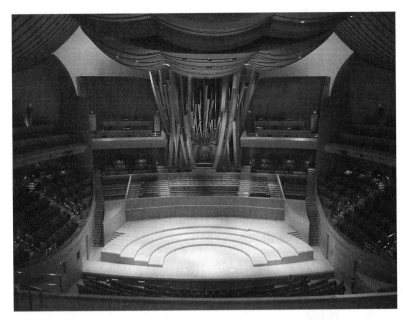

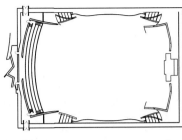

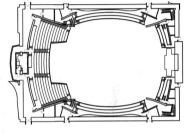

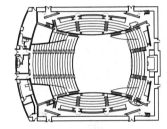

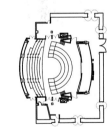

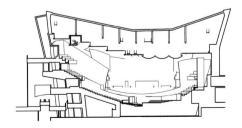

theatrical issues must also be considered. A three-dimensional space adds visual and acoustical intimacy to the performance. Various types of musical performance require flexibility of the platform and its surroundings, while stage lighting, sound, and video installations are also needed.

These projects demonstrate different acoustic design approaches and different three-dimensional audience configurations, but all require the flexibility of stage, backstage, and equipment to accommodate a range of performances.

AUDIENCE SEATING

Once the form of the theater has been determined, the next fundamental issue is the number of seats required. More seats provide more income and thus are required for those activities that are more expensive to present or produce. But often the financial sums are not so simple. More seats are of little benefit unless they are

▲ ▶ *Walt Disney Concert Hall, in Los Angeles, is headquarters to the Los Angeles Philharmonic. Frank O. Gehry Associates, architect. Theatre Projects Consultants, theater consultant. Drawings and photo courtesy of Theatre Projects Consultants, Inc.*

actually sold, and marketing those seats can add significant expense (see Chapter 12). In principle, the fewer the seats in a theater, the better the experience for performer and audience. This principle, of course, runs contrary to every manager's views. But a sold-out house has always been (one suspects since the time of Aeschylus) the surest way to guarantee success.

The scale of the human body—and spirit—dictates (or should dictate) the size of any theater and thus the seat count. The human eye cannot discern the details of facial features if the spectator is seated beyond 65 feet from the stage.[1] Simple geometry demonstrates that for the proscenium end-stage of a certain width only a limited number of viewers can be seated on a single level with reasonably acceptable sight lines and still have feelings of contact with the performer. To fit more people within the same distance, overlapping balconies can be added.

Seat Count

Each variant of each art form has its proper limits of seating capacity. Small community or experimental theaters may find 150–200 seats sufficient, regional drama theater 400–700, drama theaters in a major community 600–900, small-scale dance or opera 500–1,500, large-scale opera, ballet, and multipurpose theaters for touring musicals 1,800–2,500. There is pressure to build ever-larger auditoriums, as evident in the barnlike civic centers that have been constructed to house

large-scale productions. The decision to build more than 2,500 seats must be made with great care. While a blockbuster Broadway hit or a popular entertainer may sell out for a few days or even weeks, bringing in much-needed profit, for the remainder of the year other performances and local presentations in half-empty houses seem second-rate.

(These comments on seating capacity exclude buildings, such as amphitheaters and stadiums, specifically built for larger assemblies of people. Popular music, church ceremonies, and sports events frequently demand upward of 5,000 seats.)

The Seat Itself

At the heart of any auditorium layout is the seat itself: its dimensions, spacing, and construction. Comfort is clearly a high priority. Audience members everywhere, with each generation, seem to be getting physically larger. But the architect must strive for a balanced design. If every seat were to be a spacious armchair with unlimited legroom, the theater would be enormous and a failure. Some cinema seats recline, allowing audiences to face a screen hung above stage level, with between-seat cup-holders and generous row-to-row spacing to encourage a relaxed yet passive experience. Live theater requires an alert, participating audience, so seats must be as close together and as upright as comfort allows. The smaller the comfortable seat can be, the more people can be clustered close to the actor and the greater the chance of an exciting theater experience.

---

[1]A dimension established by Sir Laurence Olivier in experiments conducted for the design of the Royal National Theatre of Great Britain.

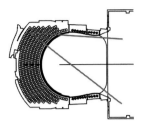

◀▼ *Sight line simulation from balconies. Drawing courtesy of Theatre Projects Consultants, Inc.*

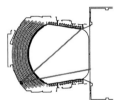

Sight Lines

Sight lines vary for each form of theater. Hard for the layperson to understand is that if every seat had a perfect view of the stage, the resultant theater would be imperfect. To achieve intimacy—and success—some seats must be placed at the sides of the room. If an ideal seat were one that could see uninterrupted the whole width of the stage, the whole height of the proscenium, the forestage or conductor in the orchestra pit, and all the scenery onstage, the resultant theater would be the undesirable fan-shaped auditorium built through much of the twentieth century. Today a rule of thumb might be that two of these criteria might be modified for 5–10 percent of the audience. Acceptable compromises vary with each discipline. For example, dance requires optimum horizontal sight lines; opera usually needs a more vertical space than drama.

For a proscenium theater the side seating can extend to a line that is 30 degrees out from the proscenium. Vertically, each seat should be able to see to a point near the front of the stage (or forestage), between the heads of those in the row in front. The exact aiming point varies with the intended discipline.

Orchestra Seating (Stalls)

Seating on the main floor of the theater is generally seen as the most popular, and accordingly as high a proportion of seats as possible are positioned on this level. However, as the orchestra seat count is increased, the balconies must be pushed farther from the stage to avoid excessive overhangs, which makes the whole theater too large. Audiences like to mingle before a performance, during intermission, and afterward, so generous seat-ways and aisles are popular. But overgenerous spacing makes audience density too diffuse.

Balconies and Boxes

Balconies bring audiences closer to the stage, but extreme care must be exercised in their design. Poor sight lines will result at the upper levels if balconies are positioned too close to the stage. If they are too close together, acoustics will be adversely affected; if there is too steep a rake, the topmost rows become vertiginous. Performers should feel as though they were at the center of their own universe. The audience should be balanced both in plan and section around the space. An auditorium with multiple balconies should place the first balcony 7–10 degrees above the actor's eye line. A topmost seat higher than 30 degrees seems too steep for audience members.

Sidewalls

To obtain the desired clustering of the audience and embracing of the performer, an auditorium's sidewalls should be wallpapered with people. Audiences seated to the sides provide a vital link between each vertical level and between balconies and the stage. The greater the percentage of the audience that sees fellow audience members in their peripheral vision the more alive the space will be. Audiences seeing each other in profile on the side-walls enhance that sense of togetherness. The highest side boxes may have restricted views, but they must be modestly priced accordingly, as should the seats high in the house and farthest from the stage. Broadening the range of ticket prices is one way to make live performance accessible to a wider audience.

Interior Architecture and Design

When the layout of seating, stage, balconies, boxes, and side ledges is set, what else contributes to a great theater? A theater needs fine architecture. To enter the auditorium should be an uplifting experience, one of anticipation. The humanity that lies at the heart of theater should always be the architect's guide. The proportions of the space, the architecture of the sidewalls—sloping or stepping boxes, vertical columns—must magnify the performers and make them seem closer while bringing the audience together. The color and decoration must underscore the sense of occasion. The architecture, though important to creating a suitable preperformance atmosphere, should recede into the shadows when the performance begins, leaving the attentive faces of the audience reflected in the light from the stage. Every auditorium should possess a strong sense of place. Ceiling, walls, balcony fronts, columns, floor, seats, carpeting, lighting, and house curtain, all contribute to a room in which audience and actor come together.

FLEXIBILITY, ACOUSTICS, AND TECHNOLOGY

A successful theater is a complex mix of theater design, architecture, acoustics, and performance technology. A balance must be struck to provide unrestricted possibilities for tomorrow's unknown stagecraft within a human-scale space that allows performance to take flight.

Flexibility

Contemporary buildings are constructed of steel and concrete, designed to stand for centuries. In the past, built of wood and plaster, though prone to destruction by fire, they could be altered. The master carpenter and scene painter could change the theater to reflect current needs or theatrical fashion. Theaters were innately flexible; a proscenium could be rebuilt, a forestage reconfigured, or balconies reshaped as style or ticket sales demanded. Though this versatility is hard to achieve now, modern technologies, such as the air pallet, moving floor systems, and construction techniques, promise a new freedom.

In the past, acoustics and theater design were disciplines often seen in conflict, but they have now found common ground. The theater designer needs multiple levels and side-seating ledges to create visual, emotional, and theatrical intimacy, while the acoustician needs them to support early acoustic reflection.

Technology

As it has in every age, theater employs contemporary technology to enhance performance. Nowadays, computerized scenery-handling systems, automated lighting, digital sound, and new audiovisual technologies are available, with more to come. A great deal of that technology is in the auditorium. Dozens of lighting instruments, loudspeakers, and control and projection rooms have to be integrated. Sophisticated infrastructure—lighting, sound and video cable systems, fiber optics, computer links, and communications—must be seamlessly built into every modern auditorium and must anticipate future needs.

THE FUTURE OF AUDITORIUM DESIGN

The English director Michael Elliott, prime creator of Manchester's Royal Exchange, said: "The modern theatre building is a hyper-sophisticated and very expensive architectural, mechanical and electronic monument, all designed to conjure up a rainbow. But a rainbow that shifts and fades, and reappears in unexpected places. Sometimes it appears ridiculous to hope that so heavy and inert a piece of real-estate can catch a rainbow as it moves rapidly over the landscape of society's dreams."[2]

The only purpose of a theater is to serve the arts of drama, music, opera, and dance. These arts are in a state of rapid, sometimes chaotic, and continuous change. The challenge for those involved in designing performing arts buildings is to capture the illusive magic that brings life to a performance space; to incorporate all the changing technical and acoustic needs; to make them architecturally inspiring and yet flexible and sufficiently malleable for future generations to mold to their needs. Our theaters exist for our audiences; only by enriching their participation in the creativity on the stage will the arts thrive.

---

[2] Michael Elliott, "On Not Building for Posterity," *TABS* 31, no. 2 (June 1973): 41.

CHAPTER 4
STAGE DESIGN: TECHNOLOGY AND FLEXIBILITY

LEONARD AUERBACH, STEVE POLLOCK, AND STEVEN FRIEDLANDER
Auerbach Pollock Friedlander

HISTORICAL PERSPECTIVE

Modern stage technology traces its roots to the Renaissance, when scene painters used single- or multiple-point perspective to render theatrical scenes, giving stage design a new, pictorial focus.

A New Scenography

In the late 1800s, electricity permitted new stage-lighting fixtures to illuminate performers and scenery at levels far beyond the brightness of candles or oil lamps. As a result, flat, painted canvases could be displaced by three-dimensional scenic elements to produce real, not painted, shadows. As this new scenography took hold, a new kind of venue evolved in which the subtleties of this approach could be showcased. The modern proscenium theater was the result. In 1876, Wagner's Festspielhaus opened with the opera *Parsifal* in Bayreuth, Germany. It was a seminal moment.

A New Theater Form

The composer Richard Wagner and the designer Adolph Appia's new form of dramatic opera, with its modernist multilevel staging and projected images, was unlike anything previously seen in the theater. The Bayreuth Festspielhaus abandoned the popular courtyard form that had relied on a shallow, sloped floor, surrounded by stacked galleries. The social hierarchy of gallery seating and boxes was supplanted by a more egalitarian arrangement of theater chairs set in shallow, curvilinear rows that faced the separate stage picture. Walls were simple and unadorned. A simple proscenium opening and a deeply overhung orchestra pit did away with visual distractions at the front of the room. As the lights dimmed, there was only one focus: the stage picture. The influence of Bayreuth would ripple throughout the design of theaters for more than 100 years.

Changing Perception

In the twentieth century, cinema and television redefined how audiences receive the spoken word. The close-up and the proliferation of moving images have changed our perception of what constitutes a live performance. Large-format imaging, video gaming, the Internet, and computer imaging have changed our way of seeing, making our homes into live-in venues, filled with all types of performance.

TECHNOLOGY AND ARCHITECTURE

Technology responds to the need for an architecture that serves today's audiences. Good seeing and good hearing go hand in hand; perception involves both aural and visual senses.

Good Sight Lines

Proper attention to sight lines aids the room's acoustic design. A clear view of the audience and performers, without obstruction from other audience members, is critical. If the audience feels well-connected with the room environment and enjoys a full view of the performer, the auditorium will be more intimate. No matter how large the venue, architects must continue to design for intimacy, making the performer seem larger than life-size.

New Technical Requirements

As venues continue to increase in size and complexity, arranging the seating environment for intimacy must be reconciled with the presence of new technologies. Audio- and lighting-control positions and camera locations have become basic elements within the auditorium landscape. The Americans with Disabilities Act (ADA) also poses design challenges. Distribution of accessible seating, often with elevated sight lines for disabled audiences and systems operators, can become a key issue in planning and design of media- and technology-sensitive facilities. These design considerations are basic planning issues; they are not negotiable.

Accommodation of technology both in the audience chamber and backstage requires flexibility, room for growth, and ease of maintenance. Fire-rated plenums, cable trays, and raised access floors offer great opportunities for changing wire and fiber pathways over time with minimal disruption. Integration of these systems must be part of planning from the outset.

Flexible Enclosure

Theater designers have used the technology employed in heavy manufacturing and assembly-line environments to move large scenic elements and monolithic architectural elements. Since the theater designer George Izenour's seminal work on multiuse theaters in the 1960s, architects have been moving walls and ceilings as well as rotating and lifting large volumes of audience seating. The architectural environment has therefore become pliable.

The mechanically assisted multiuse hall of the late twentieth century has allowed architects to blur the lines between venue, audience, and performance. Today, theatrical staging and effects of significant magnitude occur in close proximity to the audience. These newly indistinct boundaries occur at theme parks, popular-event centers, and purpose-built performance sites. An example is the permanent homes for Cirque du Soleil's newest productions, where staging includes fire, water, elevators, moving architectural elements, and performance-specific stage machines as part of a unified stage and audience experience.

Proscenium Area

Flexible theatrical infrastructure—especially over the audience—has given rise to new rigging loads in front of the proscenium, overhead stagehand access, and new data and power requirements. These forestage and over-audience rigging grids are found in many touring venues as well as in a new breed of theater space that houses televised events. As the audience chamber is now very much part of the performance, the pro-proscenium area is the pivot point where architecture meets production in ever more complex ways. The pro-proscenium is the area immediately downstage (on the audience side) of the proscenium. This is a complicated zone that requires attention to both audience arrangement and technical systems.

Until the national tour of *Phantom of the Opera,* forestage grids were not considered in the design of most multiuse touring halls. Forestage rigging was limited to simple hang points for lighting trusses and speaker arrays. Now, however, no touring facility is complete without an aggressive forestage infrastructure that includes a grid and fall-protection systems. Tons of scenic, lighting, and audio-system elements must be accommodated in a robust building environment, clear of obstructions imposed by heating, ventilating, and air-conditioning (HVAC) ductwork, plumbing, and drains. Ample three-phase power distribution at several voltage levels as well as signal networks and standardization of elements to accommodate touring productions are critical.

Flexibility

Flexibility must also be programmed within the seating arrangement, especially toward the pro-proscenium area. Control and camera positions, circulation paths, and ADA seating, along with moving walls and positioning of temporary equipment and cameras, make the public exit plan all the more important. Exit schemes must be carefully developed to portray an accurate flow-based accounting of audience traffic related to the egress path and rated exit corridors.

Flexible room design and moving architectural elements also affect HVAC systems within the audience chamber. Supply and return air must pass through ductwork on a variety of room reconfigurations. Architectural elements have direct impact on the configuration of overhead duct paths and must not block low-level register devices.

HVAC

A number of facilities now use low-supply or displacement HVAC systems, which rely on the delivery of air from a plenum below audience seating and create a temperate stratum at the seating plane, with warmer air rising into the return-air domain above. This green-building approach to cooling also offers significant operation

cost savings and Leadership in Energy Efficient Design (LEED) opportunities. Displacement system temperatures are as much as 10 degrees higher than the required temperature for traditional high-overhead supply. Moreover, the system is much less complicated than the overhead return-air ductwork, which enhances planning of flexible performance-systems infrastructure.

Multiuse Costs

For the owner, conversations about cost are often reduced to offsetting operating cost against capital expense. Multiuse theaters are most affected by systems that mechanically manipulate architectural elements. The expense of changing a theater from proscenium to thrust or arena stage or from road house to symphony hall may be justified by the greater income from a judicious operating and staffing strategy. Technology (automated theatrical machinery and rigging, network wiring, automated lighting fixtures, audio, video, and communications systems), if properly incorporated into a facility's design, can dramatically increase flexibility without dramatically increasing labor costs.

LIGHTING, SOUND, AND MEDIA TECHNOLOGY

Lighting, which used to be measured in only two dimensions, time and intensity, is now multidimensional.

Lighting

Automated fixtures have become commonplace, adding physical movement and numerous other visual attributes. Light sources continue to grow smaller and brighter. Ever more powerful and affordable computer-control systems are available, running quieter, more efficient dimmers. Never before has the lighting designer had such conceptual freedom. Today, the extent of the designer's imagination is limited only by the number of devices that can be plugged into a system. In 20 years, the conventional number of lighting circuits and theatrical lighting fixtures has multiplied exponentially. While this increase may be attributed to reduced equipment and systems costs, one cannot discount the effect that touring entertainment, MTV, and videos have had on our hunger for greater visual impact.

Electrical Power Requirements

Greater numbers of fixtures, devices, and dimmers tax the capabilities of the computerized control systems that monitor them. Network infrastructure continues to evolve at speeds that surpass the rate of new construction and building renovations. Intelligent planning must therefore accommodate clean power (free of interference), expandable network pathways (theatrical computer network wiring systems with expansive data location capacity), distribution of data and switch points, and the ability to speedily send control data and receive equipment feedback from any location in the theater.

Audio Systems

Audio and video systems are advancing similarly, with even greater effect on audiences and artists. We live in an age where the ready availability of sophisticated consumer electronics has made us all videographers and sound engineers in our own right. In the theater, controlled sound consists of everything from simple reinforcement to electronic acoustic enhance-ment. It is even possible to overlay acoustic characteristics of one building type on another, simply at the touch of a control board. Contemporary acoustics can make a live performance sound like a studio recording with a precision that could not have been envisioned just a few years ago.

TECHNOLOGY AND THE AUDIENCE

Audience perceptions are ever more influenced by the computer as its programs become ever more sophisticated.

Interactive Environments

In corporate and government facilities, such as board and public presentation rooms, media systems have been expanded to include audience or participant input, such as voting. Interactive technology continues to captivate media designers, and with the advent of wireless control and greater bandwidth, it may well become commonplace in the live performance environment.

It may soon be possible to manipulate space with a version of virtual technology. Three-dimensional cinema has evolved into more sophisticated digital environments, especially in contemporary planetariums and themed attractions. It may be only a matter of time before this technology finds its way into the live theater. Whether in a domed space with floating actors or on an open stage where performers move magically through space or emerge from water, technology can assist our perception of live performance in new ways. The restrictions of proscenium theaters can now be ignored as new venues with new audience-performer relationships are created.

CASE STUDIES

The following case studies touch on three new theater spaces. Judy and Arthur Zankel Hall at Carnegie Hall in New York City portrays the latest concepts in flexible space, application of technology, and music in a subterranean hall. Cirque du Soleil's new facility at the New York, New York Hotel and Casino, for *Zumanity, Another Side of Cirque du Soleil,* explores the interaction of technology and the audience in the built environment. The California Nanosystems Institute, at the University of California, Santa Barbara, is a twenty-first-century take on *The Fantastic Voyage,* where scholars explore submicroscopic and atomic structures within an interactive visual environment.

Judy and Arthur Zankel Hall at Carnegie Hall

In 1997, Carnegie Hall, one of the country's preeminent music performance centers, began exploring Andrew Carnegie's original vision of three great halls under one roof.

Technology underground

The place for Zankel Hall was created by reclaiming space below street level that was originally a 1200-seat recital hall and later, the Carnegie Hall Cinema. (See Color plate 6.) The process was spearheaded by Carnegie Hall's executive director, Judith Aaron, Isaac Stern, and Marilyn Horne, and was embraced by the board of trustees.

The project's goal was to provide a venue that would present a variety of performances, from classical chamber recitals to jazz and world music. Carnegie Hall also wished to provide distance learning capabilities, enabling Zankel to become a center of music education. The wide range of uses necessitated an equally inventive design.

Work on Zankel Hall by Polshek Partnership, architect, and Auerbach Pollock Friedlander, theater consultant, began in 1997. They collaborated on the design and flexible architecture that would fulfill the Hall's mission. Seating arrangements for the various room configurations and the technical systems to support them were developed early in the process, to enable the project team to determine the extent of excavation. In the end, 6,300 cubic yards of granite were removed. The design work included careful coordination of services within the auditorium and its support spaces, with early input on backstage, performer, and technical areas as well as lobby spaces and patron circulation areas.

The stage machinery, lighting, audio, and video systems that support Zankel's musical programs were designed to meet Carnegie Hall's specific requirements, allowing the Hall not only to meet current programs but also to expand to meet future needs.

The application of technology to the design was carefully considered. In certain situations well-established systems were chosen over newer devices. In other cases, the most up-to-date equipment was utilized. For example, the nine platform lifts at the heart of the reconfigurable audience-seating and stage areas rely on mechanical screw-jack driven lifts instead of more recently developed machinery. The choice was based on their proven reliability, low maintenance cost, and safety.

The lighting and audio systems, on the other hand, employ the most up-to-date technology available. The sound reinforcement system has a digital mixing console with wireless control technology.

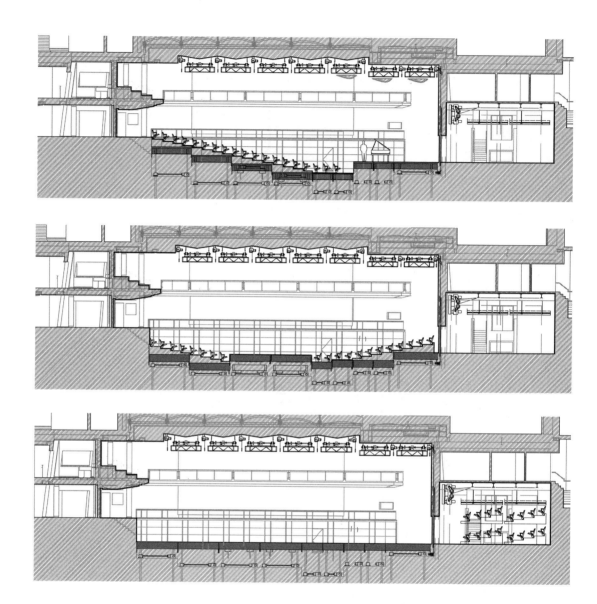

Lighting systems use wireless Ethernet networking for control and include a dual network capable of permitting the use of two completely separate control consoles.

The careful choice of technologies for each system was based on the Hall's goal of avoiding down time between events. The dynamic schedule limited time for setup and changeover, so systems had to work efficiently, supporting a wide variety of functions. Innovative technologies were called for only when the opportunity to use them supported these goals. The bottom line, however, always balanced innovation with reliability and Carnegie Hall's maintenance requirements.

◄◄ Section view, end-stage, center-stage, and flat-floor configurations, Polshek Partnership, architect; Auerbach Pollock Friedlander, theater consultant. Drawings courtesy of Auerbach Pollock Friedlander.

◄ Judy and Arthur Zankel Hall, New York City, chair-wagon being moved during commissioning. Polshek Partnership, architects; Auerbach Pollock Friedlander, theater consultant. Photo courtesy of Auerbach Pollock Friedlander.

◄ 1089-platform lift, side view. Polshek Partnership, architects; Auerbach Pollock Friedlander, theater consultant. Photo courtesy of Auerbach Pollock Friedlander.

Cirque du Soleil

Founded in 1984 by Guy Laliberté and a group of fellow street performers in Montreal, Cirque du Soleil is now a major company of 3,000 employees and is recognized as one of the world's most innovative performing arts groups. In 2003, as many as seven million people saw one of nine Cirque du Soleil productions. From their original tent shows, which still tour the world, the Cirque du Soleil has established five permanent shows in the United States. These productions, four in Las Vegas, Nevada, and one in Orlando, Florida, are housed in purpose-built theaters, each with technology designed specifically for the show.

Intense infrastructure

The design and construction process for a Cirque du Soleil venue is as exceptional as the productions themselves. Everything is possible, including a one-million-gallon pool with stage lifts, lighting, and sound for the production of *O* at the Bellagio Hotel Casino in Las Vegas.

Cirque du Soleil venues typically have thrust-stage components that allow performers, both on the stage and above it, to move out into the theater, where they are surrounded by the audience. Unlike most performing arts facilities, even those designed for specific resident companies, each Cirque du Soleil venue is designed around one specific production. The

◄ Cirque du Soleil. Zumanity, New York, New York Hotel and Casino, Las Vegas, Nevada. Marnell Corrao Architects; Auerbach Pollock Friedlander, theater consultant. Photo courtesy of Cirque du Soleil.

◀ Cirque du Soleil. Stage machinery under construction. Marnell Corrao Architects; Auerbach Pollock Friedlander, theater consultant. Photo courtesy of Auerbach Pollock Friedlander.

challenge of this kind of design effort is that during design and construction, the show's final details are still being worked out.

Each Cirque du Soleil show evolves through an extended rehearsal process in a theater once it is occupied. In many ways, Cirque du Soleil's own design and technical teams are the designers of the systems rather than the traditional situation, in which theater consultants design the systems. For *Zumanity, Another Side of Cirque du Soleil,* at the New York, New York Hotel and Casino, and for *Kà,* a

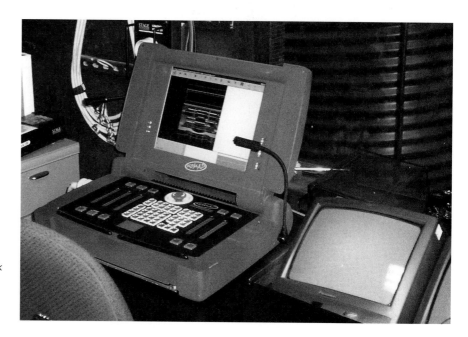

▶ *Cirque du Soleil. Stage-machinery automation controller. Marnell Corrao Architects; Auerbach Pollock Friedlander, theater consultant. Photo courtesy of Auerbach Pollock Friedlander.*

new production for the MGM Grand, the venues and systems were developed in close collaboration between Cirque du Soleil, MGM Grand, consultants, and architects. In each case, the theater consultant's role centered on the coordination and detailing of concepts developed by Cirque du Soleil staff.

Cirque du Soleil productions all have unique unifying story lines and designs into which the show's director weaves individual acrobatic performances. The need for facilities that can accommodate development over the rehearsal process calls for intense flexibility and latitude within their technical infrastructure.

For example, the creative rehearsal process places heavy demands on the feedback and interactivity capabilities of sound and lighting systems; it is not sufficient to design quantitatively. Furthermore, innovative approaches are essential to allow the flexibility required by a final production.

California Nanosystems Institute, University of California, Santa Barbara (UCSB)

Nanotechnology, the study and development of molecular-sized machines and materials, is at the cutting edge of technological development. Though not strictly a performance space, the Nanosystems Institute's Media Arts and Technology spaces, especially the domed presentation space called Media Users Space for Education (MUSE), represent the future of presentation systems' design.

Accommodation for technology of the future

The MUSE space is a flexible and immersive blank palette, on which virtual-reality systems will support visual and performing artwork, scientific research, and discovery. Used collaboratively by the UCSB California Nanosystems Insti-

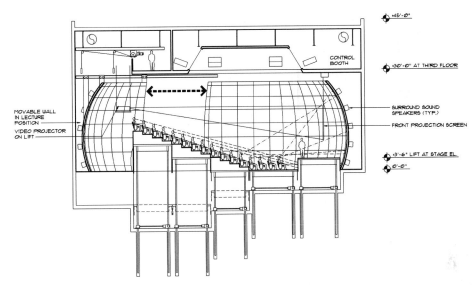

① DIGITAL MEDIA AUDITORIUM - SECTION AT LECTURE CONFIGURATION
⅛" = 1'-0"

UCSB - CNSI
DIGITAL MEDIA AUDITORIUM

tute and its Media Arts and Technology Program, MUSE will bring together scientists and artists in a virtual world of their own creation.

The architecture of the dome allows researchers to experiment as audio and video display technology expands. The audience chamber is defined by a 360-degree surround consisting of a 30-foot-high spherical projection screen of perforated metal. Edge-blended images are projected from above and below a viewing bridge at the dome's meridian line. The bridge is designed to fly up and down, changing the viewer's orientation within the dome. It also expands laterally, accommodating events requiring a larger viewing platform.

Audio sources can be placed at any location behind the perforated dome surround, above or below the floor deck. The architecture and infrastructure of the room allows for future development of audio, video, and computer processing technology.

The MUSE will also have direct digital connection with support facilities within the California Nanosystems Institute (CNSI) as well as an uplink to other such institutes around the world. The CNSI machine room will house the clusters of computers required for MUSE's signal processing as well as the broader needs of the CNSI community.

Although the intent is to outfit the MUSE with the latest technology, the facilities are tailored expressly for human experience and human interaction by observers, performers, and explorers within the virtual world. The MUSE will bring a new, dynamic teaching and research tool to the University of California, Santa Barbara.

As of this writing, specifications for the MUSE systems are still in progress. However, an extensive structural, mechanical,

▲ California Nanosystems Institute, University of California, Santa Barbara. Digital media auditorium, concept sketch, lecture configuration. Altoon + Porter Architects with Venturi Scott Brown + Associates, architects; Auerbach Pollock Friedlander, theater consultant. Drawing courtesy of Auerbach Pollock Friedlander.

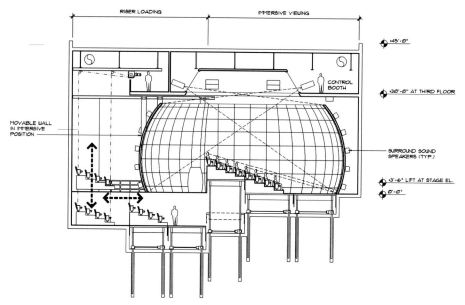

RISER LOADING   IMMERSIVE VIEWING

+45'-0"

CONTROL BOOTH

+30'-0" AT THIRD FLOOR

MOVABLE WALL IN IMMERSIVE POSITION

SURROUND SOUND SPEAKERS (TYP.)

+3'-6" LIFT AT STAGE EL.

0'-0"

1 DIGITAL MEDIA AUDITORIUM - SECTION AT IMMERSIVE CONFIGURATION
1/8" = 1'-0"

UCSB - CNSI
DIGITAL MEDIA AUDITORIUM

▲ *California Nanosystems Institute, University of California, Santa Barbara. Digital media auditorium, concept sketch, immersive configuration. Altoon + Porter Architects with Venturi Scott Brown + Associates, architects; Auerbach Pollock Friedlander, theater consultant. Drawing courtesy of Auerbach Pollock Friedlander.*

and electrical infrastructure has been installed to support the ever-changing technology that is anticipated over the life of the facility.

The CNSI MUSE project is a prime example of the emphasis placed on the infrastructure of a technologically advanced facility. We encounter these issues, of technological infrastructure and flexibili-

ty, in every performing arts facility we design. Providing owners with a vessel into which they can efficiently place a show with distinct requirements is a challenge we face daily. Careful assessment of uses, as well as thorough knowledge of current technology and trends are the essential components of appropriate and forward-looking design.

1. Hult Center, Eugene, Oregon. Hardy Holzman Pfeiffer Associates. The Silva Concert Hall, in Eugene's Hult Center, includes a 2,500-seat multipurpose theater and a 515-seat drama theater. Since it opened, in 1982, the Center has been credited with playing a significant role in revitalizing Eugene's economy. Photo by Norman McGrath.

2. The Soreng Theater at the Hult Center is a trapezoidal room designed for a variety of production types. Because there is no permanent proscenium, a range of presentations and scenic arrangements is possible. Catwalks and ladders for lighting and rigging form a partial enclosure for both auditorium and stage, visually tying the two together. Photo by Norman McGrath.

3. The Glyndebourne Opera House, East Sussex, England. Sir Michael Hopkins and Partners. The Glyndebourne Opera House, with 1,200 seats, is an exquisite contemporary reworking of the classic opera house, with fine architecture, acoustics, and theater design. Photo by Richard Davies.

4. New Jersey Performing Arts Center, Newark. Barton Myers. The New Jersey Performing Arts Center includes a 2,750-seat multipurpose house, one of two halls designed by Barton Myers with Fisher Dachs Associates and Artec (acoustics). A catalyst for redevelopment of downtown Newark, it is shown here in symphony mode. Photo by Jeff Goldberg/Esto.

▲ **5.** *Whitaker Center for Science and the Arts, Harrisburg, Pennsylvania. Hardy Holzman Pfeiffer Associates. Lobbies are unpopulated during performances and whenever the theater is unused, so it is wise to design in a second lighting "scene" that emphasizes decorative features. Photo by Michael Moran.*

◀ **6.** *Carnegie Hall, Judy and Arthur Zankel Hall, New York City. Polshek Partnership. The project's goal was to provide a venue that would present a variety of performances, from classical to chamber music recitals to jazz and world music. Auerbach Pollock Friedlander, theater consultant, and Jaffe Holden Acoustics. Photo by Jeff Goldberg/Esto.*

◀ **7.** *Ohio Theater, Columbus, Ohio. Hardy Holzman Pfeiffer Associates. The theater's lobby stairs light the way to the performance space. Light can be a prime tool for clarifying circulation. Photo by Cervin Robinson.*

◀ **8.** *Radio City Music Hall, New York City. Hardy Holzman Pfeiffer Associates. Radio City Music Hall was intended to be simple and modern, without traditional ornament. When it was built it was unlike any other theater in the world. Each restored surface was reconditioned or replicated exactly, but lighting levels were increased, to convey to contemporary audiences the brilliance and grandeur of the original design. Photo by T. Whitney Cox.*

◀◀ **9.** *Radio City Music Hall, New York City. Hardy Holzman Pfeiffer Associates. Radio City Music Hall's soaring lobby is an intensely social space, where audiences enjoy seeing and being seen. Because the space is also used for stand-alone events (banquets, exhibitions, etc.), the chandeliers and wall sconces have been supplemented with theatrical lighting in ceiling slots. Photo by T. Whitney Cox.*

10. New Amsterdam Theatre, New York City. Hardy Holzman Pfeiffer Associates. Aurora is one of numerous hidden treasures at the New Amsterdam. The light bulbs surrounding her face provide fanciful decorative lighting.

11. New Amsterdam Theatre. Contemporary restoration can retain fixtures made with exposed light bulbs, but it cannot make them the principal source of illumination without glare. Here, pin-spot down lights add missing illumination. They are incorporated into the restoration of the foyer so that it feels as if the original fixtures were the principal source of illumination.

12. The New Amsterdam Theater is awash in colorful excess. Its color scheme has been softened to complement higher lighting levels and a large proscenium mural. Photos these two pages courtesy of Disney Enterprises, Inc.

▲ **13.** *Joyce Theater, New York City. Hardy Holzman Pfeiffer Associates. During conversion of this movie house into a fully equipped dance theater, the interior was gutted, and a single steeply raked seating level was inserted to provide excellent sight lines throughout. The stage is built to the site's full width, with support functions below. Two slightly elevated tiers along the hall's sidewalls enclose the seating and permit patrons to view both the stage and each other. Photo by Norman McGrath.*

▶ **14.** *Joyce Theater. This staircase connects the two audience gathering areas and administrative offices. It joins the below-ground level to the theater's street-level lobby. It is wide enough to accommodate the public ascending and descending at the same time and follows the curve of the landing. Patterned carpet and indirect lighting lend drama to this small lobby. Photo by Norman McGrath.*

▲ **15.** *The addition of air-conditiong equipment may require structural modifications
to a theater's roof. These modifications may
call for an acoustic enclosure to prevent
noise from disturbing neighbors as well
as theater patrons. At the Joyce Theater,
a 10 ft metal-panel enclosure has been
placed around two rooftop units to reduce
airborne noise. Photo by Timothy Hursley.*

▲ **16.** *Harvey Theater, Brooklyn Academy of Music, Brooklyn, New York. Hardy Holzman Pfeiffer Associates. Although this altered configuration brought the stage forward into the auditorium, the theater's decorative surfaces remained, without restoration, scarred by water, disintegrated from the passage of time. The result is a contemporary performance place that resonates with the past. Photo courtesy of 83 Durston Saylor.*

17. *Overture Center for the Arts, Madison, Wisconsin. Cesar Pelli & Associates. Overture Hall, the new 2,257-seat multipurpose proscenium theater, was the focus of the first design phase of the Overture Center for the Arts. In this room, the collaboration between architect and acoustical consultant can be seen in every detail and every wall surface. Photo by Frans Swarte, Kirkegaard Associates.*

18. *Proctor & Gamble Hall, Aronoff Center for the Arts, Cincinnati, Ohio. Cesar Pelli & Associates. The Proctor & Gamble Hall is the centerpiece for the Aronoff Center for the Arts complex in downtown Cincinnati. This 2,700-seat space has an intimate feel that belies its size. The ceiling is constructed of perforated metal in a cascading geometry that draws the focus of the audience to the stage. Photo by Dawn Schuette, Kirkegaard Associates.*

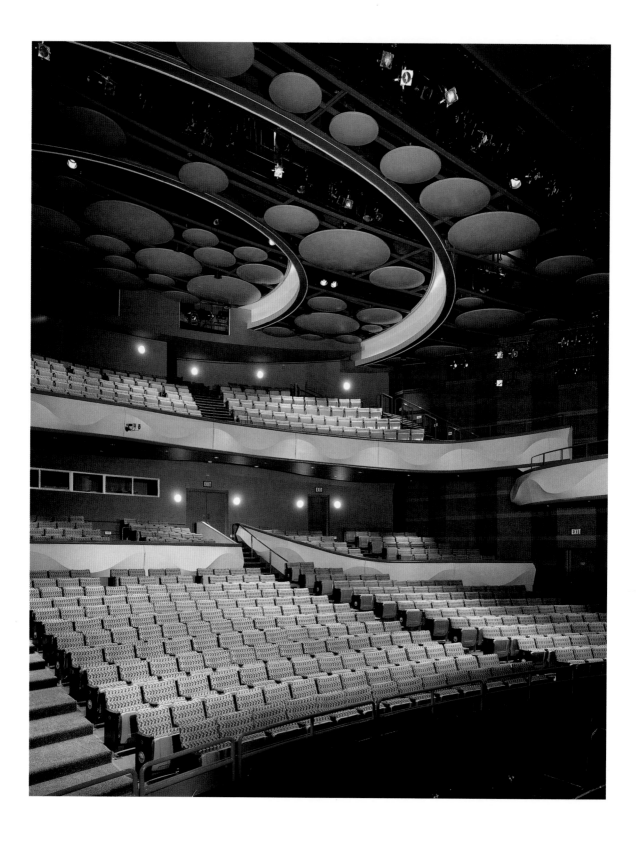

◀◀ **19.** *Alaska Center for the Performing Arts, Anchorage. Hardy Holzman Pfeiffer Associates. Each of the three auditoriums in the Alaska Center for the Performing Arts has its own entrance, lobby, and roof. This is the Discovery Theater, designed for drama, with unamplified acoustics. Its 800 seats are divided into two tiers, and it features a "pro-proscenium" production area that connects performer to audience and provides scenic and staging flexibility. Its open ceiling offers almost unlimited access to lighting equipment. Photo by Christopher Little.*

▲ **20.** *Alaska Center for the Performing Arts. Modern theaters often employ transparency between the exterior and the public lobbies, using the gathering audience to animate the exterior at night, thus heightening audience anticipation. Here, the theater's walls are transparent and include both patterned glass and integral artwork, with views of interior activity. Photo by Christopher Little.*

21. *Alice Busch Opera Theater, Cooperstown, New York. Hardy Holzman Pfeiffer Associates. The Alice Busch Opera Theater, home of the Glimmerglass Opera Company, takes full advantage of its arcadian setting. Patrons reach the theater by walking from their cars across a meadow and around a small pond. Parking disappears across the highway. The theater is an open-air pavilion, whose screened sidewalls are rolling doors that close when the performance begins.*

22. *Alice Busch Opera Theater. The hall interior is an abstraction of a small Italian opera house. A patterned wooden ceiling, inspired by domestic quilts, complements its sprightly interior. The theater has 600 seats on the orchestra floor and 300 on the balcony. The large stage and the high fly loft provide ample space for handling scenery. The orchestra pit accommodates 80 musicians. Photo by Elliott Kaufman.*

23. *Boettcher Concert Hall, Denver, Colorado. Hardy Holzman Pfeiffer Associates. The undulating face of each balcony is lined with a gold strip that reflects light from the stage. These fascias have a feeling of great intimacy, set against the room's dark walls. Photo by Norman McGrath.*

▲ **24.** *New Victory Theater, New York City. Hardy Holzman Pfeiffer Associates. Contemporary codes call for fire separation between the auditorium, lobby, and stage areas, together with smoke dampers in ductwork to prevent the spread of toxic air in a conflagration. In restoration work, the integration of piping and sprinkler heads, even if they are concealed, requires great care to ensure they do not interfere with the decorative character of the existing auditorium. Here, piping and sprinkler heads have been invisibly integrated in flat ceiling areas. Photo courtesy of Elliott Kaufman.*

CHAPTER 5

BACKSTAGE PLANNING

KEITH GERCHAK *Theatre Projects Consultants*

Design efforts for a theater invariably concentrate on the lobby and the auditorium. Not that this focus is totally unwarranted. First, these areas encompass the audience experience, providing the comfort and enjoyment so essential to attracting patrons. Second, donors expect their financial gifts to yield publicly visible results. Third, these public areas offer the greatest opportunity to create a visionary architectural statement. Fourth, the patron areas are more familiar to the architect than the areas behind the curtain.

BACKSTAGE DESIGN

Backstage design can be lost in the wake of such considerations, reducing much of the back-of-house program to little more than a list of rooms with square-foot assignments. These rooms are often shoehorned into a predescribed geometry, without full appreciation for what they contain, who uses them, or how they relate to each other. Backstage spaces are work spaces, and like any other, their usefulness relies on minimum dimensions, optimum proportions, adequate height clearances, sufficient electrical and mechanical capacity, and efficient adjacencies.

DESIGN-TEAM REVIEW

Architects are problem-solvers by training and, along with the rest of the design team, should be walked through the backstage process from pre- to post-production. Usable and efficient backstage spaces are created through careful planning, and low-cost solutions are rooted in a clear understanding of how things work backstage.

A production house mounts its own shows, casting and rehearsing, designing and constructing the sets, designing the costumes or pulling them from stock, designing and positioning the lighting. While resident artistic and technical staff members often collaborate with jobbed-in production teams of directors, choreographers, musical directors, and designers, they remain consistent users of the facility and are readily accessible to inform a production house's programming and planning. Each house has its own artistic mission, season selection, audience demographics and subscriber base, operational and production budgets, and artistic and technical staff preferences. Therefore, the design of a production house is specific to the needs of a particular theater and its staff.

A road house, on the other hand, does not mount its own shows but rather hosts self-contained touring productions, each with its own cast of players (performers, stage and company managers, department heads) and its own scenery, lighting instruments, sound equipment, and costumes. This autonomy ensures consistent production values from San Jose, California, to Bangor, Maine, and aspects of the production process common to all tours dictate the fundamental physical requirements of the facilities that house them. While an administrative director and resident head carpenter are available to inform programming and planning decisions at a road house, the process does not have the same level of representation in the touring production staffs that use the facility.

BACKSTAGE PLANNING

The following outlines basic backstage planning needs for a touring production, from load-in to load-out. While the road house is used as the basis of discussion, many of the principles outlined here apply to production houses as well. The hope is that, for those theaters contemplating either building a new facility or renovating an existing one, the information provided here can serve as a catalyst for discussion by technical, artistic, and administrative staff, trustees, and the architectural team.

LOAD-IN

Ease-of-access is the single most important factor in backstage planning. Efficient load-in means fewer people are required, which translates to a reduction in labor time and therefore labor costs. While load-in is a one- or two-day process, depending on the size of a production, the first few hours are the most critical, as they involve coordination of many people from different departments. Carpenters, electricians, sound operators, props crew, hair and makeup staff, wardrobe masters and mistresses, and dressers have their own load-in responsibilities, which must be met simultaneously to finish preparations in time for the first performance.

Personnel

Each department of the touring production has its own head and assistant(s), who are intimately familiar with the re-

quirements of the production but unfamiliar with the intricacies of the venue. There are correlating department heads, resident at the house, that hire a local crew of twenty or more, and they, conversely, are familiar with the venue but not the specifics of the production. Include the visiting stage- and company-management teams, and there are as many players unseen backstage as there are actors and musicians in front of the audience.

Loading Dock

Backstage planning begins with the overall site planning, which should provide an accessible dock area that clearly resolves the turning radii required for semitrailers to back into a row of dock spaces. Minimizing slope grades at the dock avoids dangerous situations inside the trailer as equipment that shifted during transport is unloaded. A single production can involve eight to twelve semitrailers or more, with drivers who have been on the road for hours, so a minimum of three truck docks at a bed height of 4 ft above grade expedites unloading. An additional overhead door at grade can accommodate production vans for smaller road shows.

Load-In of Stage Equipment

First priority is the load-in of electrics, soft goods, and all flown items onto the stage. A straight path from the loading-dock's overhead doors to the stage's load-in access doors is best, because trusses and set pieces as long as 20 ft cannot make sharp turns. As soon as these items have been loaded onto the stage, the electricians tie into the temporary power and the work of hanging items off the rigging-line sets begins.

◀ Oversized doors to the stage are immediately off the scene dock. A storage loft, behind the pair of doors overlooking the scene dock, takes advantage of the double-height space.

▲ A dock leveler is provided to accommodate bed heights of semitrailers and production vans at the same dock, while a separate man door is immediately adjacent to the overhead load-in door. All photos, this chapter, courtesy of Keith Gerchak.

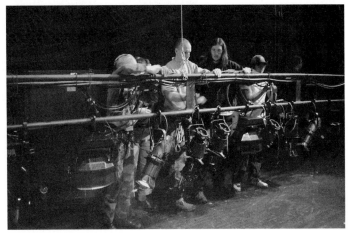

◀▲ Electricians hang performance lighting from the rigging line sets on stage.

▲ *House sound equipment is flown by motorized chain winch from strong points immediately in front of the proscenium.*

All other photos, these two pages: Carpenters hang scenery drops and flats from the rigging line sets on stage.

Load-In of Back-of-House Equipment

While this work is being done on stage, workboxes for props, wardrobe, hair, and makeup, and the company- and stage-

management teams are rolled off the next truck and into the scene dock, which is between the stage and the loading dock. Access routes to the backstage support spaces for these departments

should not cross—or interfere with work being done on—the stage. The scene dock's size and layout should facilitate flow of equipment off the truck to department destinations. Quick distribu-

tion of the workboxes should be accommodated via direct, clear circulation paths that have flat floors and are at least 8 ft wide, so that workboxes, once emptied, can be stored along the corridor

▶ *The freight elevator is visible at the opposite end of the dock, so that the flow of traffic to the stage and other program spaces at stage level remains unobstructed. Depending on wing space, the scene dock becomes storage space for set pieces as well as road boxes.*

▶▶ *Backstage corridors should be finished in durable materials to withstand abuse. The niches created by structural columns become places to store emptied workboxes, thus maintaining clear circulation paths. Pairs of doors accommodate wide theatrical equipment.*

walls and still allow minimum clear-passage widths.

Where required for security or fire separation, pairs of 3-ft doors should be provided within these backstage corridors as opposed to a single 36-in.-wide leaf, whose clear opening, reduced by projection of hardware and door thickness, cannot accommodate some equipment. Transitions between finished floor materials and between floor elevations must provide clear paths that allow large, heavy equipment to be rolled from dock to destination.

Where site restraints require distribution of backstage program spaces on multiple floor levels, a freight elevator should be clearly visible and accessible to the scene dock. However, it should allow a large enough staging area in front, so as not to disrupt the flow of equipment onto the stage or down the corridors leading to rooms on stage level.

Load-In of Front-of-House Equipment

While equipment is distributed to the stage and various points backstage, front-of-house lighting and sound elements are being loaded in. Because theatrical equipment is being hung on stage, there should be controlled, direct access that does not cross the stage to the front-of-house from the scene dock. Connections from both sides of backstage should be wide and level, as equipment is heavy and will be rolled a distance from the dock to the lobby and then into the rear of the house. These means of access also link front-of-house and back-of-house crew and staff during performances without their having to pass in front of the audience.

Access to front-of-house catwalks and the follow-spot booth should be as easy as physical and budgetary restraints allow. If one of the lobby passenger elevators cannot be extended to the catwalk level, theater planners must recognize that lighting

equipment, including follow spots, can take as many as four crew members to carry up stairs or to lift over a catwalk rail with a rope and pulley.

Load-In of Pit Equipment

Next, the props crew brings in instruments, music stands, the conductor's platform, and other items for the orchestra pit. Loading these onto a pit lift (which allows flexibility in stage depth or audience capacity when not used in the orchestra-playing position) requires access to the stage while equipment is being hung from the rigging. Extending the backstage freight elevator down to the basement level, with direct, ramped access to the pit, provides greater efficiency.

Load-In of Sets

Set pieces are last to load in, including the deck, which serves as the actual performance-stage floor. Touring productions often bring their own deck to

accommodate a specific rake, trap-door location, turntable, or other stage-floor effect critical to the production design. Anything that must cross the stage during load-in should do so before the deck is mounted over the stage floor.

BACKSTAGE ROOMS

Temporary Storage

For efficiency and therefore operational cost savings, touring-production storage space should be provided for empty workboxes, dollies, and racks once load-in is completed. Otherwise, these items will have to be loaded back onto the trucks, only to be unloaded again at the end of the production run.

Offices

Offices for touring productions include one for the company-management team, usually the manager and an assistant, and one for the stage-management team, usu-

▲ Locating the freight elevator immediately adjacent to the overhead dock door can obstruct the unloading of trucks if equipment for other floors is staged in front of it.

ally the production stage-manager and first and second assistants for a Broadway-type musical. These offices need two phone and data lines, a fax line, and high-speed Internet access, to facilitate communication with the production home office and arrangements with the next venue. Centrally locating the stage-management team office gives it accessibility not only to the stage but also to company management, department heads, and performers.

Other than a touring production's head carpenter, who often works out of the theater's stage-management office, touring productions' department heads work out of road boxes. However, each resident department head for the house has an office, a workshop, and a storage room for house equipment. Immediate adjacency to the stage or to each other is not critical.

Wardrobe

Wardrobe should have immediate access to laundry facilities, including three washers and dryers or at least hookups for rented equipment, consisting of 220V power and direct venting to the exterior. A service sink should be provided, along with shelving above for detergent and related items. The room should be sized to

▼ Carpenter's road box.

accommodate as many as twenty work-boxes, two 8-ft-long work tables for sorting laundry, and three 8-ft-long tables for costume maintenance. Since dressers collect costumes after shows for laundering or to be sent out for dry cleaning, convenience to both the scene dock and dressing rooms is essential.

Costumes travel in as many as thirty rolling gondolas, each accommodating the needs of two actors and measuring 6 ft long by 6 ft high by 18 or 24 in. deep. For efficiency, except for the stars of the production, costumes usually remain hung on these gondolas, which therefore need to be accommodated in the planning of dressing rooms.

Hair-and-Makeup and Props

The hair-and-makeup department is separate from wardrobe; but it, too, should be accessible to the dressing rooms and provided with a service sink and 220V power for traveling wig ovens. Props should have a kitchen near the stage with a counter, sink, and refrigerator to facilitate preparation of perishables used in the production.

Dressing Rooms

Dressing rooms should be convenient not only to the stage and green room but also to wardrobe, laundry, and hair-and-make-up as noted. Ideally, dressing rooms are at stage level. Star dressing-room suites should be near the stage in an area of little traffic. They should be near the conductor's dressing room, sized to accommodate a small, quick rehearsal. Multiple two- to four-person dressing rooms for principals should be the next closest to the stage, followed by chorus dressing rooms, all with their own toilet and shower facilities en suite. Where site restrictions preclude locating all dressing rooms at stage level, stairs must be easy to find and have direct access to both stage left and stage right. Even then, there should be at least one star dressing room at stage level.

To avoid clutter, damage to personal property, and possible injury, particularly in crowded chorus dressing rooms, the designer must carefully consider where to store performer street clothes and bulky personal belongings. Umbrellas, coats, hats, scarves, boots, shoes, socks, trousers, shirts, makeup kits, backpacks, purses, and dance bags must all be accommodated, in addition to production costume gondolas and personal props, such as umbrellas and purses. Shelves or cubbies installed above the makeup mirrors easily accommodate some accessories, and a fixed niche with a coat rod and shelf should also be provided. Stage-management staff collects small valuables, such as watches and wallets, which remain inaccessible in a locked road box for the duration of the show. However, there is not enough storage to secure larger items of value: purses, cameras, backpacks, and laptops. Therefore, individual lockable accommodations are recommended, which means either sizing the dressing room to accommodate a row of two-tier lockers or increasing each makeup station's width to accommodate an undercounter cabinet with a clasp on the door for a padlock.

The makeup station is the performer's work station and is ideally 3 ft wide, with a pinup corkboard for notes, reminders, and contact numbers. Incandescent lights along the top and sides of the mirror should be provided; they become extremely hot and should be caged to avoid accidents. Sinks with mirrors should be immediately accessible within the dress-

◀◀ *Lighting equipment workshop for the resident department head.*

ing area as well as in attached restrooms. A ratio of one sink per two performers and one toilet and shower per four performers is a good standard. Sinks should have enough surface area, or the mirror should have a shelf, to accommodate makeup, cold cream, shaving cream, and other general hygiene items, with a ground-fault-interrupt (GFI) outlet conveniently located. There should be a full-length mirror near the door, as well as an intercom monitor to allow the stage manager to communicate from the booth. The dressing rooms and the green room should have windows to allow natural daylight, with provisions for privacy as appropriate. Again, backstage is a work environment, and those behind the scenes for many hours a day should not be deprived of this basic amenity.

Break Rooms

Locating the green room, complete with kitchenette, between the stage and stage door allows it to function before, during, and after a performance as the cast's formal and informal gathering place. The room can also serve as a greeting area for guests, who enter through stage-door security.

Musicians usually come dressed ready for the show, as union guidelines require only a five-minute call before curtain. However, a musicians' lounge, accessible to the orchestra pit, should provide toilet facilities, an electric water cooler, a mirror, a service counter, and somewhere to sit. Lockers should also be provided, not only for backpacks, coats, and purses, as valuables are not collected by stage management, but also as secure instrument storage during nonperformance hours for those musicians not needing to carry an instrument back to a hotel room and not

wishing to leave smaller instruments unattended in the orchestra pit.

A break room for the touring and local crews should provide toilet facilities, including showers, an electric water cooler, a mirror, a kitchenette with sink and refrigerator, and tables and chairs. Also, while the crew usually comes dressed ready for the show, lockers should be provided for backpacks, coats, and purses, as their valuables are not collected by stage management.

Rehearsal Spaces

A mirrored rehearsal room with a sprung wood floor serves several functions. Cast-replacement and understudy rehearsals for the tour often take place during the week. Because of union regulations, which require crew to prepare the stage for use, rehearsing on stage can be an unnecessary labor cost, depending on the rehearsal's nature and length and the number of performers involved. A room that approximates the size of the playing area on stage avoids this cost and has the added benefit of mirrors and barres. However, if simultaneous rehearsals are needed, the rehearsal room and the stage can be used at the same time.

Also, as the dressing rooms and backstage corridors are crowded and chaotic, the rehearsal room can serve as a warm-up space, where dancers can stretch and singers can vocalize before a performance. When not in use by a touring production, the rehearsal room can generate revenue as a rental space to local arts producers.

Stage Adjacencies

Other elements essential to backstage planning include a crossover corridor that connects stage left to stage right and sound- and light-locks at the stage entrances from the crossover. There should be restrooms immediately off stage left and stage right, as well as electric water coolers. Full-length mirrors with barres near the stage sound and light locks can offer last-minute costume checks and stretching. Space to set up a table for physical therapy, whether dedicated or shared as a warm-up room, is essential for addressing dance injuries. A service sink should be accessible to the stage, but it should be in a nearby janitor's closet instead of directly on stage, where the proximity of electrical cables and the potential of spilled water on the crossover floor pose dangers.

All of the program spaces mentioned should be organized along direct, straightforward circulation paths, not only for efficiency of load-in but also for ease of navigation by those unfamiliar with the facility, who must function in a hurried state under the low light-level conditions of a performance.

BACKSTAGE DESIGN PARITY

Most professional work environments are designed with clear circulation patterns, natural light, appropriate task lighting, proper work surfaces, lockable cabinets, pinup space, kitchen facilities, adequate and convenient toilet facilities, water coolers, sufficient power outlets, and the like. Backstages are peopled with performers, musicians, crew hands, and technical and production staff, who deserve the same work environment considerations. In the end, backstage planning should comprise simple, logical layouts that ease rather than hinder navigation, that facilitate the efficiency of a production, and that provide a comfortable work environment.

INCORPORATING BUILDING CODES

JACK MARTIN *H³ Hardy Collaboration Architecture*

The intent of all building codes is to protect the health, safety, and welfare of the public. Nowhere is this protection more critical than in places of public assembly, like theaters, especially those for live performance. Their compact occupant loads and large stage areas containing sets and props are fire hazards. Relaxed code enforcement and minimal life-safety features have led to tragedies, such as the Iroquois Theater fire in Chicago in 1903, in which 602 people died in 15 minutes.

High hazards in performance venues consist of congestion, chaotic conditions caused by fire, low illumination levels, and mass exiting in short durations. These perils have resulted in special sections of building codes. Designers must thoroughly understand code issues in both the early planning and final contract documentation stages of any theater project.

JURISDICTION AND ENFORCEMENT

The Tenth Amendment of the United States Constitution states, "The powers

◀ *The charred interior of the Iroquois Theater, Chicago, 1903. Photo by Chicago Daily News, 1904, courtesy of the Theatre Historical Society of America, Elmhurst, Illinois, and the Chicago Historical Society.*

not delegated to the United States by the Constitution, nor prohibited by it to the states, are reserved to the states respectively, or to the people," leaving it to each state to decide how to enforce building regulations. To this end each state has either adopted one of the three model codes—International Building Code (IBC), Standard Building Code (SBC), or Uniform Building Code (UBC)—or prepared its own. The 2000 International Building Code unifies the other two. Many states have adopted the IBC, with each jurisdiction making it consistent with local ordinances and conditions. New York City has always used its own code, one of the nation's oldest, but it has begun adapting it to the IBC. Code citations in this chapter are based on the 2000 IBC.

Process

Though a theater's design varies according to the approach taken by architect and client, code requirements are constant. They are an essential part of the program provided by the architect prior to conceptual or schematic design, and they define many elements of a project's scope of work, among them seating configurations, circulation routes, accessibility, public floor area, and location of entries and exits. If these basic planning issues are not addressed and thoroughly understood from the beginning of a project, redesign is inevitable, and will cause great difficulty for the architect and cost issues for the client.

The architect's first task is to contact the local code-enforcement agency to determine the site's code jurisdiction. Careful investigation of all local ordinances is essential and should be done as early as possible, while the program is being developed with the client.

Code Analysis

Once the model code has been identified, a theater code analysis is made in two parts. The first takes place in the theater's schematic-design phase, and its components are discussed in IBC—Chapter 3, "Use and Occupancy Classification"; Chapter 4, "Special Detailed Requirements Based on Use and Occupancy"; Chapter 5, "General Building Heights and Areas"; and Chapter 6, "Types of Construction." The second part of the analysis is performed during the design-development phase and covers fire protection, occupant needs, building envelope, structural systems, structural materials, nonstructural materials, building services, special services, and conditions and standards. Having completed the analysis, the architect incorporates these considerations into the construction documents. For complex projects, the architect should retain the services of a code consultant.

Documentation Plan Approval

The architect must submit plan sets to the building department early in the design process, not only because deviations from the code require a meeting with code officials but also because alternative safety features may be mandated to compensate for deviations. Once code officials accept an approach, the architect sets a schedule that allows time to coordinate and follow up plan reviews. Upon acceptance of code variances, the architect completes the process by filing all the construction documents. Their approval allows the client's contractor to obtain the necessary permits.

USING THE CODE

The American Institute of Architects (AIA) suggests the following steps in Section 3.72, Building Codes and Regulations, of the *Architect's Handbook of Professional Practice*.

Step 1

Establish building occupancy

Theaters usually have fixed seating, which produces buildings with high-occupancy densities. As a result, a separate classification has been established called Assembly Group A-1, Theater. However, if a space holds fewer than fifty people and is an accessory to another kind of occupancy, then it can be classified under that occupancy (IBC 303.1). If a building has mixed uses with different classifications, such as A-1, Theater, and E, Educational, fire walls must be provided to separate them. Ratings of fire walls can be found in the code's Table 302.3.3. One of the benefits of the IBC is that if the building conforms to the building type, area, height, and fire protection requirements of the most demanding occupancy, occupancy separations may not be required (IBC 302.3.2).

IBC Chapter 3, "Use and Occupancy Classification," outlines these requirements.

Step 2

Establish building height, area, and type of construction

Three elements of a theater that are interrelated in the code are height, area, and type of construction. The architect must be aware of the critical impact these elements have on the theater's design. Height and area define a theater's massing. Depending on the size of a theater's program area, seating capacity, and volume, several construction types can be considered. Large theaters, especially those with a fly tower more than 100 ft tall, require a more expensive Type I construction, because Type I has higher fire-resistive ratings than Type V construction, which has much less resistance to fire. The added investment of the high-rated construction assemblies allows larger seating capacities and enhances production opportunities provided

▼ *2000 International Building Code Table 503 (Groups A-1 through A-5). Allowable height and building areas. Above and remainder of tables and illustrations, this chapter, from 2000 International Building Code Commentary, Volume 1. © 2001. Falls Church, Virginia: International Code Council, Inc. Reproduced with permission. All rights reserved.*

TABLE 503
ALLOWABLE HEIGHT AND BUILDING AREAS
Height limitations shown as stories and feet above grade plane.
Area limitations as determined by the definition of "Area, building," per floor.

GROUP		TYPE I A	TYPE I B	TYPE II A	TYPE II B	TYPE III A	TYPE III B	TYPE IV HT	TYPE V A	TYPE V B
	HGT(feet) Hgt(S)	UL	160	65	55	65	55	65	50	40
A-1	S	UL	5	3	2	3	2	3	2	1
	A	UL	UL	15,500	8,500	14,000	8,500	15,000	11,500	5,500
A-2	S	UL	11	3	2	3	2	3	2	1
	A	UL	UL	15,500	9,500	14,000	9,500	15,000	11,500	6,000
A-3	S	UL	11	3	2	3	2	3	2	1
	A	UL	UL	15,500	9,500	14,000	9,500	15,000	11,500	6,000
A-4	S	UL	11	3	2	3	2	3	2	1
	A	UL	UL	15,500	9,500	14,000	9,500	15,000	11,500	6,000
A-5	S	UL	UL	UL	UL	UL	UL	UL	UL	UL
	A	UL	UL	UL	UL	UL	UL	UL	UL	UL

by the fly tower. A fly tower provides greater flexibility in staging and set design. Construction types I through IV have graduated height ratings and area limitations, shown in IBC Table 503.

Structural frame components, walls, partitions, and floor and roof elements have fire-resistance ratings that vary greatly by the degree of protection needed for the theater's massing height and area, shown in IBC Table 601.

▼ 2000 International Building Code Table 601, Fire-resistance rating requirements for building elements (hours).

IBC Chapter 5, "General Building Heights and Areas," outlines these requirements, and IBC Chapter 6 addresses "Types of Construction."

Step 3
Determine the location on the property
Eliminating the spread of fire both inside and outside a building is the building code's primary objective. Two precautions

TABLE 601
FIRE-RESISTANCE RATING REQUIREMENTS FOR BUILDING ELEMENTS (hours)

BUILDING ELEMENT	TYPE I		TYPE II		TYPE III		TYPE IV	TYPE V	
	A	B	A[d]	B	A[d]	B	HT	A[d]	B
Structural frame [a] Including columns, girders, trusses	3[b]	2[b]	1	0	1	0	HT	1	0
Bearing walls Exterior[f] Interior	3 3[b]	2 2[b]	1 1	0 0	2 1	2 0	2 1/HT	1 1	0 0
Nonbearing walls and partitions Exterior Interior[e]	See Table 602 See Section 602.4.6								
Floor construction Including supporting beams and joists	2	2	1	0	1	0	HT	1	0
Roof construction Including supporting beams and joists	$1\frac{1}{2}$[c]	1[c]	1[c]	0	1[c]	0	HT	1[c]	0

For SI: 1 foot = 304.8 mm.

a. The structural frame shall be considered to be the columns and the girders, beams, trusses and spandrels having direct connections to the columns and bracing members designed to carry gravity loads. The members of floor or roof panels which have no connection to the columns shall be considered secondary members and not a part of the structural frame.

b. Roof supports: Fire-resistance ratings of structural frame and bearing walls are permitted to be reduced by 1 hour where supporting a roof only

c. 1. Except in Factory-Industrial (F-1), Hazardous (H), Mercantile (M) and Moderate-Hazard Storage (S-1) occupancies, fire protection of structural members shall not be required, including protection of roof raming and decking where every part of the roof construction is 20 feet or more above any floor immediately below. Fire-retardant treated wood members shall be allowed to be used for such unprotected members.

   2. In all occupancies, heavy timber shall be allowed where a 1-hour or less fire-resistance rating is required.

   3. In Type I and Type II construction, fire-retardant-treated wood shall be allowed in buildings not over two stories including girders and trusses as part of the roof construction.

d. An approved automatic sprinkler system in accordance with Section 903.3.1.1. shall be allowed to be substituted for 1-hour fire-resistance-rated construction, provided such system is not otherwise required by other provisions o the code or used for an allowable area increase in accordance with Section 506.3 or an allowable height increase in accordance with Section 504.2. The 1-hour substitution for the fire resistance of exterior walls shall not be permitted.

e. For interior nonbearing partitions in Type IV construction, also see Section 602.4.6.

f. Not less than the fire-resistance rating based on fire separation distance (see Table 602).

that must be taken in theater design are preventing fire and smoke within the building and preventing them from spreading to or from adjacent buildings. Fire-resistance ratings vary by the theater's proximity to the property line of an adjacent site. Once a theater has been sited on its property, basic fire-resistive-rated building elements address these two code concerns. These ratings are based on construction type as discussed in step 2 above. Fire-resistance ratings of such building components as structure, walls, floors, and roofs can be determined by following the procedures enumerated in sections 703.3, 719, and 720 of the IBC. The fire-resistance ratings listed in Section 719 were established by actual tests of the wall assembly and cannot be altered. For material assemblies that have not been tested, see Section 720 of the IBC.

IBC Chapter 7, "Fire-Resistance-Rated Construction," outlines these requirements.

Step 4

Determine whether a fire-suppression system is required

Fire-suppression systems consist of automatic sprinklers, standpipes, fire alarms, detection systems, and portable fire extinguishers. A theater's capacity determines which of these and how many it will include. An automatic sprinkler system is required if the fire area is more than 12,000 sq ft or has an occupant load of more than 300 persons or a fire area at an elevation different from the exit doors discharging at grade level to a public way, such as a street or alley (903.2.1). An automatic sprinkler system permits increased exit-travel distances and reduction of required fire-resistance ratings of some structure components (IBC Table 601,

noted). A standpipe system is required if the highest story is more than 30 ft above or below a level that provides accessible right-of-way for fire-department vehicle access (IBC 905.3.1). Additional suppression systems are required for stage areas and are described in Step 6.

A manual fire-alarm system is required if the occupant load is more than 300 persons. However, fire alarm boxes are not required if the theater has sprinklers and if its notification appliances (bell, horn, speaker, light, or text display) activate upon sprinkler flow (IBC 907.2.1). Activation of a fire-alarm signal must use an emergency voice-alarm communication system if the occupant load is more than 1,000 persons (IBC 907.2.1.1). Emergency power is mandatory for voice-alarm communications systems (IBC 907.2.1.2).

IBC Chapter 9, "Fire Protection Systems," outlines these requirements.

Step 5

Establish parameters for the egress system

Occupant load calculation

The calculation of a theater's occupant load is based on Table 1003.2.2.2. Increased occupant loads, beyond Table 1003.2.2.2, are allowed when sufficient egress capacity is provided and when a density of 1 occupant per 5 sq ft is not exceeded (IBC 1003.2.2.4). The occupant load of an assembly area with fixed seats and aisles is determined by the actual number of seats configured in an architect's layout. Occupancy loads must be calculated for the stage area as well as the audience area. The maximum occupant load permitted on the stage is 15 sq ft per occupant. Once the occupant load has been fully calculated, the width of the means of egress as well as the capacity, number, and location of exits in an assembly area can be designed.

Capacity, number, and location of exits in an assembly area

Because a theater has unique safety issues, exit access, the exit itself, and the exit discharge (stairs and doors at grade level to a public way, such as a street or alley) require special compliance. IBC Section 1008 guides theater-code design. It is written specially for places of assembly, and its calculations for means of egress are more restrictive than those for other occupancies.

The distribution and number of exits establishes the overall egress circulation pattern in theater auditoriums at all lev-

els. Exit-distribution requirements in Section 1008 provide exit capacity for auditoriums whose occupant load exceeds 300 people in the Group A occupancy classification (IBC 1008.1) established in Step 1. Each level requires a main exit—sized for one half the occupant load that either directly accesses a street or fronts on an occupied space—at least 10 ft wide adjacent to street. Because most occupants are not familiar with the theater, this requirement assumes that in an emergency they would take the same route leaving the theater they used when they entered.

In addition to the main exit, other exits must be evenly distributed, sized for the other half of the occupant load, as shown in IBC Figure 1008.1.

▶ *2000 International Building Code Figure 1008.1 Group A-1, With waiting space.*

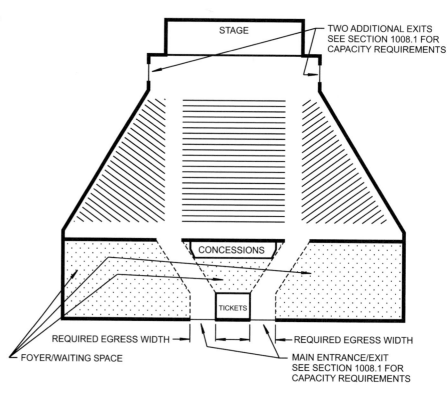

Should a main exit not be well defined, as in a stadium or a large arts center, the aggregate width of all exits must be sized for 100 percent of the theater's occupant load.

Balconies with a capacity that exceeds 50 people require two means of egress, one on each side. One egress path must connect to an exit. The other can consist of open stairs between the balcony and the orchestra level (IBC 1008.4).

Escalators provide an efficient method of moving large numbers of people in a short time. They are especially effective when a theater is one or two stories above grade level, and they are preferable to stairs or elevators. However, IBC 1003.2.9 does not allow escalators to be counted as a legal means of egress. They provide only convenience.

Travel distance

The organization and number of exit locations and placement of aisles leading to exits is always determined by travel distance. The maximum distance from any seat in the house to the exit door is 200 ft unless the building has a full sprinkler system, in which case an increase to 250 ft is permitted (IBC 1008.6). Travel distance is calculated along pathways and is never measured diagonally over seats in an enclosed theater. Travel distances can also be extended if smoke-protected assembly seating is provided (IBC 1008.6.1). Smoke-protected assembly seating is defined as seating with egress that is not subject to smoke buildup. Methods of providing smoke-protected seating are described below.

Features of a smoke-protected environment include a smoke-control system or natural ventilation designed to keep smoke 6 ft above the floor of the means

of egress (IBC 1008.5.2.1). In addition, the lowest part of the roof height must be maintained at least 15 ft above the highest aisle (IBC 1008.5.2.2), and an automatic sprinkler system (IBC 1008.5.2.3) is required.

Aisles

The width of an aisle depends on the seating configuration and catchment area it serves. The catchment area is the occupant load served by the aisle and is calculated by the number of seats feeding into the aisle. A balanced positioning of egress doors, aisles, ramps, vomitoriums, and pathways must be configured in proportion to the capacity of the seating area served as shown in IBC Figure 1008.7.2.

The width of egress aisles utilizing stairs and ramps varies depending on whether or not a smoke-protection environment is provided in seating areas. Compliance with IBC 1008.5.2 is required when smoke-protected seating is provided. Features of a smoke-protected environment include a smoke-control system or natural ventilation designed to keep smoke 6 ft above the floor of the means of egress (IBC 1008.5.2.1). In addition, the lowest part of the roof height must be at least 15 ft above the highest aisle (IBC 1008.5.2.2), as shown in IBC Figure 1008.5.2.2 (1), and an automatic sprinkler system (IBC 1008.5.2.3) is required. IBC 1008.5.2 permits reduced aisle widths when smoke-protected seating is provided, but then a life safety evaluation is required that complies with the National Fire Protection Association's (NFPA) code 101. A life safety evaluation is a written review that considers the adequacy of life-safety features and is required where occupancy load exceeds 6,000 people (National Fire Protection Association Life

▶ *2000 International Building Code Figure 1008.7.2, Typical aisle catchments.*

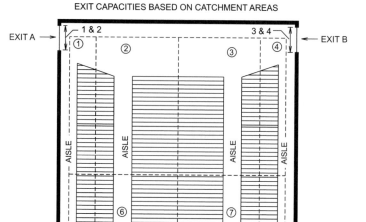

EXIT CAPACITIES BASED ON CATCHMENT AREAS

NOTE: FOR MINIMUM AISLE WIDTHS, SEE SECTION 1008.7.1.
EXIT A IS DESIGNED FOR OCCUPANTS
IN CATCHMENT AREAS ① AND ②.

◯ INDICATES A CATCHMENT AREA

Safety Code 12.1.7.3.) Safety measures are analyzed for the type of venue being designed, access and egress movement, crowd-density problems, fire hazards, and building systems (NFPA 12.4.1.)

Aisle widths are based on two calculations. The first is the number of occupants served in the seating catchment area. The second is the type of aisle needed in the theater as determined by sight lines. If a shallow, raked, sloped-ramp aisle is used, then 0.2 in. per person of aisle width is required, as shown in IBC Figure 1008.5.1 (2). If steps are used in the aisle, then 0.3 in. per person of aisle width is required (IBC 1008.5.2), as

shown in IBC Figure 1008.5.1 (1). Steps will result in greater widths than ramps, because it takes more time to exit the space and more people per area must be accommodated.

The illumination level of all means of egress may not be less than 1 footcandle (fc) at floor level. To enhance the experience of theater performance, this illumination level can be reduced at aisle access ways in Group A to 0.2 fc if the required illumination is automatically restored when the fire-alarm system activates (IBC 1003.2.11).

In no case may aisle widths be designed under the code minimums. Most typical is

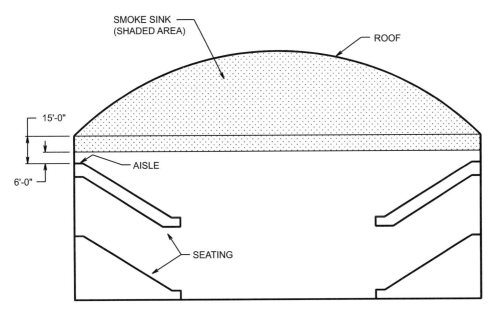

SMOKE SINK
(SHADED AREA)

ROOF

15'-0"

AISLE

6'-0"

SEATING

For SI: 1 inch = 25.4 mm, 1 foot = 304.8 mm.

the 48-in. minimum aisle (IBC 1008.7.1), provided when there is seating on both sides of an aisle. This width may be reduced as follows:

- Aisle is subdivided by a center rail: 23 in.
- Aisle serves fewer than five rows on one side: 23 in.
- Aisle serves fewer than 50 people: 36 in.
- Seating is on only one side of an aisle: 36 in.
- Seating is on both sides of an aisle, with no steps that are either ramped or level, that serves fewer than 50 people, typically occurring at the orchestra level: 36 in.
- Seating is on one side of an aisle with no steps that are either ramped or level, typically occurring at the orchestra level: 36 in.

- There is seating on both sides of an aisle, with no steps that are either ramped or level, typically occurring at the orchestra level: 42 in.

Seating capacity in rows
The critical limitation in the number of seats permitted in a row is the horizontal clearance between chairs. Once rows have been established, the number of seats in a row determines the placement of aisles in a theater auditorium. A maximum of 100 seats is permitted in a dual-access row with direct passage to aisles or doors and with sufficient horizontal clearance between chairs (IBC 1008.8.1). The minimum clearance of 12 in. (as measured from the back of the row ahead and the nearest projection of the row behind) is the basis for calculating the number of seats in a row as shown in IBC Figure 1008.8.

▲ *2000 International Building Code Figure 1008.5.2.2 (1), Roof height (convex dome roof).*

▸ *2000 International Building Code Figure 1008.5.1 (2), Computation of width for level aisles or for aisles with ramps.*

▸▸ *2000 International Building Code Figure 1008.5.1 (1), Computation of width for stepped aisles.*

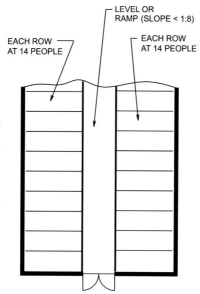

LEVEL OR RAMP (SLOPE < 1:8)

EACH ROW AT 14 PEOPLE

EACH ROW AT 14 PEOPLE

9 ROWS PER SIDE
252 PEOPLE PER CATCHMENT AREA
252 × 0.2 PER PERSON = 50.4" REQ'D AISLE WIDTH

For SI: 1 inch = 25.4 mm.

STAIR AISLES (7" MAX. RISE, 11" MIN. TREAD DEPTH)

EACH ROW AT 14 PEOPLE

EACH ROW AT 14 PEOPLE

9 ROWS PER SIDE
252 PEOPLE PER CATCHMENT AREA
252 × 0.3" PER PERSON = 75.6" REQ'D AISLE WIDTH

For SI: 1 inch = 25.4 mm.

▸ *2000 International Building Code Figure 1008.8, Minimum required row width clearance.*

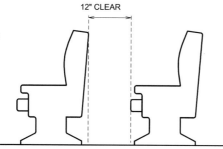

12" CLEAR

FIXED SEATING

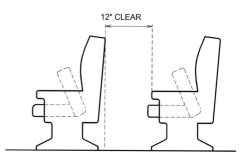

12" CLEAR

AUTOMATIC OR SELF-RISING SEATS

For SI: 1 inch = 25.4 mm.

TABLE 1008.8.1
SMOKE-PROTECTED GRANDSTAND
ASSEMBLY AISLE ACCESSWAYS

TOTAL NUMBER OF SEATS IN THE SMOKE-PROTECTED ASSEMBLY OCCUPANCY	MAXIMUM NUMBER OF SEATS PER ROW PERMITTED TO HAVE A MINIMUM 12-INCH CLEAR WIDTH AISLE ACCESSWAY	
	Aisle or doorway at both ends of row	Aisle or doorway at one end of row only
Less than 4,000	14	7
4,000	15	7
7,000	16	8
10,000	17	8
13,000	18	9
16,000	19	9
19,000	20	10
22,000 and greater	21	11

For SI: 1 inch = 25.4 mm.

◀ 2000 International Building Code Table 1008.8.1, Smoke-protected grandstand assembly aisle accessways.

▼ 2000 International Building Code Figure 1008.8.1, Typical dual access row—minimum accessway width.

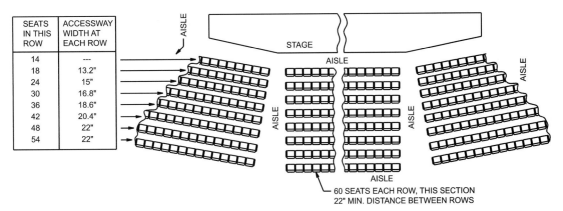

SEATS IN THIS ROW	ACCESSWAY WIDTH AT EACH ROW
14	---
18	13.2"
24	15"
30	16.8"
36	18.6"
42	20.4"
48	22"
54	22"

60 SEATS EACH ROW, THIS SECTION
22" MIN. DISTANCE BETWEEN ROWS

For SI: 1 inch = 25.4 mm.

Smoke-protected assembly seating permits an increase in the number of seats per row, as shown in Table 1008.8.1, and varies with an auditorium's total occupancy. Also, automatic self-rising chairs efficiently increase the number of seats permissible in a row, because this measurement is used when seats are in the upright position. Clearance must be increased for every seat that exceeds 14 in a row, up to 22 in. The increase is based on 0.3 in. for each seat beyond 14 seats. For example, 15 in. is required for a dual-access row with 24 seats (12-in. minimum clearance for the first 14 seats and 0.3 x 10, or 3 in. for the additional 10 seats.)

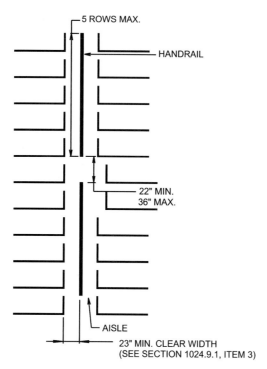

5 ROWS MAX.

HANDRAIL

22" MIN.
36" MAX.

AISLE

23" MIN. CLEAR WIDTH
(SEE SECTION 1024.9.1, ITEM 3)

For SI: 1 inch = 25.4 mm.

▲ *2000 International Building Code Figure 1008.11.1, Discontinuous aisle handrails.*

Steps, ramps, and sight lines

The architectural cross-section of a theater is the result of careful sight-line relationships between the stage acting area and the eyes of the audience at every row. Once sight lines have been determined in the cross-section, the floor elevation of each row can be established. Coordination with aisle walking surfaces (that are slip resistant) must then be considered in accordance with IBC 1008.9. To accomplish these elevations, ramps at aisles can be used up to a slope of 1 in 8 units of measurement (12.5 percent slope.)

When sight lines dictate a slope steeper than permitted by ramps, steps can be used at aisles. Treads must be a minimum of 11 in., with the treads immediately above and below within $\frac{3}{16}$ in. (0.188). Risers can vary between 4 and 8 in., as long as they are uniform within each flight of steps. The riser requirement is a crucial consideration of the IBC code, because it allows riser-height nonuniformity to accommodate theater sight lines, which vary geometrically in cross-section as the rows recede from the stage. To compensate for uneven riser heights, which can be tripping hazards especially in low lighting, contrasting marking stripes, 1 to 2 in. in width, are required at all nosings.

Handrails

Handrails must be provided at ramped aisles exceeding a slope of 1 in 15 units of measurement (6.7-percent slope) and at all aisle steps (IBC 1008.11). This requirement is waived if ramps do not exceed a slope of 1 in 8 (12.5-percent slope), and seating is on both sides of the aisle. Handrails can be placed at intervals of 5 rows or less, providing easier access to the patron's seat, as shown in IBC Figure 1008.11.1.

Guards and sight lines

The design of a guard is usually a low wall or an open-pipe railing system. It is important for the architect to understand where and how guards can be configured so they do not block sight lines, as shown in IBC Figure 1008.12.2.

Guard heights of 42 in. at mezzanines, stairways, ramps, and landings are required where there is an elevation change of 30 in. or more to a floor adjacent to the seating area (IBC 1003.2.12). To accommodate sight lines, guards as low as 26 in. can be provided at cross aisles with an elevation change of 30 in. or less to an adjacent floor. A guard at the cross-aisle

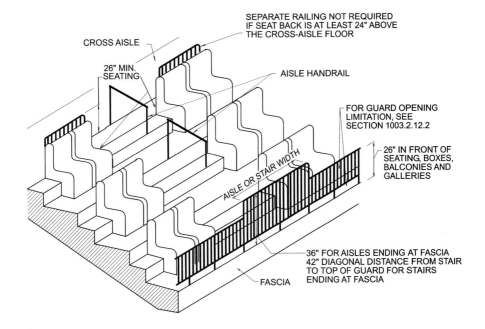

CROSS AISLE

SEPARATE RAILING NOT REQUIRED
IF SEAT BACK IS AT LEAST 24" ABOVE
THE CROSS-AISLE FLOOR

26" MIN.
SEATING

AISLE HANDRAIL

FOR GUARD OPENING
LIMITATION, SEE
SECTION 1003.2.12.2

26" IN FRONT OF
SEATING, BOXES,
BALCONIES AND
GALLERIES

AISLE OR STAIR WIDTH

36" FOR AISLES ENDING AT FASCIA
42" DIAGONAL DISTANCE FROM STAIR
TO TOP OF GUARD FOR STAIRS
ENDING AT FASCIA

FASCIA

For SI: 1 inch = 25.4 mm.

floor is eliminated if the seat-back height along the cross aisle is 24 in. or greater.

To further enhance sight lines, 26-in.-high guards can be provided at seating areas with an elevation change of 30 in. or less to an adjacent floor. This can occur at parterres, which are used at the orchestra level, and at side boxes stepping down at the upper-balcony levels.

High guards of 36 in., with open railing systems, are permitted at the ends of aisles if there is clearance of 42 in. as measured on the diagonal between the railing member and the nearest tread nosing.

Accessibility
The IBC requires buildings and their sites to be made accessible to persons with physical disabilities. American National Standards Institute (ANSI) A117.1, referenced in IBC Section 1101.2, is similar in scope to the Americans with Disabilities Act Accessibility Guidelines (ADAAG). IBC addresses exterior accessibility for parking, loading zones, pathways to building, and, for theaters of varied capacities, interior seating accommodations for the physically disabled.

Table 1107.2.2 in the IBC code outlines the ratio of wheelchair spaces to assembly capacity. It does not completely correspond to ADAAG and is compared to ADA (7-1-99 Edition) guidelines below. Where there is a discrepancy between the two, as in number of accessible wheelchair spaces, it is recommended

▲ *2000 International Building Code Figure 1008.12.2, Typical balcony guards at fascia.*

ACCESSIBILITY REQUIREMENTS: ONE ROUTE CONNECTS ALL ACCESSIBLE SPACES*

Width	3'0" minimum clearance at accessible-route lengths greater than 24" 2'8" minimum clearance at accessible-route lengths less than 24"
Doors	2'8" minimum clearance
Headroom	6'8" minimum clearance of protruding object
Floor slope	1:20 units of measurement maximum permitted (if steeper, floor must be designed as a ramp)
Ramp slope	1:12 maximum permitted

*ICC/ANSI A117.1, 1998: Chapter 4.

ACCESSIBILITY REQUIREMENTS: ONE PASSENGER ELEVATOR SERVES EACH LEVEL*

Automatic operation	6'8" W × 4'6" D (center 3'6" door opening)
Minimum dimensions of car	5'8" W × 4'6" D (off-center 3'0" door opening)

*ICC/ANSI A117.1, 1998: Chapter 4.

that the more restrictive requirement be followed. Two features to plan in the layouts consist of one seat for an able companion next to each wheelchair position and wheelchair clusters in the minimum numbers stated in Table 1107.2.2.1. IBC allows theaters to achieve sight lines by reducing the number of wheelchair clusters by half (see IBC 1107.2.2.1, Exception) when row-elevations have more than one step between them. The IBC and ADA share the requirement that wheelchair clusters be dispersed. IBC bases dispersal on availability of accessible routes to various levels, while ADA requires that wheelchair positions be provided for all ticket prices. This may create another discrepancy between ADA and IBC stipulations should ticket prices vary at theaters with two balconies, because IBC does not require access to the second balcony (see IBC 1107.2.3.1).

Other accessibility features addressed in IBC are toilet facilities and elevator requirements.

While there is a high level of requirements to be coordinated between ADAAG and the IBC code, the ADA guidelines include several areas (public telephones and signage) not included in the IBC code.

A summary of key International Code Council and American National Standards Institute (ICC/ANSI) A117.1-1998 requirements for areas outside the auditorium is given in the tables above.

Not all accessibility requirements are the same in the IBC and ADA guidelines. See the tables on the opposite page. To avoid liability problems, the architect would be wise to use the more restrictive of the two accessibility requirements.

An exception in the IBC code allows the number of space clusters to be re-

REQUIRED WHEELCHAIR-ACCESSIBLE SPACES: IBC VS. ADA			
Theater Capacity	IBC Table 1107.2.2	ADA 7/2/99 Edition	Use
4–25 seats	1	1	1
26–50 seats	2	2	2
51–100 seats	4	4	4
101–300 seats	5	4	5
301–500 seats	6	6	6
More than 500 seats	6+1 additional space per increase of 200 seats	6+1 additional space per increase of 100 seats	6+1 additional space per increase of 100 seats

REQUIRED WHEELCHAIR SPACE CLUSTERS: IBC VS. ADA			
Theater Capacity	IBC Table 1107.2.1	ADA (7/1/99 Edition)	Use
Up to 300 seats	1	1	1
300–600 seats	2	*	**
601–900 seats	3	*	**
901–1,500 seats	4	*	**
1,501–2,100 seats	5	*	**
More than 3,000 seats	6 + 1 additional cluster per 1,000 seats or portion thereof	*	**

Provide more than one location or one location for each ticket-price area.

** *Provide per IBC cluster count. This must include one location for each ticket-price area.*

duced by one half where more than one step between rows is required to accommodate sight lines (IBC: 1107.2.2.1, Exception). This exception pertains only to areas with multiple steps, typically at balcony levels.

Another exception to the number of space clusters in balcony areas is provided in the code. If the balcony contains 25 percent or less of the theater's total capac-ity, and if the balcony contains fewer than 300 seats, no access is needed. All wheelchair spaces and clusters are permit-ted by code only at the orchestra level (IBC: 1107.2.3.1, Exception 2). However, this may conflict with ADA guidelines should there be a choice of admission price at upper-balcony areas that vary from lower and orchestra areas. ADA guidelines require one location for each ticket-price area. The more restrictive requirement should be used.

- Size: 3'0" W × 4'0" D (with forward or rear access) or 3'0" W × 5'0" D (with side access). Width can be reduced to 2'9" in. when multiple wheelchair spaces are adjacent to each other (ICC/ANSI A117.1-1998: Section 801 and 802).

- At least one companion fixed seat shall be provided next to each wheelchair-seating area (ICC 2000: 1107.2.2).

- Access to performing areas requires a minimum 60-in. wheelchair turning space (ICC/ANSI A117, Section 803).
  a. Fitting rooms
  b. Locker rooms
  c. Dressing rooms

- Accessibility is not required at following areas (ICC 2000: 1103.2.8 and 1103.2.9):
  a. Nonoccupiable spaces accessed by ladders, catwalks, and freight elevators (used for load-in).
  b. Spaces used by service personnel
  c. Elevator pits
  d. Elevator penthouses
  e. Piping catwalks
  f. Equipment catwalks

IBC Chapter 10, "Means of Egress," outlines these requirements, and Chapter 11 addresses "Accessibility." References are made to ICC/ANSI A117.1 (1998 version). The ADA (whose guidelines generally match ICC/ANSI A117.1-1998) is a law that was enacted by Congress in July 1990.

Step 6
Check detailed fire-performance requirements that apply to the specific occupancy and construction type

Requirements for the stage house
Stage design creates code challenges that must be carefully considered to avoid disaster. Because of performance demands, which may have combustible scenery, stages are treated separately in the code. A stage is considered a large room that can be completely separated from the rest of the theater complex with rated-wall construction that must extend from foundation to roof.

Two stage elements that trigger special code features are height and floor area. Once the stage exceeds a height of 50 ft and a floor area of 1,000 ft, fire-prevention construction enhancements are required. A two-hour fire-resistive wall is required at the proscenium wall between the auditorium and stage at all levels of the theater. Either a material fire curtain or a water-curtain sprinkler system must protect the proscenium opening (IBC 410.3.4). A material fire curtain is generally preferred by theater companies, because the sprinkler system of a water curtain may be activated accidentally, causing tremendous damage not only to the theater facility but also to expensive sets. When water curtains are activated, performances will be cancelled for weeks, even months, until damaged areas and sets are rebuilt.

Two means of egress are required, one on each side of the stage. Back-of-house actor areas adjacent to the stage must be separated by fire-rated walls to maintain a safe facility, especially when the stage is fully loaded with scenery and sets. Direct stage access is provided by fire-rated doors in the fire-rated walls separating stage and back-of-house actor areas. The challenge of providing both emergency egress and back-of-house access is easily met when they are planned so they use common pathways that lead to an approved exit.

Only one means of egress is required to provide access to the fly galleries, gridiron, and catwalks that service the technical stagecraft demands of a performance, including rigging and stage-lighting systems.

Automatic sprinkler systems are required at all stage areas. Fixed projections (fly galleries, gridiron, and catwalks) must have sprinklers both above and below. Installation of a sprinkler system allows for enhanced theater performances and for utilization of a stage house with a full fly tower. If sprinkler systems are not used, no trap areas can be built below the stage deck, the floor area must be less than 1,000 sq ft, and the stage height cannot exceed 50 ft. Also, scenery is limited to props that cannot be flown from above the stage. Only simple hangings, curtains, and borders can be used. Placement of scenery is restricted to the stage deck.

A standpipe system is required for stages greater than 1,000 sq ft. If a theater has a sprinkler system, hose connections on both sides of the stage can be made from sprinkler piping, per IBC 905.3.5.

Interior finishes

Interior finish types allowed in Assembly Group A-1, Theater Occupancy, depend on whether or not the building has sprinklers and are shown in Table 803.4. The finishes are separated into three classes that establish their flame-spread index. This index is a measurement of each finish type's relative burning characteristic. Class A has a flame spread of 0–25 and consists of such finishes as masonry and gypsum board; Class B has a flame spread of 26–75 and consists of certain types of carpet; Class C has a flame spread of 76–200 and consists of such finishes as untreated wood paneling. Class B and C flame-spread finishes are permitted in buildings with sprinklers. The more restricted Class A and B flame-spread finishes are permitted in buildings without sprinklers.

IBC Chapter 4, "Special Detailed Requirements Based on Use and Occupancy," outlines these requirements, and Chapter 8 addresses "Interior Finishes."

Step 7

Determine compliance with interior environment requirements

IBC addresses many interior nonfire protection issues, such as ventilation, temperature control, lighting, yards and courts, sound transmission, room dimensions, and surrounding materials. IBC section 1207 provides the minimum dimensions of spaces that are habitable. Minimum room width is 7 ft. Room heights must be at least 7 ft 6 in. However, theater areas such as bathrooms, toilet rooms, kitchens, storage rooms, and laundry rooms are allowed a minimum height of 7 ft.

IBC Chapter 12, "Interior Environment," outlines these requirements.

Step 8

Determine compliance with exterior envelope requirements

The architect must consider the energy required for a theater's large volumes. Energy-efficient envelopes, mechanical, lighting, and power systems that emphasize performance are essential to the successful operation of a theater, whose intermittent operating hours allow this kind of expenditure. The International Energy Conservation Code (IECC) regulates the design scope of public-assembly building components (IECC 101.4), such as exterior envelopes, mechanical systems, lighting, and power systems by positing prescriptive and performance requirements. Outdoor design temperature, degree-days (units of measure used to calculate heating and cooling loads of a building), and climate zone are the basis for code energy calculations (IECC 302.1). These three parameters establish design criteria, and they vary depending on site location of the theater.

Once the design criteria have been established, the building components can be developed in compliance with the total building performance (IECC 806.0). Two important considerations in the design of theaters are the exterior building envelope and interior lighting design.

A theater's exterior appearance is affected by the amount of glazing used. Glazed areas that are no more than 50 percent of the exterior skin are controlled by the energy code (IECC 802.1). However, should this percentage be greater than 50 percent, guidelines issued by the American Society of Heating, Refrigerating, and Air-Conditioning Engineers (ASHRAE) and the Illuminating Engineering Society (IES) are used.

Interior lighting power calculations for theaters with live performance permit 1.4 watts per sq ft for the building or 1.5 watts per sq ft for the portion of the building used as a theater (IECC Table 805.4.2). An additional 1.0 watts per sq ft can be provided for lighting equipment, such as stagecraft lighting, which requires enormous amounts of energy during performance.

IBC Chapter 13, "Energy Efficiency," outlines these requirements (with reference made to the International Energy Conservation Code). Technical requirements of the exterior envelope are provided in IBC's Chapter 14, "Exterior Walls," and Chapter 15, "Roof Assemblies and Rooftop Structures."

Step 9

Determine compliance requirements for structure and materials

The code establishes the engineering criteria for the structure. The structural engineer must consider the live loads permitted (Table 1607.1) for places of assembly, which greatly vary in different occupied areas of a theater. For example, spaces whose density is undefined (lobbies and theaters with movable seats) must be designed to a minimum of 100 pounds per sq ft (psf) and cannot be reduced (1607.9.1.3) in public-assembly occupancies. An even greater live load is required at the stage area. This requirement enhances flexibility of various staging configurations by the set designer. As a result, it must be designed to a minimum of 125 psf. However, well-defined areas have reduced live load requirements. Auditorium areas with fixed seats fastened to the floor can be designed to a minimum of 60 psf. Theater auditorium support spaces, such as follow spot, projection, and control rooms can be designed to a minimum of 50 psf, catwalks to a minimum of 40 psf.

Seismic considerations vary by location, and a significant portion of IBC Chapter 16 is dedicated to earthquake loads and site ground motion. Coordination with the structural engineer is critical for this building type.

IBC code requirements for structural materials (concrete, aluminum, masonry, steel, and wood) and nonstructural materials (glass, glazing, gypsum board, plaster, and plastic) must also be met.

IBC Chapter 16, "Structural Design," outlines these requirements; IBC Chapters 19–23 address "Structural Materials"; and Chapters 24 to 26, "Non-Structural Materials."

Step 10

Determine compliance with building services systems requirements

As the design development is advanced and the engineering of a theater's design progresses, code requirements for electrical, mechanical, plumbing, elevator, conveying, and special construction, such as marquees, must be adhered to.

Toilets

The design and location of public toilets at the front of the house greatly influence a theater's operation. Their resolution has a considerable impact on the patron's enjoyment of the theater. Pedestrian movement in a theater needs to address the congestion often created by peak use of toilet rooms during intermission. It is of such consequence that many of New York's historic Broadway theaters and older theaters in other cities have enjoyed rejuvenation in the past decade. Historic landmarked theaters in Boston, Washington, D.C., Los Angeles, Chicago, and Baltimore have been significantly altered to increase the number of toilets. These modifications have been especially important for women's restrooms and have resulted in much shorter waiting lines.

While the code minimum of 1 lavatory per 200 occupants is adequate, the number of water closets in the IBC code does not minimize waiting periods. Unfortunately, the IBC does not recognize the intermission peak demand in stipulating the minimum number of plumbing fixtures (Table 2902.1) for theater occupancy. The code requires 1 water closet per 125 males and 1 per 65 females. The Broadway experience demonstrates that 1 water closet per 40 men and 1 per 20 women are reasonable ratios that shorten intermission waits. Urinal fixture counts should be maximized for males, to improve traffic flow. Toilets must be no more than one story above or below the level of occupancy and must be within a 500-ft travel distance (IBC 2902.6).

Marquees

The IBC defines a marquee as "a permanent roofed structure attached to and supported by the building that projects into the public right of way" (IBC Section 202). It must be noncombustible and 3–9 ft in height. A maximum height of 3 ft is permitted when the marquee projects more than two-thirds of the distance from the property line to the curb line. A maximum height of 9 ft is permitted when the marquee projects less than two-thirds of the distance from the property line to the curb line (IBC 3106.2.) Marquee signs are not allowed to project beyond the marquee perimeter (IBC Appendix H113.3). Signs cannot extend more than 6 ft above nor 1 ft below a marquee. However, the maximum vertical sign dimension permitted is 8 ft (IBC Appendix H113.4).

IBC Chapters 27–30 outline requirements for engineering building service systems, including electrical, mechanical, plumbing, and elevators.

CODE ISSUES IN EXISTING BUILDINGS

The International Existing Building Code (IEBC) has been developed to consolidate international codes involving upgrades of existing buildings. The IEBC specifically addresses code requirements for repair, alteration, additions, and change of occupancy.

Classification of Work and Code Upgrades

The code implications of the IEBC vary depending on the extent of work required in an existing building. Work involving basic repair has minimal code impact. Work involving more than 50 percent of the building's aggregate area (IEBC 305.1) or changes to the occupancy classification of an existing building impose a significant upgrade to various life-safety features, such as exhaust systems, elevators, enclosures of mechanical-equipment rooms, stairways, automatic sprinkler systems, and fire alarm systems. In addition, upgrades to all means of egress (number of exits, egress doorways, doors, dead-end corridors, lighting, exit signs, handrails, and guards) are required. Unless technically infeasible, accessibility (entrances, elevators, platform wheelchair lifts, ramps, performance areas, toilets, and dressing rooms) upgrades are required to the maximum extent possible (IEBC 706.1).

Changes in Building Use

Any change of use that adds a stage in an existing building must comply with all new building requirements of the International Building Code (IEBC 802.1). Areas of specific impact include building materials, fire protection, means of egress, accessibility, structure, electrical system, light, and ventilation.

Building Additions

Additions to an existing building must comply with the code. However, code upgrades within existing buildings are not required. The new addition shall not be designed to increase the degree of code noncompliance of the existing building's accessibility, structure, fire safety, means of egress, capacity of mechanical, plumbing, or electrical systems (IEBC 901.2).

Historic Buildings

The IEBC recognizes the importance of preserving historic buildings for the type of work and code changes described above.

Any historic building being planned for theater use or undergoing repair or alteration must meet the requirements of Chapter 10 of the IEBC. A written report is prepared and filed with local code officials, identifying safety features in existing buildings that comply with IEBC. The report also requires a listing of safety features not provided that would damage the building's historical features (IEBC 1001.2). The architect should meet with the code official to discuss these issues prior to starting the report. The extent of noncompliance will determine the need to file a report and will be based on the opinion of the code official.

COMPLIANCE ALTERNATIVES

The IEBC permits existing buildings to be evaluated through the use of performance-related provisions instead of the prescriptive requirements of chapters 4 through 10. Chapter 12 outlines the compliance alternative process of evaluating an existing building's performance.

The evaluation considers three essential categories: fire safety, means of egress, and general safety (IEBC 1201.5).

Safety parameters are identified in table 1201.7, and each is scored under these three categories. Safety parameters consist of building height, building area, compartmentation, tenant- and dwelling-unit separations, corridor walls, vertical openings, HVAC systems, automatic fire detection, fire-alarm system, smoke control, means-of-egress capacity, dead ends, maximum exit access travel distance, elevator control, means-of-egress lighting, mixed occupancies, automatic sprinklers, standpipes, and incidental-use area protection.

Once all building data is entered, a total building score is determined. The existing building complies if the scores equal or exceed the mandatory safety scores of Table 1201.8.

INCORPORATING BUILDING CODES

Understanding the theater code mandated by the IBC is essential to ensuring that life-safety demands placed on high-density assembly buildings are met. The code needs to be analyzed and followed step by step to ensure its comprehensive, accurate integration into this complex building type. The IBC code can be obtained at technical bookstores or through the International Code Council (ICC) Web site: www.iccsafe.org/e/category .html.

CHAPTER 7

PRINCIPLES OF ACOUSTIC DESIGN

DAWN SCHUETTE AND LAWRENCE KIRKEGAARD *Kirkegaard Associates*

SHAPING A SPACE FOR SOUND

When theater acoustics are right, audiences rarely remark upon them.

There is no simple formula for the architecture of theater acoustics. A theater's form, height, width, and depth are governed by its program, site conditions, architectural design expression, and construction budget. Because theaters comprise such intricate juxtapositions of elements and systems, including acoustic and theatrical consultants early in the process is of great benefit to the designer.

Direct Sound

Outdoors, sound level drops quickly with distance. Of great importance in outdoor theaters is the need for all audience members to have a clear line of sight to the sound source. The most extreme examples of an arrangement for best line of sight are the Greek amphitheater or Roman coliseum. This configuration pro-

vides audience members with not only ample views of the production but also full access to the sound. While such exaggerated viewing angles are not usually found in contemporary theaters, good sight lines are fundamental to good acoustics in any performance space.

Creating the Acoustic Signature of a Space

Unlike open-air acoustics, sound in an enclosed space is enhanced by adding reflected sound to the direct sound. The shaping of wall and ceiling surfaces controls sound reflection into all seating areas. As sound strikes the walls and ceiling of a performance space, some portion of the sound energy is reflected from that surface. The direction reflected sound energy will travel (reflection angle) can be determined in relation to the angle with which the sound strikes the surface (incidence angle).

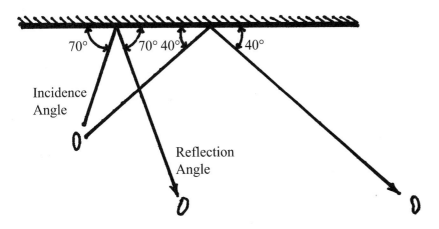

70°   70° 40°   40°

Incidence Angle

Reflection Angle

◀ *Reflection angle. Drawing by Kai Orion, Brian Bellie, Kirkegaard Associates.*

PRINCIPLES OF ACOUSTIC DESIGN

▶ *Direct vs. reflected sound. Drawing by Kai Orion, Brian Bellie, Kirkegaard Associates.*

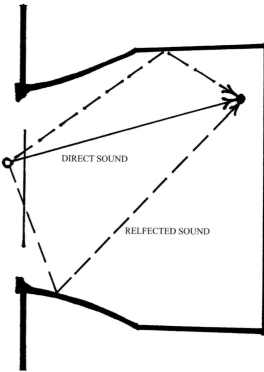

DIRECT SOUND

RELFECTED SOUND

▼ *Ceiling shaping. Drawing by Anthony Shou, Brian Bellie, Kirkegaard Associates.*

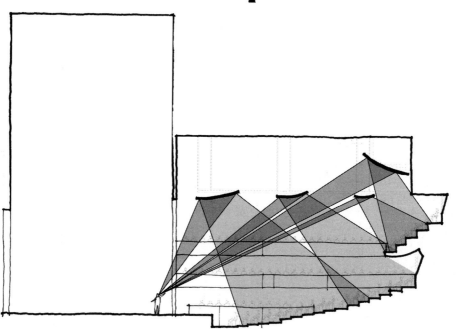

Human hearing is a complex system in which distinct reflections can be perceived $\frac{1}{20}$ of a second after the original sound has been heard. To avoid cacophony, wall and ceiling geometries incorporate angles and curves to reflect sound to listeners quickly after the direct sound. This control of reflection prevents late sound from being perceived as echoes, which result in a lack of clarity. In controlling echo conditions, acoustic shaping of sidewalls and ceiling elements should distribute sound evenly within the seating area as illustrated below.

The acoustic intimacy of a space is largely based on the delay between the direct sound and the first reflections. A short delay provides a greater sense of intimacy. This quality comes naturally in a small space, where the walls and ceiling are relatively close to the audience, but it is harder to achieve in a large room. A long delay between the direct sound and first reflections results in a more spacious but less intimate sound. If the delay is too great, the result can be an unwanted sense of acoustic distance and separation between the performer and listener.

Room Width

Width requirements for a performance space that provides natural acoustic support vary with size of space and performance type. An intimate theater or a flexible black box should be 40–60 ft wide to keep reflections within an appropriately short delay range. Midsize theaters, containing 600–1,200 seats, can increase in width to a maximum of 80 ft, but the front of the room should be narrowed to avoid late reflections. Similar narrowing at the front of the space is needed for a large venue for orchestral music and opera performance (2,000–2,400 seats), with room width limited to 90 ft for support of reverberant, sustained sound. Large rooms for amplified performances *only*, such as Broadway road houses, can be 100 ft wide or more. In this latter case, the sidewalls do not provide substantial acoustic support, and echo control becomes the primary concern.

Sidewall Boxes and Galleries

As the width of a space increases, sidewall boxes or galleries can both increase acoustic reflection to lower seating areas

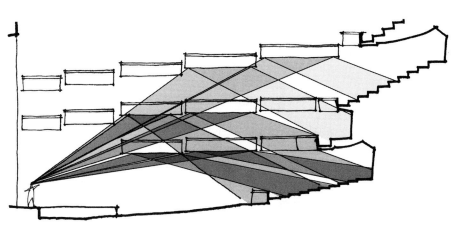

◀ *Sidewall boxes. Drawing by Anthony Shou, Brian Bellie, Kirkegaard Associates.*

and provide visual scale at the front of the space. The underside of boxes above the main level redirect a portion of the sound that is moving upward in the room down to lower seating levels at the center of the main floor and first balcony. At the main floor, boxes also provide a mechanism for reducing the acoustic width of the room if their fronts extend high enough above the seating plane, so they, rather than the more distant wall behind, provide the primary reflections.

Room Height

Supportive reflections for unamplified performances should be provided both from the sides and from overhead, so the principles that guide room width also apply to room height.

The use of the space and the ceiling's visual character have a significant impact on acoustic shaping. For unamplified music and speech, the ceiling must be low enough to provide reflections within the time delay required for clarity and support. If a space is designed for amplified use only, the acoustic requirements for the ceiling are primarily to control delayed reflections that could become distracting echoes from the sound reinforcement system.

In a small room, the architectural ceiling can integrate all acoustic and technical functions. However, if a room is large and if its program calls for a long reverberation time, acoustic ceiling reflectors low in the front of the room are often required to provide natural acoustic support. The choices available to the architect when faced with the latter situation are:

- Expose the technical catwalks visually to the house and provide acoustic

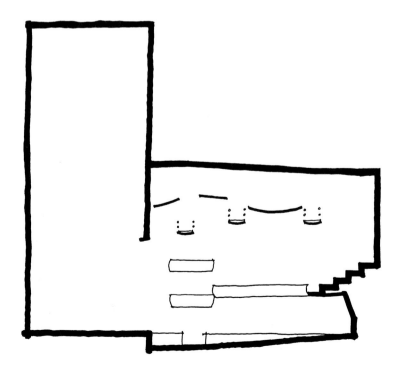

▶ Reflectors above catwalks, Wilson Center, Florida Community College, Jacksonville, Florida. Thompson, Ventulett, Stainback + Associates, architect. Drawing by Anthony Shou, Brian Bellie, Kirkegaard Associates.

shaping above them that is not visually prominent;

- Use acoustic reflector elements to par-
  tially shield the technical catwalks
  from view;

- Provide a finish ceiling that is acoustically transparent to allow sound to
  move freely to the higher volume and
  integrate acoustic reflectors and catwalks directly above the visual ceiling.

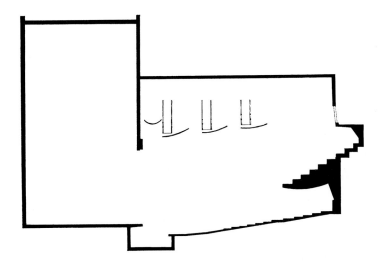

◀ *Reflectors below catwalks,
North Shore Center for the
Performing Arts, Skokie,
Illinois. Graham Gund,
architect. Drawing by Kai
Orion, Brian Bellie,
Kirkegaard Associates.*

▼ *Acoustically transparent
ceiling, Aronoff Center for
the Performing Arts,
Cincinnati, Ohio. Cesar Pelli
& Associates, architect.
Drawing by Kai Orion, Brian
Bellie, Dawn Schuette,
Kirkegaard Associates.*

▶ *Room shape and reflection. Drawing by Anthony Shou, Brian Bellie, Kirkegaard Associates.*

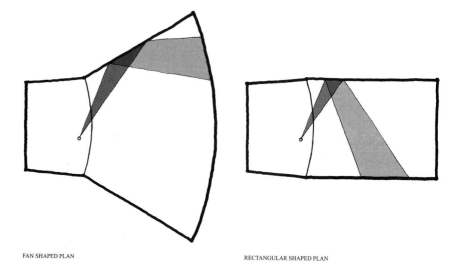

FAN SHAPED PLAN   RECTANGULAR SHAPED PLAN

▶ *Flexible space with overhead reflectors. Drawing by Anthony Shou, Kirkegaard Associates.*

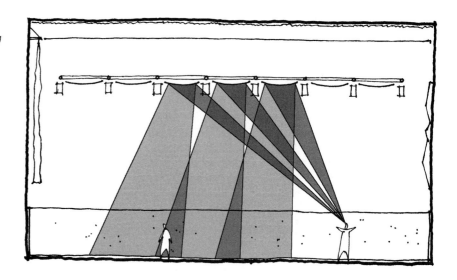

In the challenging combination of symphonic orchestra performance within a space that otherwise houses amplified musical theater or popular music performances, a sound-reflective ceiling is required only for the orchestra. A ceiling element or series of panels may be rigged to be exposed only for orchestral use and removed for other performances. These acoustic adjustments for performance type cause the room's visual character to change, an issue for the architect to address.

Other circumstances affect the acoustic design of overhead elements. If the room shape or width does not allow sidewall re-

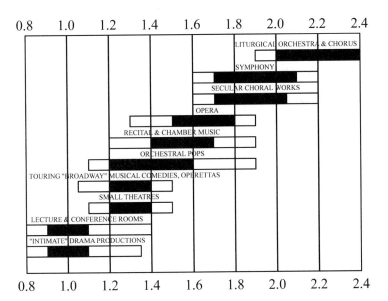

| 0.8 | 1.0 | 1.2 | 1.4 | 1.6 | 1.8 | 2.0 | 2.2 | 2.4 |

LITURGICAL ORCHESTRA & CHORUS

SYMPHONY

SECULAR CHORAL WORKS

OPERA

RECITAL & CHAMBER MUSIC

ORCHESTRAL POPS

TOURING "BROADWAY" MUSICAL COMEDIES, OPERETTAS

SMALL THEATRES

LECTURE & CONFERENCE ROOMS

"INTIMATE" DRAMA PRODUCTIONS

| 0.8 | 1.0 | 1.2 | 1.4 | 1.6 | 1.8 | 2.0 | 2.2 | 2.4 |

◀ *Reverberation time and use. Drawing by Brian Bellie, Kirkegaard Associates.*

flection, the ceiling or hung acoustic reflectors become the only means of acoustic support. This is typical of a fan-shaped space, where the walls provide reflection to only a limited area of audience seating. In this case, ceiling height and shaping are critical and often drive the design.

Another special situation is a flexible theater with a variety of stage locations. Because there is no single room orientation and walls are often covered with drapery or scenery, primary acoustic support may be provided from overhead.

The coordination of acoustic reflectors, catwalks, overhead ductwork, structure, and front-of-house rigging is a complex puzzle. Theatrical and acoustic elements inevitably want to occupy the same space. This zone of the room remains in development throughout the design, for any slight shift in one element has a domino effect on all of the others. Designers should take this as a challenge, not a limitation.

Reverberation Time and Volume

Reverberation time (RT) refers to the length of time the sound is sustained after the direct sound has stopped. A room is considered "dead" or "dry" when the time that sound is sustained is short, often less than 1.2 seconds. A room is considered "live" when the reverberation time is long, 2.0 seconds or more. Reverberation gives fullness to the sound and is a desired component of any room, but its length and level must be appropriate to the performance type.

The acoustic volume of a space must accommodate the longest anticipated reverberation time required for a room's use. For symphonic music, the house volume may need to be 400 cu ft per seat or more. For purely dramatic presentations, volume can be as low as 200 cu ft per seat. Room volume requirements relate to overall room shape. A space that is rectangular in plan supports sound better and is more reverberant than one that is fan-shaped or semicircular.

Variable Acoustic Elements

A room designed for one kind of performance or performances requiring similar acoustic conditions can have a fixed acoustic environment. For example, Broadway theaters that present a given production type are fixed acoustic environments.

However, most contemporary spaces must accommodate a variety of performance types. The most common means of varying the acoustic condition of a theater is through moveable, sound-absorptive elements, such as tracked curtains, vertically moving banners, or horizontally or vertically moving rigid sound-absorp-

tive panels. Through early discussions with users, the acoustical consultant determines the maximum and minimum reverberation times required to serve a theater's program. Volume is established by the maximum reverberation time requirement, and variation between the maximum and minimum reverberation times establishes the amount of moveable absorption needed.

Moveable acoustic elements may be installed to operate automatically or manually. Users prefer motorization, as it allows the elements to be deployed or retracted quickly and easily, though a tight construction budget may mandate manual operation. Initial versus long-time operational costs should be considered carefully when this design decision is made.

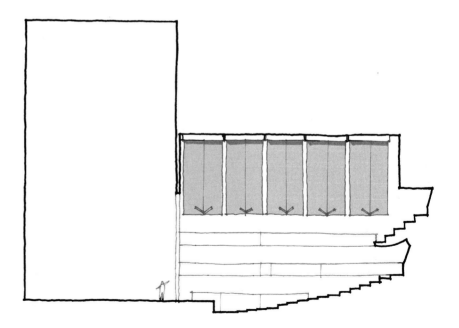

▶ *Acoustic banners.*
Drawing by Anthony Shou,
Kirkegaard Associates.

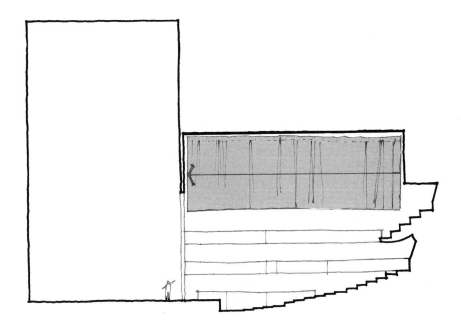

THE FINER DETAILS

Once overall geometry is established, designers must focus on the more subtle shaping and material selections that equally influence the room's sound.

Acoustics Under Balconies

Seating under a balcony overhang differs acoustically from the middle of the main floor or the openness of an upper balcony, but the shaping under balconies can enhance the sound in those areas. Working with the architect, acousticians can help sculpt the underside of the balcony overhang and the rear wall of the seating area to give the impression of a more open sound that surrounds listeners.

If height allows, spacing between the floor and underside of an overhanging balcony should be equal to or greater than the depth of the farthest seating row below the balcony. It is most critical for orchestral music that the balcony overhang be limited and the opening height maximized. Six rows below an overhang is the functional acoustic limit for unamplified performances. In small rooms, the overhang should be limited to only three or four rows.

Control of Echoes and Other Anomalies

In addition to providing support of sound, room geometries control or diffuse unwanted acoustic conditions, such as:

- Echo: Sound that arrives $1/20$ of a second or more after the direct sound that is noticeably louder than the reverberant energy in the room.

- Focus: A concentration of sound resulting in reflections that can be as loud as or louder than the direct sound.

- Flutter: Sound becomes trapped in a repetitive pattern, resulting in a harsh quality.

▶ *Underbalcony shaping.*
Drawing by Anthony Shou,
Kirkegaard Associates.

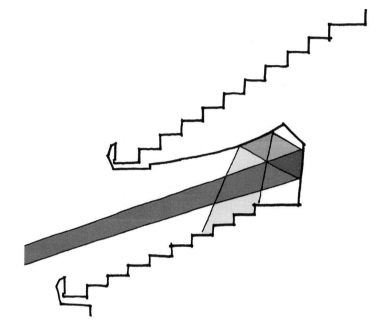

▶ *Flutter and echo. Drawing*
by Anthony Shou,
Kirkegaard Associates.

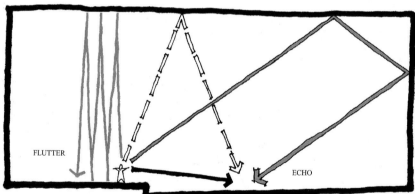

FLUTTER

ECHO

Late, strong reflections or harsh coloration of the sound from these conditions may be avoided through:

- Reorientation. This is simple if done early in design. Slight reconfiguration of walls may be all that is needed to eliminate a flutter condition between parallel surfaces.

- Diffusion. The application of sound-diffusive elements reduces the effect of focus and flutter. But diffusive shaping that may work well on the rear wall to control echoes may not be effective at sidewall or ceiling surfaces. The orientation of the diffusive geometry relative to the sound source and listeners dictates the depth and type of diffusion to be used.

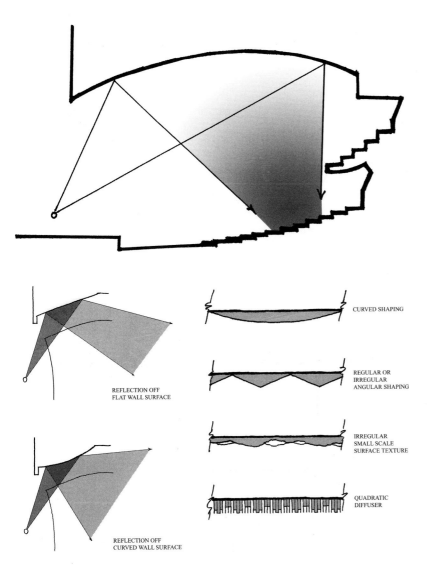

◀ Focus. Drawing by Kai Orion, Brian Bellie, Dawn Schuette, Kirkegaard Associates.

◀ Diffusion examples. Drawing by Laurie Kamper, Dawn Schuette, Brian Bellie, Kirkegaard Associates.

REFLECTION OFF FLAT WALL SURFACE

REFLECTION OFF CURVED WALL SURFACE

CURVED SHAPING

REGULAR OR IRREGULAR ANGULAR SHAPING

IRREGULAR SMALL SCALE SURFACE TEXTURE

QUADRATIC DIFFUSER

- Absorption. Sound-absorptive materials are widely used and often incorrectly labeled "acoustic products." (All materials have acoustic properties; some just happen to absorb sound, while others reflect it.) Use of fixed sound-absorptive materials in performance spaces is appropriate and necessary at times to control loudness, echoes, or focusing conditions, but the location and amount of material in the room has a profound impact on overall sound. Too much absorption near audience members makes a space feel lifeless. Sound-absorptive materials should not be a substitute for reorientation or diffusion if those options are available and acoustically preferable. Additional information on absorption can be found in Chapter 8.

DESIGN COLLABORATION: OVERTURE HALL, MADISON, WISCONSIN

Madison, Wisconsin, needed a large, multipurpose space that would better serve the community arts groups and touring shows that had been performing in the 2,200-seat Oscar Mayer Theater, a renovated 1920s movie palace. The symphony needed a more acoustically appropriate space than the cavernous old vaudeville house, and the opera and touring shows needed a stage house with greater depth and capacity.

The solution was a new, expanded facility that surrounds the existing theater. Altogether, the construction fills a full city block to create the Overture Center for the Arts. Overture Hall, a 2,257-seat, multipurpose performing arts venue, was constructed first, along with rehearsal and public spaces to en-

courage use of the complex throughout the day. A new facility for the Madison Museum of Contemporary Art, renovation of the 330-seat Isthmus Theater (created in a 1980 renovation), and renovation of the Oscar Mayer Theater into the more intimate 1,000-seat Capitol Theater occurred in the second phase. Challenges included operating the existing theater during construction of the new facilities and providing acoustic isolation that would

▶ *The Acoustics of Overture Hall. Illustration by Laura Sparks,* Wisconsin State Journal.

THE ACOUSTICS
OF OVERTURE HALL

The 2,257-seat concert auditorium, shaped like a horseshoe, is designed to offer the best possible sound for a variety of performances, from the Madison Symphony Orchestra to touring Broadway shows.

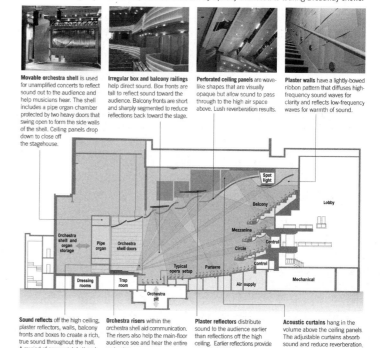

Movable orchestra shell is used for unamplified concerts to reflect sound out to the audience and help musicians hear. The shell includes a pipe organ chamber protected by two heavy doors that swing open to form the side walls of the shell. Ceiling panels drop down to close off the stagehouse.

Irregular box and balcony railings help direct sound. Box fronts are tall to reflect sound toward the audience. Balcony fronts are short and sharply segmented to reduce reflections back toward the stage.

Perforated ceiling panels are wave-like shapes that are visually opaque but allow sound to pass through to the high air space above. Lush reverberation results.

Plaster walls have a lightly-bowed ribbon pattern that diffuses high-frequency sound waves for clarity and reflects low-frequency waves for warmth of sound.

Sound reflects off the high ceiling, plaster reflectors, walls, balcony fronts and boxes to create a rich, true sound throughout the hall. A myriad of appropriately timed reflections make a room sound pleasant. Carpet and other soft materials absorb sound; hard surfaces reflect it.

Orchestra risers within the orchestra shell aid communication. The risers also help the main-floor audience see and hear the entire orchestra.

Structural framework is made with special joints that isolate the hall from outside noise and vibrations.

Plaster reflectors distribute sound to the audience earlier than reflections off the high ceiling. Earlier reflections provide support and clarity.

Air-handling system is designed to move fresh air into the hall slowly and silently from below.

Acoustic curtains hang in the volume above the ceiling panels. The adjustable curtains absorb sound and reduce reverberation, particularly for amplified performances. They can retract into pockets for orchestral concerts.

Illustration by Laura Sparks

◀ *Balcony front shaping.*
Photo by Frans Swarte,
Kirkegaard Associates.

▼ *Sidewall diffusion panels.*
Photo by Frans Swarte,
Kirkegaard Associates.

allow all spaces to operate simultaneously once complete.

The Overture Center's design had been under way for more than six years before phase one of the full city-block redevelopment was realized, in September 2004. The new museum and renovation of the existing theaters will be another two years in construction. The design team, including Cesar Pelli & Associates, Kirkegaard Associates, and Theatre Projects Consultants, will have worked together on this project for nearly nine years before it is finished.

Overture Hall, the new 2,257-seat multipurpose proscenium theater, was the focus of the first design phase. In this room, the collaboration between architect and acoustical consultant can be seen in every detail and every wall surface:

- The shape of the sidewalls began as a sketch by the acoustical consultant to define the narrow, nearly parallel walls required at the front of the seating area. The designers saw a motif for their design in this series of stepping planes: a "lightning bolt," as it became known. The architects further developed the shaping and, working with Kirkegaard, achieved both the visual effect and the acoustic shaping desired.

- Theatre Projects originated the room's seating layout, which distributed the audience at various levels to achieve good sight lines and a sense of intimacy. Within the framework of the seating planes, Kirkegaard established the volume and ceiling shaping to achieve the reverberation time and natural acoustic support needed for the symphony and opera. The architects integrated the acoustic shaping, theatrical lighting, and rigging requirements into a wavelike series of sound-transparent ceiling planes that visually scale the room yet allow full acoustic access to the volume above.

- The under-balcony geometry is a complex series of bowed shapes in a stepping pattern. This shaping interacts with the angled rear wall, distributing sound to listeners beneath the overhanging balconies to give a greater sense of spaciousness.

- Box and balcony fronts are segmented and of varying size to control reflection. The architect and acoustician worked closely through sketches and finally a full-size mock-up to achieve the desired acoustic and architectural shaping. The stepped planes scatter sound vertically to counteract the horizontal focusing of the balcony fronts. The box railings at the sidewalls are taller than the balcony fronts, especially at the first two seating levels, to provide useful sound reflections to the audience in the lower balconies.

- Side- and rear-wall surfaces are covered with cast plaster panels. Kirkegaard defined an area where diffusive wall treatment would be needed at the side and rear walls of the room. Pelli desired that the pattern be regular to achieve the architectural finish they favored, but too much regularity would present acoustic problems. To meet both critera, two somewhat random patterns were chosen. Rear- and sidewall diffusion has a similar vocabulary but provides varying depth for acoustic performance.

Throughout the design process, every system in the room—including structural isolation, mechanical air supply, stage orchestra shell, seating—was discussed and carefully detailed.

Frequency Balance: Construction Materials

Every surface plays a role in determining the acoustic signature of a theater. The discussion thus far has focused on orientation of elements, but construction materials are of equal importance.

"Warmth" is a term that describes sound rich in low-frequency energy. Amplification systems can produce the low-frequency energy needed for a performance, but unamplified voice and instruments have limited strength at these frequencies. For unamplified sound, surfaces within the room must be heavy to resist being set into vibration by sound waves 4–60 ft long. Wall or ceiling surfaces of ½-in.-thick drywall provide little resistance to

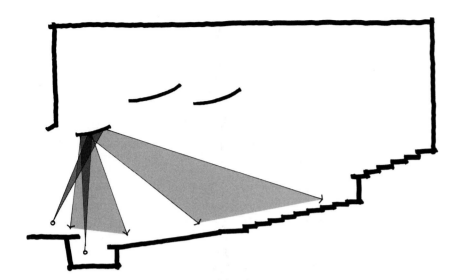

◀ *Pit vs. stage support. Drawing by Anthony Shou, Dawn Schuette, Kirkegaard Associates.*

this sound energy. Full-frequency reflection requires the use of filled masonry, concrete, or many layers of gypsum board.

Finish treatments in a space, including sound-absorptive materials, also affect the balance of sound within it. Sound within a room should have a vibrant quality but not be shrill or scratchy. Without any high-frequency control, a room can sound harsh. On the other hand, excessive amounts of sound-absorptive materials eliminate all shimmer or vibrancy. A common example of too much high-frequency absorption is the use of unsealed concrete block. Integrally colored block is a good, economic material to provide the heavy construction needed for warmth of sound, but its surface is often extremely absorptive of high-frequency energy. A large space built entirely of unsealed block sounds dull and muted.

A significant amount of surface area within a theater consists of audience seating. In a space designed for unamplified performance, foam thickness of the chairs should provide patron comfort but not allow excessive sound absorption.

Balance

The shape of the room, particularly the area directly around the stage, affects the balance of sound from various areas of the stage or between the stage and orchestra pit. In a space programmed for unamplified musical theater and opera, the shaping at the front of the room must allow communication within the pit but not emphasize pit sound over support for the stage.

The sound within the room varies in each seating area and often even within one large seating area. It is neither feasible nor desirable for the sound to be the same at each seat. The front of the main floor receives a stronger direct sound than any other space in the room. The upper balcony receives considerably more supportive reflection than other seating areas and is closely linked to the upper acoustic volume of the room, with the result that the cheapest seats often have the best acoustics. The goal is not for all seats to be the same acoustically but for patrons to have a good listening experience appropriate to their position within the space.

ACOUSTIC CONSIDERATIONS FOR PERFORMERS

What the Performers Hear

What performers hear is as important as sound for the audience. "Acoustic response" is both the return of a performer's own sound to the stage or the orchestra pit and how the sound of the audience is conveyed to the actors and musicians.

To feel comfortable in a space, performers must be able to judge their own sound within the context of the performance. For unamplified performances, the room must provide performers with a sense of their balance or strength of voice. Intimate drama relies on the rapport between stage and audience, with the actor judging his pacing from the mood of the moment. Even for amplified events, where stage monitors provide performers information about their own sound, audience participation can be critical to boosting the energy of the entertainers. A room without *any* support does not create a satisfying experience for either audience or performer.

Direct response of a performer's own sound can be provided through overhead ceiling shaping, properly shaped balcony fronts (if opaque), and, most critically, the rear walls of the seating area(s). The upper rear wall must be shaped not only to avoid strong echo conditions but also to provide reflection for unamplified music events. In multipurpose venues, such reflection must be controlled by moveable, sound-absorptive curtains or banners when amplification is in use.

▶ *Response to performers. Drawing by Anthony Shou, Kirkegaard Associates.*

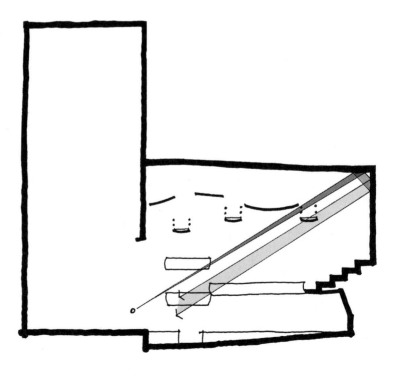

Orchestra-Pit Design

Projected use of a space dictates the acoustic and theatrical needs of an orchestra pit or whether one is required at all. Musical theater, particularly touring Broadway, is relying on fewer musicians in the pit with each passing year. Grand opera and ballet may require space for 100 musicians or more. For accurate assessment, programming discussions must focus on the theater's short- and long-term use.

Acoustically, the minimum dimension required at the centerline of a pit can vary, from 8–12 ft, to allow good acoustic access from the pit into the room. A considerably larger pit opening dimension, of 18 ft or more, is required for unamplified opera and ballet, to control loudness buildup within the pit for large numbers of musicians, to provide good projection of sound to the audience, and to assure good acoustic connection with the singers or

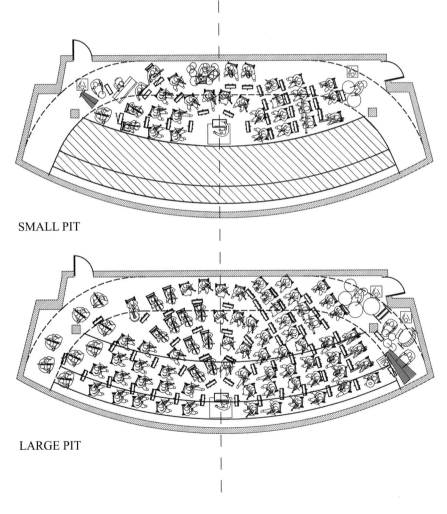

SMALL PIT

LARGE PIT

◀ *Orchestra pit, size. Drawing by Anthony Shou, Dawn Schuette, Brian Bellie, Kirkegaard Associates.*

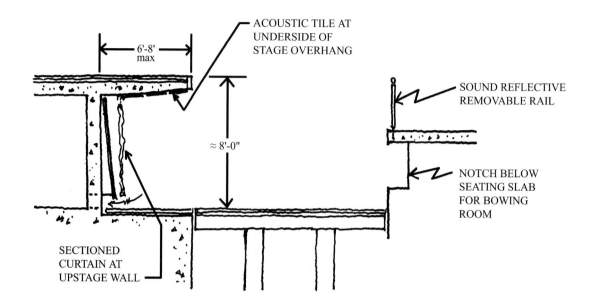

ACOUSTIC TILE AT
UNDERSIDE OF
STAGE OVERHANG

6'-8'
max

≈ 8'-0"

SOUND REFLECTIVE
REMOVABLE RAIL

NOTCH BELOW
SEATING SLAB
FOR BOWING
ROOM

SECTIONED
CURTAIN AT
UPSTAGE WALL

▲ Orchestra pit, section.
Drawing by Dawn Schuette,
Brian Bellie, Kirkegaard
Associates.

dancers on stage. Pit size may be made adjustable.

The orchestra pit normally extends below the stage. This provides sufficient area for musicians while limiting seat loss in the house and keeping the audience as close as possible to the stage when the pit is in use. A rule of thumb for an orchestra pit's overhang is 6–8 ft, to avoid the musicians' experiencing extreme loudness. The pit should be as close to the stage elevation as possible while providing the minimum required clearance below the overhang. This allows the conductor to have a good line of sight to the stage as well as to the musicians. A distance of 8 ft below the finished stage floor is appropriate in most cases.

Orchestra-Shell Design

A moveable orchestra shell enclosure within the stage house is a requirement if symphonic orchestra performance is integral to a multipurpose theater program. An orchestra shell creates an

acoustic and architectural extension of the theater into the stage house to give the visual and aural impression of a single room volume. Shell towers and ceiling elements provide the required supportive shaping on stage to project the sound of the orchestra to the audience and permit the communication between musicians so critical to accurate judgment of timing and tone. The shell also separates the orchestra from the sound-absorptive stage drapery within the fly tower, conserving as much of the sound within the room as possible.

Of shell enclosure designs, the two most common approaches are:

- Freestanding orchestra-shell towers with individual, hung ceiling panels. This system is quite flexible, as the towers can be arranged in a variety of positions to accommodate small or large ensembles. Towers typically nest in a storage area on stage, and movement of these large elements must be carefully coordinated with rigging materials, stage galleries, and stage mechanical, electrical, and plumbing (MEP) systems. Ceiling panels are often stored within the fly tower, but they may also track to a rear-stage storage position or lower for manual removal.

- A unitized shell enclosure consisting of sidewalls and ceiling, integrated into a single structure. Flexibility is slightly limited in this case, with the smallest stage performance area based on the size of the unit. Depth can be extended via only a few moveable tower units and flown ceiling panels. This solution requires a larger storage area just offstage, but deployment time can be cut significantly with little or minimal loss of rigging lines for ceiling elements.

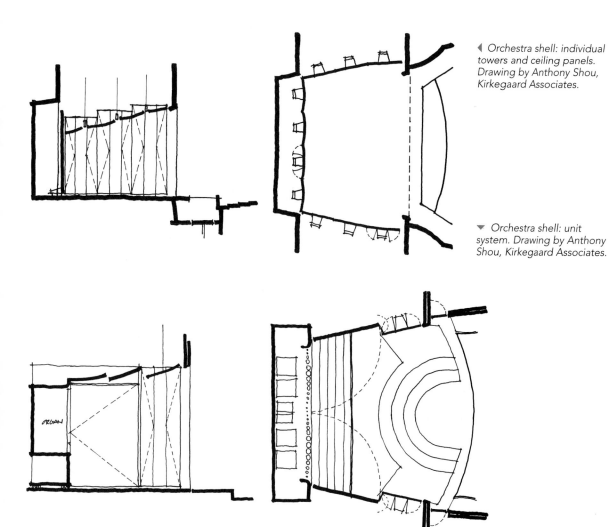

◀ *Orchestra shell: individual towers and ceiling panels. Drawing by Anthony Shou, Kirkegaard Associates.*

▼ *Orchestra shell: unit system. Drawing by Anthony Shou, Kirkegaard Associates.*

Final Thoughts on Room Shaping

It is not possible when planning a facility to know with certainty where the performers will be at any given time. A performance may begin with spoken dialogue across the room, performer entry from a side balcony, or loudspeakers surrounding the audience. Designers cannot anticipate all uses, but good planning should provide the best acoustics possible for a variety of conditions.

SOUND ISOLATION

Keeping unwanted sound out of a performance space is as important as supporting the sound within the room. Noise can ruin the effect of a quiet pause. Excessive noise limits dynamic range, the variation between silence and loudness that a performer can control for theatrical or musical impact. Control of noise—whether from exterior traffic, from other spaces within the facility, or from the building's heating, plumbing, and electrical systems—is a critical consideration for any theater.

Background Noise

Ambient sound within a space is referred to as background noise; its level determines the lower limit of the dynamic range available to performers. For unamplified speech or music, the background-noise level must be low, as there is only so

▶ Background noise: RC (room criteria) graph. Drawing by Dawn Schuette, Laurie Kamper, Kirkegaard Associates.

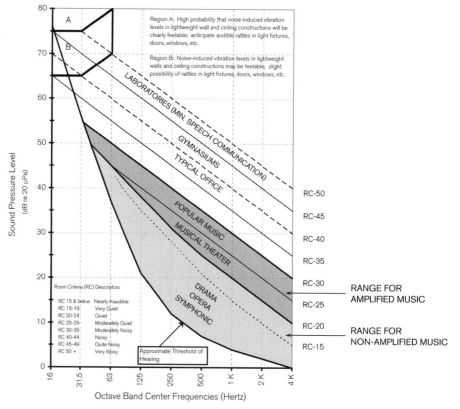

much energy available to the human voice or instrument. Competition with excessive background noise is tiring and unsatisfying for performers and audience members alike.

Allowable sound level varies with frequency, because the human ear is not as sensitive to lower frequencies, which provide warmth of tone but do not contribute to clarity. Designers of performance spaces must work closely with the acoustical consultant, structural engineer, and MEP engineers to control unwanted noise.

Isolation from Surrounding Spaces and Exterior

A building's layout determines the isolation construction that will be needed between the performance space and loud or other acoustically sensitive spaces within the facility. As the concept plans develop,

even as early as bubble diagrams take shape, isolation between sensitive areas should be established so that the building layout can provide acoustic buffer space between critical areas. Careful planning early in the design process can save substantial isolation costs later in the detailing stages.

At times, site restrictions, space limitations, or owner requirements dictate adjacencies that cannot be avoided. In these instances, spaces must be separated by an acoustically separated inner "box" within the building structure (often termed "box-in-box" construction).

Isolation between spaces within a facility and between the performance space and the exterior can be provided through careful structural-system design. A through-building acoustic isolation joint (similar to a building-expansion joint) be-

▼ *Isolation plan: Overture Center for the Arts, Madison, Wisconsin. Cesar Pelli & Associates, architect. Drawing by Polyanna Frangetto, Brian Bellie, Dawn Schuette, Kirkegaard Associates.*

THEATRES - HIGH ISOLATION
LOBBY / NOISY SPACES
BUFFER ZONE

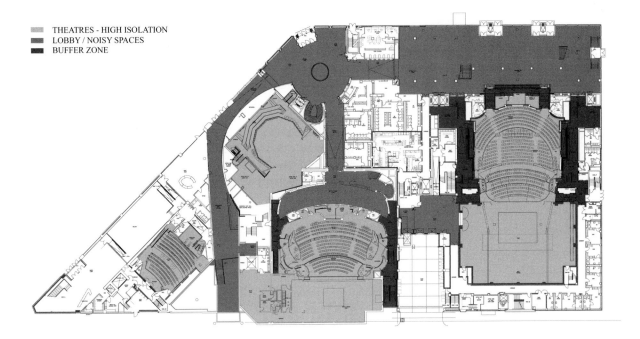

▶ *Box-in-box diagram.*
Drawing by Anthony Shou,
Kirkegaard Associates.

tween the major performance space and other critical areas is effective, because it prevents the transfer of structure-borne vibration. If isolation is designed into the project early, its cost can be low.

Upper sidewalls and roof of the performance space may be the only isolation between the theater and the exterior. Double-wall systems and separate internal ceiling constructions are often required for buildings in noisy surroundings, such as airport flight paths, train lines, or major roadway systems. In extreme situations, transportation lines around or under buildings generate such high levels of ground-borne vibration that the only solution is special foundation isolation systems.

Rain noise can shatter the mood or emotion within a theater if a storm suddenly erupts outside during a performance. The drumming of rain on the roof is typically the biggest concern, but driving rain along wall systems can also

present noise problems. Particular attention should be paid to roof systems and the inclusion of acoustic-isolation detailing in metal roofs and wall panels.

Doors and Vestibules

Entry points into a theater for the audience, performers, and theatrical equipment are the weakest links in the acoustic isolation of the performance space. Every entry should be designed with vestibules that incorporate sound-absorptive finish materials. The quality of door construction is critical. Sound-rated door assemblies should be selected when vestibules are not feasible or isolation of loud noise is required. An example is the large loading door that connects the theater with noisy shop or loading areas.

Panic hardware and latches on doors within a theater can be quite disruptive to the performance. Ideally, fire-separation lines are designed to locate these devices outside the theater envelope.

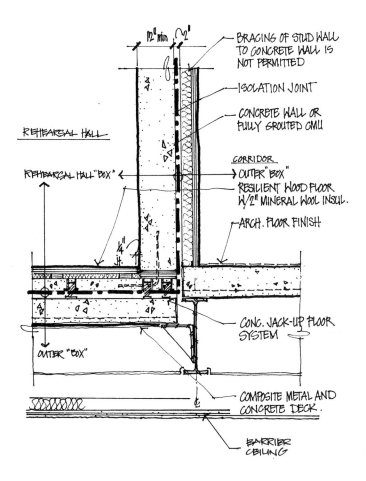

12" min ∩ 2"
— BRACING OF STUD WALL TO CONCRETE WALL IS NOT PERMITTED

— ISOLATION JOINT

— CONCRETE WALL OR FULLY GROUTED CMU

REHEARSAL HALL

REHEARSAL HALL "BOX" ←

CORRIDOR
→ OUTER "BOX"
— RESILIENT WOOD FLOOR W/2" MINERAL WOOL INSUL.

— ARCH. FLOOR FINISH

¼" H.

— CONC. JACK-UP FLOOR SYSTEM

OUTER "BOX"

— COMPOSITE METAL AND CONCRETE DECK.

— BARRIER CEILING

◀ Box-in-box detail. Drawing by Louise Sunga, Kirkegaard Associates.

Isolation of Theatrical Equipment

Equipment that generates noise within the performance space can include:

- Video projectors
- Amplifiers for loudspeakers
- Computers and cooling fans for sound- and light-control equipment
- Automated lighting, automated gel changers, automated gobos
- Motors and lifts for automated scenery elements
- Follow spots and associated power supplies
- Light-dimming equipment

Some equipment, such as follow spots, should be housed in dedicated control areas, while others, such as amplifiers and light-dimming equipment, should be located in rooms outside the auditorium. Projection equipment can be housed in sound-isolating enclosures with powered, low-level ventilation as needed. However, it is not possible to remotely locate the sound operator and associated equipment or to remove or enclose moveable lighting and rigging equipment.

For some equipment there is as yet no solution to noise. Broadway productions tour with automated lighting that generates noise. Fortunately, these shows are usually amplified, which helps the performers rise above the level of the equipment noise, but that, too, colors the experience. Designers should do whatever they can to contain or remotely locate noisy house equipment. The sound-control position, for instance, can incorporate sound-absorptive finish materials to contain fan noise.

MEP-Systems Noise Control

The basic acoustic requirements that influence the design of a performance space are:

- Ductwork should be large enough to control turbulence noise within the air-handling system. Air-handling-unit rooms also are oversized to accommodate large ductwork and sound-reducing plena and attenuators.

- Rooms for air-handling units (AHUs) must be some distance away from the main space to attenuate system noise.

- Major plant equipment and even AHUs should be on grade for cost-effective isolation. Alternately, this equipment can be placed across structural isolation lines from the theater.

- Rooftop equipment should be avoided, not only because it is unsightly but also because noise of these systems is harder to control.

- Isolation of all vibrating equipment is required within the facility.

- Lighting fixtures or lamps that have low noise output must be selected.

- Rain leaders within the performance space require acoustic enclosure or must be routed outside acoustically sensitive areas.

The acoustic design of a performance space is integrated into every discipline of the construction. Look to your consultants to help you along the way.

PERFORMANCE TYPES

The following is a brief discussion of performance types and their effect on the acoustic and architectural design of a theater.

Dramatic Work or Play

A dramatic work is an intimate exchange between actors and audience. Most dramatic work is performed without vocal amplification, but sound reinforcement is often utilized for music playback and sound effects.

The room should be small to provide acoustic intimacy and contain the acoustic energy of the performance. Strong direct sound must be provided to all audience members, which can be achieved only if the sight lines are good. Background noise levels must be low to assure that subtle voice inflections are easily heard by all audience members.

The space should be shaped to provide good support for performers and acoustic envelopment of the audience. Echoes must be controlled to assure a high level of clarity, and reverberation should be relatively low.

Musical Theater and Broadway Productions

Musical theater introduces sung dialogue to accompany spoken passages, with music providing accompaniment to singing and dancing. The music is generated by live musicians or recorded playback. Musicians typically perform from a recessed orchestra pit directly in front of the stage, but small ensembles may be on the floor in front of the stage or on stage with the actors.

The size of the house, type of instruments used, and number of musicians determine whether or not amplification is required. If it is the user's intent not to amplify, the pit area must accommodate enough musicians to acoustically fill the hall. A larger room requires more musicians to provide enough musical impact. A small number of musicians either limits the size of the house or requires sound reinforcement. Amplification of small pit orchestras is typical for touring Broadway productions.

In musical theater, the music should not distract from the action on stage, so the balance between the pit and stage is a primary acoustic concern. For unamplified performances, actors should be well supported and sound from the pit not overemphasized. Reverberation in the theater should be low to moderate.

Opera

In operatic productions, the music is continuous, and all performer dialogue is sung. Most opera is performed without reinforcement of either the instrumentalists or singers. This tradition has resulted in the special operatic singing style performers employ to acoustically fill the large volume of opera halls. There is a limit, however, to the size of hall that opera singers can fill. The Metropolitan Opera House, in New York City, is one of the largest of its type and challenges even the most experienced and powerful voices in the opera world.

The size of the orchestra pit and the acoustic shaping in the front of the room is of great importance. Opera orchestras can number between 30 and 100 musicians, so the playing area is often variable.

Acoustic communication within the pit is critical. Room shaping should provide response to pit musicians but not emphasize the orchestra over solo singers on stage.

For opera, the room should have a moderate reverberation time, long enough to provide fullness to the sound and audience envelopment but not so live that it interferes with clarity of the sung dialogue.

Ballet and Dance

For most dance productions, instrumental music is the primary accompaniment, provided by live orchestra, band, or percussion ensemble or as prerecorded music.

Like opera orchestras, ballet orchestras perform in an orchestra pit immediately in front of the stage and vary in size, although most number 30 to 60 musicians. Providing good acoustic support of the orchestra to the audience is the primary emphasis. Unlike opera, orchestra-pit sound for ballet should be supported more than sound from the stage to assure the impact of dancers' feet is masked by the music. When opera and ballet share a venue, balancing their respective needs is an acoustic challenge. Reverberation requirements for classical ballet are often similar to those for opera.

Unamplified Symphonic and Choral Music

Symphonic music requires a connection with the audience that can be provided only when the musicians and audience are in the same acoustic space. Dedicated concert halls are built as one room for this purpose. In a multiuse venue, an orchestra shell provides the needed enclosure.

An orchestra's size varies with the type of music presented: from chamber music, with 20–30 instruments, to choral and orchestral repertoire, with up to 100 instrumentalists and 150–200 chorus members. Orchestra-shell depth must be variable to reduce or expand as required. The width of the proscenium opening to accommodate full symphonic orchestra must be 60–65 ft, wider than that for dramatic or musical theater.

Reverberation may vary with the type of music performed, from moderately live to very reverberant. Orchestra needs are the driving factor in determining the room's volume if unamplified symphonic music is a major component of the building's program.

Orchestral Pops

Orchestral pops is an integral part of the season for many orchestras in the United States. Programs typically include light classical pieces, film scores, and pop arrangements and performances with popular guest stars. The presentations may be amplified or not, depending on the guest artist or type of music.

An orchestra shell is required for unamplified presentations. In amplified performances, the enclosure may be only partial or absent altogether to control loudness and echoes from monitor loudspeakers onstage. Reverberation time is usually at the low end of the range for orchestral use or as low as musical theater requirements.

Popular Music

Popular-music presentations include jazz, blues, gospel, folk, country, rock-and-roll, hip-hop, and world music, whose groups vary in size. The acoustic setting may be amplified or not. The venue's scale often determines its amplification requirements. For example, a folksinger may perform without amplification in an intimate room that provides good acoustic support but with amplification in a large theater.

Lectures and Conferences

Lecture presentations, graduation ceremonies, product roll-out announcements, and the like all take place in any theater that serves as a community venue. Acoustic emphasis for this use is clarity for speech and multimedia presentations. Scaling a large space for a small lecture group can be done with lighting or seating arrangement if incorporated into the room design.

THE LAST NOTE

Every project has its own circumstances, opportunities, and constraints, so the designer must apply the principles of acoustic design to the situation at hand. The following is an acoustic checklist for a theater design project:

- Clarity of voice, musical instrument, and amplified sound for the audience, and ease of projection and communication for the performers. These come from:
  - Good sight lines
  - Proper shaping of wall and ceiling surfaces
  - Appropriate use of sound-absorptive materials
  - Room response that provides feedback to performers
  - Quiet background noise
- Fullness of sound provided by appropriate volume
- Variability of the acoustic environment, as needed

- Construction materials that sustain full frequency sound energy and provide isolation from the exterior

This chapter is not a detailed primer on acoustics; there are many good texts dedicated to that subject, many of which are in this book's bibliography. Rather, it is meant to arm designers with a basic understanding of acoustic design principles that allows them to make informed decisions as they approach the design of a theater.

CHAPTER 8
FLEXIBILITY IN ACOUSTIC DESIGN

CHRIS JAFFE *Jaffe Holden Acoustics*

THE ACOUSTIC DESIGN PROCESS

The development of a theater's acoustics parallels the architectural design process, discussed in Chapter 11.

Feasibility Study

A feasibility study, with appropriate team members, should be the first step taken by all clients contemplating the construction of a theater building. Such a study determines audience demographics, competing venues in the area, fund-raising possibilities, and site selection, among other items.

During this initial phase, an acoustic survey of the site and its environs is conducted. Measurements of traffic, industrial, aircraft, and emergency vehicular noise and vibration must be taken to verify the site's acceptability and to assist the acoustician in designing effective isolation constructions.

Program Study

Acousticians must be brought in as integral members of the design team at the very beginning of the program study. They must be able to discuss directly with the client the acoustic implications of the programs planned for the facility. Is the theater to be used only for straight plays? Will musicals be part of the mix? What are the client's desires in terms of audience-to-performer relationships? Will the theater be proscenium, end-stage, thrust, arena, or flexible? What support spaces are involved? Will they include rehearsal rooms, warm-up rooms, loading dock, workshop, mechanical rooms, and

control rooms? Once this information has been obtained, acousticians can contribute their insights to the architectural team.

The acoustician assists the architect in space planning by identifying those activities that work well in adjacent spaces and those that must be separated.

Basic initial criteria, such as volume requirements, rough geometry, areas of audio control rooms, amplifier rooms, and rehearsal rooms are provided during this phase.

Schematic Design

In this phase, specific acoustic criteria for performance and rehearsal rooms are determined as are all other sound-critical spaces. The criteria consist of reverberation times throughout the frequency range, background noise of mechanical systems, and transmission-loss characteristics of isolation walls, ceilings, and floors. The criteria are based on the programs of individual rooms and the noise and vibration sources in the spaces that surround them.

Working with the architect and engineering specialists, the team arrives at geometric forms that meet the acoustic requirements for the program and that enable other team members to achieve their design goals. Selection of construction materials is discussed and specified.

At the completion of the schematic design phase, the cost consultant should prepare a construction estimate. If it is close to the budget estimate, the team can start work on the next phase, design development. If the estimate exceeds the budget, either the team must revise their plans or the client must reduce the program requirements.

Design Development

Once the cost estimate has been matched to the budget estimate, the team can proceed with the design development phase. It is at this stage that more specific details of design and construction are developed.

For instance, the mechanical room must be properly isolated from the rest of the structure and duct-chase volumes identified. Materials related to internal-room acoustic requirements are further refined at this stage, and locations of theatrical equipment, such as loudspeakers, theatrical light fixtures, rigging, lift, and reflectors, are determined.

Throughout the design-development phase, the acoustic consultant reviews the architect's drawing updates and those of other members of the design team. If the acoustic firm is also responsible for designing the venue's audio systems, their electroacoustic designers will coordinate their designs with the architectural plans as they are developed.

At this point the cost consultant again checks the design construction costs against the original budget projection. Should the team be over budget at the end of this phase, further value-analysis sessions will be scheduled. During value analysis, the program value of a proposed design modification is evaluated against its estimated cost reduction.

Construction Drawings

Acousticians are very busy during this phase. The architect, the engineers, and the theater consultant are finalizing their designs and coordinating drawing sets. It is important that acoustic criteria are not compromised and that acoustic recommendations are integrated into the overall specifications. Acousticians assist the team in coordinating the drawings of the disciplines that affect acoustic recommendations.

Upon completion of this phase, the documents are submitted to the cost consultant for a final cost estimate and then to contractors for bidding purposes. If there is a discrepancy between the final cost estimate and the original budget, the design team schedules another value-analysis conference to see how they might further reduce costs without compromising the client's program.

Bid Conference

Contractor submittals are reviewed for conformity to acoustic design issues as are substitutions made by the contractors in the interests of improving the design and reducing costs.

Construction

At the start of the construction phase, the implications of critical acoustic design details, such as wall constructions, floating floors, and duct-lining, are explained to the contractor's crews, as is the necessity of caulking and sealing all conduit and duct penetrations.

The acoustician makes periodic trips to the site to make sure the contractor is constructing the acoustic elements according to specification and must have the opportunity to inspect isolation joints, floating floors, box-in-box constructions, and penetration caulking as the job progresses, not after possible flanking paths have been sealed over.

Postconstruction

The resident theater technicians are trained in the proper use of variable acoustic devices, operation of the sound system, and use of reflectors. In addition, by taking a series of acoustic measurements in the hall, rehearsal rooms, and lobby, the acoustician confirms that acoustic criteria have been met and prepares a final acoustic report and operations manual for the architect and the client.

ACOUSTIC CRITERIA

To develop the acoustic criteria for a new theater, the designer must understand the producing company's mission and its interest in specific audience-to-performer relationships.

A professional regional theater company, such as the Long Wharf, in New Haven, Connecticut, may have as its mission the mounting of the classics together with the presentation of new plays on a thrust stage to audiences of 500–800 per-sons, while a Broadway producer's main interest may be to present lavish musical extravaganzas to audiences of 1,500–1,800 in existing Broadway the-aters. The out-of-town presenter is proba-bly most interested in the lavish musical, but will opt for a 2,500–2,700-seat hall because of ticket-price limitations. He cannot charge his patrons Broadway-scaled ticket prices and therefore needs more seats to cover the cost of these large productions.

Different companies have different pre-sentation styles. Some regional or off-Broadway presenters work in the more intimate style of arena or thrust-stage productions, while others prefer to stage their events in traditional proscenium theaters with stage houses capable of fly-ing scenery.

The Broadway producer and the out-of-town presenter almost always choose the proscenium-style hall with a stage house, as every Broadway theater and almost every road house in the country is de-

◀ Long Wharf Theatre, New Haven, Connecticut. The thrust stage at this professional regional theater. Photo courtesy of Jan Berice.

▲ *Harris Theater for Music and Dance, Chicago, Illinois. A multiuse proscenium theater for unamplified music and amplified theater productions. Hammond, Beeby Rupert Ainge, Inc., architect. Photo by Jon Miller. Courtesy of Robert Shimmer, Hedrick-Blessing.*

signed in this fashion. Presenters are always hopeful that a successful New York production can be toured throughout the country, and perhaps even the world, for many years.

Another variable is whether or not the actors' voices will be amplified in straight dramatic plays or singers' voices in musicals. The acoustic characteristics of playhouses for amplified voice are quite different from those that rely on natural sound.

Small Unamplified Theaters
Acoustic design for professional regional, off-Broadway, and amateur theaters presenting straight dramatic productions and musical theater may be approached as follows.

Acoustic relationship between style of presentation and size of audience
The human voice is a highly directional instrument. The normal frequency range of human speech runs between

Speech Contours (500 and 4000 Hz)

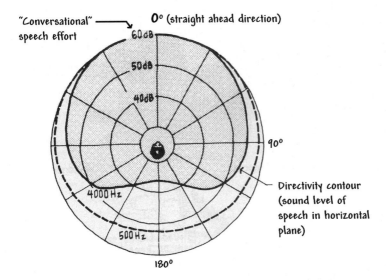

◀ Directional characteristics of the human voice in the range of the speech frequencies. From David Egan, Architectural Acoustics (New York: McGraw Hill, 1988).

150–4,000 hertz (Hz; cycles per second). Articulation information, the consonants and the plosives, such as *k, p,* or *t* sounds associated with speech intelligibility, lie in the higher-frequency range, with dispersion angles from the mouth ranging 30–60 degrees.

In an arena or thrust-stage theater, the actor's back or side faces a large number of audience members; the sound levels of intelligible speech drop off about 5 decibels (dB) at the side and 10 dB at the rear. Audience members seated to an actor's back or side have a hard time understanding speech at these levels unless they are close to the performers. Arena and thrust theaters must be kept small so that all members of the audience receive intelligible speech signals.

Acoustic criteria

A room designed for unamplified speech should have a relatively low reverberation

SEATING CAPACITIES OF SMALL UNAMPLIFIED THEATERS	
Theater Style	**Seating Capacity**
Arena stage	300–500
Thrust stage	500–800
End stage	800–1,000

ACOUSTIC CRITERIA FOR SMALL UNAMPLIFIED THEATERS	
Reverberation time (midfrequency)	0.7–1.2 seconds
Reverberation time (low frequency)	0.7–1.0 seconds
Background noise criteria	Noise Criteria 25
Initial time-delay gap	20–30 milliseconds

The Arena Stage, Washington, D.C. Harry Weese, architect; Bing Thom Architects. Photo by Scott Suchman.

time, low background noise from air-handling devices, and early first reflections to enhance and support speech intelligibility.

Noise Criteria (NC) is a numerical rating system or family of curves used to specify background sound levels over a given frequency range. Basic physical acoustic criteria for halls designed for unamplified speech transmission are given in the table on page 119.

One should be careful not to reduce the reverberation times to too low a figure, or the character of the human voice will go flat and actually sound unnatural.

Acoustic treatment

Small arena, thrust, and end-stage theaters designed for unamplified speech may be new buildings or constructions within found spaces, such as warehouses, garages, old movie palaces, and bank buildings. They should be acoustically treated accordingly.

New Theaters

In new theaters with ceiling heights of 30 ft, substantial amounts of absorption are required to control liveness; adding absorption in the form of checkerboard patches directly to the ceiling's underside is acceptable.

Some theater consultants may specify catwalks or cable grids over the performing area so that technicians can easily install and focus lighting fixtures and spot lines. Theaters designed along these lines require 30-ft or higher ceilings and incorporate a fair amount of cubic volume. Since the reflective portion of such a checkerboard ceiling may be too high to provide early speech reflections, the acoustician may recommend that the underside of a catwalk system be filled in with a hard material, such as ⅜-in. plywood. If the theater consultant specifies a walking cable net instead of catwalks, ⅜-in. plywood panels can be suspended over the lighting pipes in the cable-net design. (A walking cable net is a grid of cables over a stage platform or seating area that is erected in place of catwalks.)

Found Spaces

The amount of added absorptive material, which reduces liveness, and sound reflectors, which enhance speech intelligibility, varies on the basis of a room's ceiling height. Some theaters, particularly those in "found" spaces, have low ceilings, of 15 to 20 feet, and therefore low cubic volumes. These require less added absorption once upholstered seats and audience absorption have been factored into the equation.

If added absorption is indicated it should take the form of carpet in aisles, on floor surfaces under the audience seating area, or panels on wall surfaces behind the audience. Absorption should not be placed on the ceiling of a room with low volume, because the low hard ceilings provide the early reflections needed for enhanced speech intelligibility.

Larger Theaters, with Some Amplification

Large regional, off-Broadway, and amateur theaters presenting straight plays and musicals might still have thrust, arena, or end stages, but their larger seating capacities usually mandate some form of amplification.

From an acoustic standpoint, because the productions use amplification, there are no limits to the seating capacity of these theaters. Limitation might come from the theater-design consultant, who usually does not want patrons seated

▲ The Anspacher Theater, Public Theater, New York City, thrust stage. The Reading Room of the Astor Place Library was modified to incorporate this space. Giorgio Cavalieri, architect.

121

SEATING CAPACITIES OF LARGE THEATERS WITH SOME AMPLIFICATION	
Theater Style	**Seating Capacity**
Arena stage	500–3,000
Thrust stage	800–1,500
End stage	1,000–2,200

more than 90 feet from the stage. Here again, if large video screens are introduced as part of the production, many thousands might be accommodated in outdoor venues like the Hollywood Bowl and the Baths at Caracalla.

Indoor theaters of this style offer 1,500–3,000 seats. The thrust-stage Vivian Beaumont Theater, at Lincoln Center, New York City, holds 1,500 patrons; the arena-stage Casa Mañana, in Fort Worth, Texas, holds 3,000, and the proscenium and end-stage Schuster Theater, in Dayton, Ohio, holds 2,200.

Thrust and arena theaters of up to 1,500 seats might use a variety of electronic speech-enhancement systems, which are designed so that the portion of the audience facing the actor hears the natural sound of his voice while those to his side and rear receive an amplified signal.

Other presenters use wireless microphones in the more traditional fashion of the Broadway musical producer. However, the cross-fire system is a more natural sound, and one does not have to engage a

▶ The Casa Mañana, Fort Worth, Texas. A large arena theater for locally produced amplified Broadway musicals. Henry Kaiser, architect. Photo courtesy of Casa Mañana Inc.

◀ Benjamin and Marian Schuster Performing Arts Center, Dayton, Ohio. A large amplified proscenium theater for touring Broadway musicals. Cesar Pelli & Associates, architect. Photo by Andy Snow.

sound technician to constantly mix signals throughout the performance.

The large end-stage proscenium uses the wireless-microphone technique as the best solution for good intelligibility. If the theater is not too large, one can combine natural speech with electronic reflections, which would again provide a more natural sound.

Large theaters designed for amplified speech can have slightly higher reverberation times in both the mid- and low-frequency ranges. Background noise levels must remain low, and the initial time-delay gap is not applicable, because the sound system provides required speech intelligibility information.

Acoustic treatment

To provide the proper reverberation times throughout the frequency spectrum, quite a lot of absorption is required in these larger venues. Start with heavily uphol-stered audience seating, carpet with padding under the seats, and totally absorptive rear walls. In smaller theaters, such as the Beaumont, additional absorption can be patched onto the sidewalls. The ceiling in these smaller venues should remain hard for speech intelligibility. If the venue is as large as the Casa Mañana, one may need to add absorption to the ceiling to reach the required low reverberation times.

Fully Amplified Theaters

Professional Broadway and municipal multiuse theaters that present Broadway musicals use electronic amplification. All these theaters are proscenium-style end stages with full-height fly towers. Electronic enhancement of singers' voices and pit musicians' acoustic and electronic instruments have become an artistic as well as economic factor in the presentation of Broadway musicals. Amplification is inherent in most popular music today and is a necessity for presenting productions in large theaters. Since these shows are rehearsed and produced on Broadway in this form, road versions of these productions must use the same presentation style when they are booked into municipal multiuse theaters

The artistic use of amplification revolves around improving balance between orchestra and vocalist and developing the sonic possibilities of electronic instruments written into the score. From a financial standpoint, producers can now cast high-profile film and television actors in leading roles, even if they have not been theatrically trained to project their voices.

Early Twentieth-Century Broadway Theaters

Almost all musicals on Broadway itself are presented in theaters designed and built in the early twentieth century for straight (nonmusical) plays, vaudeville acts, and revues. Examples of such shows are *Abie's Irish Rose, George White's Scandals, Coconuts,* and the Ziegfield Follies. These old theaters contained 800–1,700 seats and were designed for natural speech and instrumental accompaniment. How was this unamplified audibility accomplished in the larger of these venues?

They were designed with relatively low volumes to reduce reverberation, and all room surfaces were hard, to furnish the early reflected high-frequency energy needed for clarity of both speech and music. The actors used exaggerated stage movements and spoke in a more declamatory fashion (slowly and loudly). Directors blocked the actors' movements so they almost always faced the audience, thus allowing for lip reading.

Moreover, in those days, there were no noisy mechanical systems providing air-conditioning. Public performance venues closed for the summer months and did not open until the fall. Long-term exposure to noise was not so prevalent, and people had not become ear lazy from listening to high levels of sound emanating from their television sets and car radios.

Newer Broadway Theaters

Only three new Broadway theaters have been built for the amplified musical in New York City in the last 70 years. Many of the older ones, such as the New Amsterdam, the New Victory, and the Ford, have been renovated for this purpose, but the return on investment of building brand new musical theaters is low.

Two of the new musical theaters, the Uris and the Minskoff, were constructed within office towers, whose owners received concessions from the New York City Planning Commission to add floors or to reduce setbacks. Both theaters were

ACOUSTIC CRITERIA FOR LARGE THEATERS WITH SOME AMPLIFICATION	
Reverberation time (midfrequency)	1.0–1.2 seconds
Reverberation time (low frequency)	0.9–1.1 seconds
Background noise criteria	NC 25

SEATING CAPACITIES OF BROADWAY THEATERS	
Vintage of Theater	**Seating Capacity**
Early twentieth-century Broadway theaters	800–1,800
Newer Broadway theaters	1,500–2,700

built with little regard for physical acoustics and have had problems with amplified speech from the start.

The third new theater, the Marriott Marquis, is on the third floor of a high-rise hotel on Seventh Avenue and Forty-fifth Street. The developer was encouraged to add the theater as part of the building because three older Broadway houses had to be demolished to clear the site for the hotel. This theater was designed specifically for amplified musical theater, and great attention was paid to physical acoustic requirements.

Acoustic Criteria for Amplified Older Broadway Theaters

Broadway theaters with 800–1,200 seats are relatively low in volume and have hard walls and ceilings. They worked well for unamplified musical theater in the 1940, 1950s, and early 1960s, but their volume was too small and the room surfaces too hard for rock-and-roll musicals like *Hair* and *Jesus Christ Superstar,* which started the amplification trend.

When renovating these theaters, acousticians added as much absorption as possible and then relied on electronic processing equipment, such as artificial reverberation, to add color to both the human voice and acoustic instruments. So that sound operators did not have to deafen people seated near loudspeakers, sound designers placed rows of loud-speakers under and above the balconies, delaying the signal so that sound from the stage and from loudspeakers near the stage arrived simultaneously to the ears of listeners in those locations.

Older Broadway theaters with 1,200–1,800 seats have the cubic volume to handle the high-decibel levels of contemporary amplified productions, and they do not require the addition of as much acoustic treatment in relation to wall area as the smaller theaters. However, in view of these theaters' greater length, absorption must be placed on the rear walls to eliminate echoes generated by loudspeakers.

In all of these theaters, it is necessary to hang lighting trusses and locate box-boom lighting positions on the sidewalls to accommodate the myriad fixtures that now light a Broadway musical. Loud-speakers must be mounted on the ornate plaster prosceniums to accommodate contemporary production styles.

One should design a new theater for amplified musical theater with enough cubic volume to absorb the loudspeakers' high power levels. However, to prevent unwanted reverberant energy from destroying intelligibility, the room's lower ceiling should be designed as a series of open reflectors positioned below the upper ceiling to provide the early reflections needed for speech clarity.

ACOUSTIC CRITERIA FOR NEW BROADWAY-STYLE MUSICAL THEATERS*	
Seating Capacity	**Acoustic Criteria**
1,800 seats	Reverberation time, 0.9–1.2 seconds
	NC 25
Proscenium with full stage house	

The upper ceiling and rear walls should be covered with enough absorption to reduce reverberant levels to the criterion of 1.0 seconds at midfrequency. If more is required, it can be laid in on the backside of the reflectors.

All Broadway producers, road-company producers, and most off-Broadway producers rent sound and light equipment for each show. Although municipal and university theaters have a complement of sound and light equipment for in-house productions, they usually use the road company's equipment when these shows are booked into their facilities. Therefore, the electroacoustician must design the electronic infrastructure and sound systems so that they will not dilute any acoustic criteria or disturb the architect's vision for the space.

Multipurpose Road Houses (Municipal and University)

Multipurpose road houses are designed for the presentation of symphony concerts and opera as well as amplified Broadway musicals. The volume that symphonic presentations require is twice that required for amplified stage productions, and a considerable amount of variable absorption must be added to the space to reduce reverberation times to reasonable levels. Most variable absorption is added in the form of soft goods or fiberglass blankets or boards. These materials are most effective at the high points and midpoints of the frequency spectrum and do not address low-frequency reverberation

Low-frequency reverberation conditions can be lowered by providing an air space

▶ *The Weidner Center for the Performing Arts, Green Bay, Wisconsin. Typical university and community theater, designed for symphony, opera, and amplified shows. Beckley/Meyers Architects, Inc. Photo courtesy of Weidner Center for the Performing Arts, Cofrin Family Hall.*

between the absorptive material and the hard walls of the theater. By adding remote loudspeakers close to listeners in and under balconies, one might not need to release as much low-frequency energy into the hall from the front-mounted loudspeakers on the proscenium wall.

Single-Purpose Broadway-Style Road Houses

Few of these theaters have been built over the years. In a hall with a limited seating capacity of, say, 1,500 people, one might follow the Marriot Marquis design approach.

However, most Broadway-style road houses are built to accommodate 2,700–6,000 people. In these instances, the room has multiple balconies and, as a result, a much higher ceiling. Like the

Marriot Marquis, it can have multiple reflective surfaces with permanent absorption systems on the rear and side walls.

Care should be taken to create a room with a flat reverberation curve throughout the frequency spectrum so that amplified low-frequency electronic instruments do not mask the intelligibility of singers' lyrics.

THEATERS OF THE FUTURE

We cannot predict the physical design of theaters of the future unless we can define the nature of the theater of the future.

Milly S. Barranger defines theater as follows:

> Theatre is a performance art that places human experience before a group of people—an audience—in the present moment. For theatre to happen, two

◄ Sarofim Hall in the Hobby Center for the Performing Arts, Houston, Texas. A large, single-purpose proscenium theater for amplified Broadway musicals. Robert Stern, architect. Photo by Frank White.

groups of people, actors and audience, must come together at a certain time and in a certain place. There, on a stage or in a special place, actors present themselves to an audience in a story usually involving some aspect of being human. The audience shares in the story and occasion. We listen, gather information, feel emotions, and actively interact with the actors and their events that define in some way what it means to be a human being in certain circumstances—both familiar and unfamiliar.[1]

Theater has been thus for at least 3,000 years, so there is reason to believe that the theater of the future will be similar to the theater of today. Arena, thrust, and end-stage theaters will be constructed with the same audience-to-performer relationships that have served for centuries.

Because participatory theater does not require a built enviroment, I have ruled out such events as happenings, where the line between performer and audience disappears and, as Jimmy Durante used to say, "Everyone wants to get into the act." For the same reason I have also ruled out guerilla or street theater.

To say that the relationship between audience and performer will remain the same does not mean that the architectural environment and production values will not change. Technological advances have already enabled architects to create innovative theatrical environments that have not had to follow the rigid rules of natural acoustics.

These spaces employ an electronic system that simulates the natural reflection patterns of acoustically successful theaters designed along natural acoustic guidelines. One might use the term "electronic architecture" to describe the process. Such systems allow architects to realize more imaginative environments for theater presentation, because the configuration of physical walls and ceilings, so critical to natural acoustic requirements, may be disregarded. They can be placed to suit the designer's vision for the space.

This technique has been used in Silva Hall, at the Hult Center in Eugene, Oregon (Color plate 2); Atwood Concert Hall, at the Anchorage Performing-Arts Center in Alaska; and the original Concord Pavilion in Concord, California. The first two represent an architect's vision for end-stage halls and Concord for an arena.

More recently, electronic architecture was employed for the 5,000-seat Hall A at the Tokyo International Forum. Electronic architecture enabled the designer to have a glass-walled hall seating 5,000 people that may be used for symphony concerts as well as musical theater.

In 1898 Adolphe Appia, the great scenic and lighting designer, wrote, "It is hardly necessary to point out that the construction of our theatres should evolve toward a freer, more flexible concept of dramatic art. Sooner or later we shall achieve what will be known as the *Salle* (hall, auditorium), cathedral of the future, which, in a free, vast, and flexible space, will bring together the most diverse manifestations of our social and artistic life."

Everyone dedicated to the theater arts should work toward realization of Appia's vision—with great acoustics.

---

[1]Milly S. Barranger, *Theatre: A Way of Seeing* (Belmont, Calif.: Wadsworth Publishing Company, 1995), p. 3.

CHAPTER 9
LIGHTING THE THEATER BUILDING

PAUL MARANTZ *Fisher Marantz Stone*

As a building created for performance, the theater should fill the arriving theater-goer with anticipation, and its design must send the message that something special is to occur within.

Consider the inviting glow of any traditional movie marquee; one glance and you can hear the corn popping. Or imagine guests arriving at the opera, conversing excitedly in the lobbies, hurrying to their seats. A theater is a place for heightened expectation; its design and lighting must reflect this.

▲ *Hult Performing Arts Center, Eugene, Oregon. The Hult Center, with its lit peaks, beckons to audiences. Hardy Holzman Pfeiffer Associates, architect. Photo by Norman McGrath.*

LIGHTING AND ARCHITECTURE

Lighting and architecture are allied disciplines. Light is the "material" that conveys the form and spirit of a building to the eye and brain of the viewer. The architecture (and the architect) drives the lighting design. If the ideas informing the architecture are clear and coherent, the lighting will naturally flow from these ideas and will be at one with them. It is, therefore, not possible to describe in abstract terms how to light a theater (or any other type of building) other than to assert that the architecture and common sense must supply the needed direction.

Stumped for a lighting solution at an early point in my career, I brashly told my architect client that there was no way to light what he had drawn and that, therefore, something was wrong with his design. After a long and, for me, uneasy silence, he replied that perhaps I might be right. A week later, a revised design appeared that beautifully considered how light and space might cooperate, and our task became simply to carry it through.

The Exterior

Lighting for a theater begins outside. A dark and hermetic building is rarely the right idea. Exterior lighting must be considered together with exterior graphics, for there is necessary information to be supplied about the building's identity and perhaps also about the events within.

Modern theaters often employ transparency between the exterior and the public lobbies, using the gathering audience to animate the exterior at night. The lighting challenge is then to design the interior lighting to serve the exterior and interior simultaneously (Color plate 20).

Keep in mind that lobbies are unpopulated during performances and whenever the theater is "dark," so it is wise to design in a second lighting "scene," which emphasizes, perhaps, the decorative features and sparkle in the space rather than its empty volume (Color plate 5).

The Lobby

The lobby is the first space intended to convey the idea that the theater represents a different reality from the everyday world outside. Historically, theaters have created a richer and more fanciful environment than almost any other building, with the possible exception of churches, to which they are genetically related in engaging life's spirit. Lighting must assist in this goal. The lobby (or lobbies) is an intensely social space, where the audience comes to see and be seen. Light must support this coming together. Designers are charged with helping people to look and feel good in every public space. As a rule this is achieved with light sources that render color faithfully, that are somewhat diffused and multidirectional (Color plate 9).

While the main lobby is programmed primarily for pretheater rendezvous and intermission socializing, it can also house such secondary activities as benefit dinners, exhibitions, preperformance snacks, and casual performances. Flexible lighting for these spaces enhances their ancillary uses.

In designing the spatial sequence from street to auditorium, the designer will consider the visual requirements for adaptation, the process by which the human vision system responds to widely variable light intensities. Inability to find a seat in a dark movie theater on a sunny afternoon is the consequence of too speedy a passage from one extreme of eye conditioning to the other. Foyers and lobbies

◀ Radio City Music Hall, New York City. The Hall's lit vertical signs and prominent marquee attract New Yorkers and tourists alike. Edward Durell Stone, architect. Photo by T. Whitney Cox.

▲ Radio City Music Hall, New York City, entry lobby. Immediately upon entering Radio City Music Hall, the audience is captivated by the high ceilings, light fixtures, and sparkling surfaces. Photo by T. Whitney Cox.

are the instruments of light adaptation in theater buildings; dark theater rooms (cinemas, black-box auditoriums) require careful attention to daytime adaptation.

Next in the entry sequence are the corridors and vestibules leading to the main hall, or halls. Many new theaters have multiple performance spaces. If these are serviced from a single lobby, wayfinding becomes a central design challenge, and light, with its ability to delineate multiple points of entry, is a prime tool for clarifying circulation (Color plate 7).

The point of connection between circulation and the performance space requires careful attention. While the audience normally passes from lighted corridors to the lighted house before and after the show and at intermissions, there is also the occasional need to enter and leave the house when it is dark and the performance is under way. Small vestibules at this point of transition serve as light and sound locks to isolate the house from the public spaces outside, and they require two modes of illumination. General lighting in these vestibules should be dimmed with the house lighting, leaving only a well-shielded aisle-light type of "floor washer" to provide safe passage. These vestibules must also be configured so that no excess daylight or, especially, direct late-afternoon sunlight can penetrate into the house from the lobbies or corridors. While one could imagine an exception to these precautions, such as a concert hall that encourages daylight as an amenity, even this kind of hall is frequently used for theatrical music events requiring complete control of exterior light.

The Performance Space

We now come to the house, the space most completely separated from the world outside, entered with anticipation and expectation. This room requires hard choices. It is the goal of every theater architect to provide each audience member with perfect sight lines and acoustics, an intimate connection with the performance, a comfortable seat, an engaging environment, and an easy route to the restroom at intermission. It is the goal of every theater manager to have and sell enough seats to pay for ever-escalating costs of production. Hence, theater rooms are often larger than anyone really wants them to be, and it is the task of the architect and his lighting colleague to provide the best possible perceived scale of the performance space, no matter what the actual volume might be.

How can we define the lighting design of a performance space? The specific lighting "task," after all, is merely to help the theatergoer find a seat safely and to read the program. The challenge, however, is to discover the way to integrate light and architecture to fashion a room that is welcoming, warm, exciting, and of a humane scale.

Size and scale are the most important considerations in the design of lighting for performance rooms. We want to feel we are close to the stage, near the action. The position, repetition, and brightness of light elements and luminous surfaces determine how we perceive size and scale. The eye is always drawn to the brightest elements in the field of vision. If they are near you and small, a room feels intimate; make them large and distant, and the room feels vast.

A simple example explains this phenomenon. There are two volumes in the traditional European opera house, the outer envelope of the room and the open space inside the horseshoe balconies. By lining the fronts of these balconies with candelabras and placing an elaborate chandelier overhead, the designer has created an intimate room, one in which only those seated in the front rows of the orchestra and in the tiers of boxes are actually contained. More than half of the audience is not sitting in this implied room, yet there is a feeling of great intimacy owing to the smaller volume defined by the collaboration of light, decoration, and color value. The real walls of the room are always dark, so that we won't see them.

This was the objective at the Hult Center in Eugene, Oregon. The designers wanted the rhythm and scale-defining qualities of classical theater balcony

133

▲ Middlebury College Center for the Arts, Middlebury, Vermont. The audience's attention is focused by the lights surrounding the stage and performers. Hardy Holzman Pfeiffer Associates, architect. Photo by Norman McGrath.

candles without the hardware, so they simply cut slices out of the balcony-front and tucked a simple lamp inside. The profile of the cut surface was thus lighted and clearly revealed. These multiple sources also gently illuminated the basket-weave ceiling, thus fixing the light balance between the focal elements (balcony lights) and enclosure (ceiling and walls).

The theater building is not a performance and should not upstage the activity it was designed to house. Nevertheless,

it should awaken the theatergoer's senses in preparation for the performance to come. In the performance room, the theater, there is that magic moment when the houselights dim and the audience grows quiet. This extraction of light from the architectural space prepares the audience to enter another space, theatrical space, where imagination is set free. Stage lighting has freely used color, the third dimension of light (the other two are intensity and direction) to energize the theatrical experience and increase emo-

tional engagement. The decision to use color in light, like all lighting decisions, must evolve from the impulse of the architecture.

DESIGN CRITERIA

Illumination Standards, Codes, and Safety

These design criteria are interrelated and should be considered together. Light levels are recommended by the appropriate national organizations: the Illuminating Engineering Society of North America (IESNA) and its European counterpart. These recommendations are only guidelines, and they are principally useful as evidence in legal actions following an accident. When an elderly audience member falls on the balcony stairs and breaks a leg, you can be certain an expert witness will arrive with a light meter.

To avoid being sued itself, the IESNA does not specify levels. Rather it recommends a range of average illuminances, 5–15 footcandles (fc) for circulation and 10–30 fc where some reading is involved. In practice, the values tend toward the low end in theaters. Common sense must be used; often, especially in educational settings, lobbies may become impromptu rehearsal or study halls and require higher levels.

▲ Hult Center, Hult Center for the Performing Arts, Eugene, Oregon. The Hult's lit balcony fronts mediate the light balance between the focal elements and enclosure. Hardy Holzman Pfeiffer Associates, architect. Photo by Norman McGrath.

The eye is a remarkable instrument. It can adapt to and see well in an extraordinary range of light conditions; daylight delivers 10,000 fc, moonlight delivers .25 fc, and one can easily walk about in either. Good lighting design begins not with numbers but with decisions about the hierarchy of seeing: what is most important, what is next, what should not be seen. If you are lighting a classroom, the blackboard and desks are primary. In a theater lobby, as a social space, the gathering audience is primary and the architectural envelope is next. This does not mean that one needs to direct a battery of spotlights or a field of down lights at the floor; one simply needs to imagine how any proposed solution will address the hierarchy of seeing.

In the United States, there are now stringent energy codes that legislate the amount of energy one can use for lighting. The values allowed are derived by calculation, and they assume that the most efficient light sources and fixtures now available will be used. The most efficient light source in general use is the high-pressure sodium lamp, for street lighting, and the least efficient is the incandescent lamp. If the designer observes these codes strictly, it is virtually impossible to design humane and engaging theater interiors; compliance using flattering, traditional light sources is virtually forbidden. In large projects it is possible to trade energy budgets between spaces, so that the energy saved by efficient lighting design of the scene shop, storage rooms, offices, and garage can be allocated to the public spaces. Only then can flattering incandescent lamps be used.

Theaters, with their attendant complexities of circulation, ramps, stairs of varying pitch, aisles, seat rows, and balconies,

invite accidents. Appropriate illumination is important here, but so is the necessity of carefully considered design and selection of materials. Seeing steps is a matter of contrast, and a patterned carpet can easily conceal this contrast, for example. Providing a safe environment is a matter of common sense.

Flexibility

Lighting is changeable and can support multiple uses. If the theater building is part of an educational setting, chances are that any space may be drafted into alternative service such as test-taking. Providing the lobby with a dimming system facilitates its use for parties and benefit events. Rehearsal studios always benefit from the addition of a simple theater-lighting rig or even a commercial track-lighting setup.

Choice of Sources

The choice of light sources, always difficult, is now complicated by stringent energy codes that favor efficiency over amenity. Fluorescent lamps of all shapes, sizes and form factors, and ceramic metal-halide lamps are all highly efficient and are certainly appropriate for all back-of-house areas. Their color rendering is good, although care must be taken when lighting scene-painting, costume-building, and other color-critical areas that alternative light sources with color appearance identical to stage lighting be available.

Traditionally, the incandescent lamp, in its myriad forms and variations (low-voltage, tungsten-halogen), has been the default choice in public areas, along with linear fluorescent lamps in coves. Only incandescent lamps can be beautifully dimmed. Fluorescent lamps can be reduced to low levels but do not extinguish or restart properly, and the color rendering and color appearance of these sources degrade when dimmed.

Thus, the performance room, the "hall," is almost always lighted with incandescent sources exclusively, as good dimming is clearly required. Sources for the lobbies and ancillary circulation need to be evaluated in terms of program and architectural design.

Maintenance

Performance rooms, with high and complex ceilings, raked floors, and fixed seating, are difficult to maintain unless catwalks are provided that give access to ceiling-mounted lighting, or unless such equipment can be lowered to the floor. In concert halls, acousticians frequently forbid porous ceilings, and setting up portable rolling scaffolds is the only option. Rentable lifts can be used in flat-floor, multistory rooms.

Incandescent sources are shorter-lived than other lamp types. Dimming radically extends lamp life and, because of the relatively short duty cycle of performance spaces, maintenance should not be onerous. By all means provide efficient, long-life "work lights" for difficult-to-maintain spaces to reduce operating and maintenance costs.

BEACONS

While the building is not the performance, it is the home for extraordinary experiences and should so inform the visitor. It is usually used at night, and so light, electric light, is the medium of this message. A great theater building is always a beacon, a luminous nimbus in urban and suburban settings.

BRINGING THE NEW TO OLD THEATERS

HUGH HARDY *H³ Hardy Collaboration Architecture*

A FINE BALANCE

This chapter offers an overview of architectural considerations for reuse of an existing theater. Because these buildings are so different from one another in their spirit and design, generalization is difficult—beyond noting the importance of first determining how they will be used, their seating capacity, and how their auditorium and stage configurations fit intended uses. Some theaters cannot expand their stage space, because they are restricted by adjacent streets or buildings. Others cannot be adapted to new uses, because they lack the appropriate performer-audience relationship. But in bringing an architectural design back to life, restoration of these buildings must first bring audiences and performers together (Color plate 13). It is possible to stage events in the auditorium even before restoration is complete, to build enthusiasm in the community and discover the distinctive characteristics of the performing space.

CHANGE

When considering restoration of an old theater the designer must first recognize how contemporary audiences and performers have changed. In the nineteenth or early twentieth centuries, theaters were known as places where fewer than 1,000 people gathered, solely to experience live performance, hear natural sound, and see a stage set with flat, painted scenery presented by simple illumination. Stagehands operated rigging mechanisms borrowed from ships. Focused, multicolored lighting with moving patterns did not exist. Movies came later. They brought amplified sound, with increasingly large auditoriums that resulted in palaces of 2,000–3,000 seats. These gigantic plasterwork fantasies made the stage a place of spectacle, not dramatic subtlety. Their projected images also changed sight lines, turning side and box seating into a liability.

NEW ELEMENTS

Contemporary theaters bristle with projected images and an electronic technology that amplifies voice and sound. The direction, color, and intensity of light can be controlled and three-dimensional scenery can easily glide on- and offstage, pulled by electric winches. Public spaces of contemporary theaters have been no less transformed (Color plate 14). Toilet use has tripled, concession stands are expected, and food, beverages, and souvenirs form part of the theatergoing experience. Building codes now mandate access to all levels via elevator or ramp. Performer unions demand space layouts whose large size was unknown two or three generations ago. Although it is a design challenge to seamlessly integrate these new elements into older buildings, a careful and respectful approach can lead to delightful results.

RESTORATION

Restoration of a theater can only interpret, not literally re-create, what was once there, but it can accurately convey the theater's original character through the sensitive incorporation of old and new elements based upon the original design. These include the character of fabrics, carpeting, plaster-work, decorative painting, and lighting fixtures. It is therefore essential that the original design be clearly understood. Many American theaters are based on those of Europe, using its traditions and associations to produce interiors that resonate with old-world culture. The style of these theaters is deliberately historical, and they suffer if reconstituted only with an eye to contemporary fashion. Nor should they be replicated to look brand new, as this approach, in which pristine surfaces deny the passage of time, robs them of their own history. Instead, traditional theaters must be interpreted and brought back to life so they convey the correct sense of their own time.

New Amsterdam Theatre

For instance, the New Amsterdam Theatre, on Forty-second Street, in New York City, is awash in colorful excess, an enchanted forest of animals, birds, faces, and ornaments, but its re-created color scheme has been softened to complement higher lighting levels and a large proscenium mural that dominates the room but is itself an interpretation of the original (Color plates 10, 12).

Radio City Music Hall

By contrast, restoration of Radio City Music Hall was a heightened replication. Conceived in 1932 as an antidote to the historicism of previous public gathering spaces, it was intended to be simple and modern, without traditional ornament, unlike any other theater in the world. Our research and the Rockefeller Center archives permitted accurate description of the various interiors so that restoration of this icon could be consistent with its

original intent — to dazzle. Every surface could be replicated exactly, mostly with brand new materials (except for the lobby mirrors, silvered in gold). Lighting levels were increased to accommodate contemporary code requirements and public expectation, so that the results convey to contemporary audiences the power and grandeur of the original design (Color plate 8).

HISTORICAL RESEARCH

Restoration starts with an investigation of written and visual material generated when each theater was built. Newspaper articles, magazine accounts, archival photographs, collections, and oral histories can offer extremely helpful insights. It is important to remember that historical photographs may not be accurate with regard to color values. Film sensitive to a given color will emphasize that hue, making it appear more dominant than it was in reality. It is therefore necessary to examine *all* historical references to a building before determining what any one of its elements will look like. Written accounts of the time can be just as telling as photographs, providing detailed impressions and descriptions of great precision. This kind of research only confirms that each restoration must be an *interpretation* — not an exact replication — of what went before. Final decisions must be a matter of judgment, not applied science.

AUDITORIUM

Seating

By contemporary standards, older theaters have small seats with tight row-to-row spacing, Their upper balconies are uncomfortable, often requiring navigation of perilously steep steps. The seat widths and back-to-back spacing acceptable in previous centuries no longer work. Minimums of 34 in. back-to-back and 23 in. side-to-side are required. Broadway theaters, for all their intimacy and historical significance, have cramped and uncomfortable seating. And Americans continue to get bigger. Although wider seats at all levels can improve comfort in older theaters, back-to-back spacing cannot be increased in balconies because the steps of the seating levels form part of the basic structure. This tightness causes discomfort in the balconies of buildings like the New Amsterdam. In the New Victory Theater, across the street, the architects were able to increase back-to-back spacing by restricting the second balcony to three rows and changing the balcony configuration so that back-to-back spacing is greater and aisles are less steep. Changes like these reduce capacity but vastly increase audience ease.

Acoustics

The acoustics of nineteenth-century theaters were dedicated to natural sound. They are therefore resonant and must be adjusted to accept contemporary levels of amplification. Movie theaters, on the other hand, have absorptive surfaces, because they are designed for amplified sound. Efforts to reuse old theaters must, therefore, include acoustic investigation to ensure new program needs can be accommodated. (See Chapter 8.)

Heating, Ventilating, and Air-Conditioning

The most difficult problems in positioning heating, ventilating, and air-conditioning (HVAC) in old theaters are finding space for concealed duct distribution and introducing the new supply-and-return registers so they do not intrude on the original design. Often, they can be made into slots and included in decorative ceiling patterns to become part of the design. This integration was accomplished with simple curving ducts in the ceiling of the restored New Amsterdam Theatre.

▼ New Amsterdam Theatre, New York City, ceiling (heating, ventilating, and air-conditioning slots). Herts + Tallant, architect; Hardy Holzman Pfeiffer Associates (HHPA), architect. Courtesy of Disney Enterprises, Inc.

▲ Mahaiwe Theater, Great
Barrington, Massachusetts.
J. Mc A. Vance, architect.
Photo courtesy of Mahaiwe
Performing Arts Center, Inc.

Architectural Lighting

Although this subject is covered in Chapter 9, it should be noted here that architectural lighting in restoration work presents challenges different from those of new theaters. Because lighting levels have increased, and there are new sources of light, with brighter, whiter levels of illumination, original lighting levels seem drab by comparison. Furthermore, building-code requirements demand more illumination in general, making it difficult to retain original lighting levels. Lighting fixtures were once all exposed, with decoration a prominent feature of their design.

Chandeliers, wall sconces, torchieres, and patterns made with exposed light bulbs were all part of the auditorium's architecture, serving to both illuminate the space and to provide an ornamental theme.

Contemporary restoration can retain these devices, but cannot make them the principal source of illumination. Subsidiary sources must be provided through concealed fixtures in ways that increase lighting levels while remaining unnoticed. Employing pin-spot down lights is one way to do this; they were successfully incorporated into restoration of the New Amsterdam Theatre's foyer. In all cases the theater must feel as if the original fixtures were the principal source of illumination (Color plate 11).

Decorative Painting

Most theaters built before the Second World War featured some form of decorative painting, and some are astonishingly elaborate, rivaling churches, banks, or state capitols. The painting techniques that made these places gleam are still practiced around the country: glazing in multiple colors, highlighting in silver and gold leaf, stencil work, and trompe l'oeil. Over the years these theaters' auditoriums were often painted several times. It is often assumed that their original decorative scheme is therefore the most authentic and should be re-created through exhaustive paint analysis or scientific investigation. But the oldest decorative work, being the farthest removed in time, is the most difficult to re-create accurately, and once restored may not appeal to contemporary taste.

Selective Restoration

It may therefore be equally authentic to reproduce a scheme from an era not of the theater's origin. This is the premise in restoring the Mahaiwe Theater (1905), in Great Barrington, Massachusetts. Here, the original scheme featured a depressing "Nile green," but the architect is restoring its second scheme, of rose and beige, chosen when it became a movie theater, in the 1930s. Contemporary lighting levels are two or three times as high as those of seventy-five years ago, and illumination is also now less amber than gas lighting or incandescent illumination with carbon filaments. Original colors and surfaces will therefore not look the same under today's lighting intensity and hues. Restoration of painted surfaces is as much a matter of what *feels* correct as it is of careful matching of hues or materials.

STAGE

In the 1920s, large-scale theaters were built for motion pictures, seating thou-

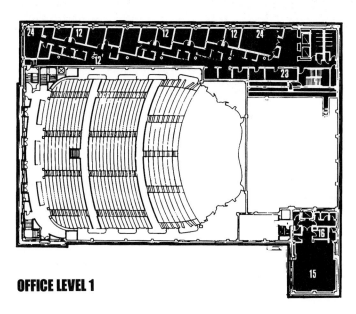

◀ Ohio Theater, Columbus, Ohio. Thomas Lamb, architect; HHPA.

OFFICE LEVEL 1

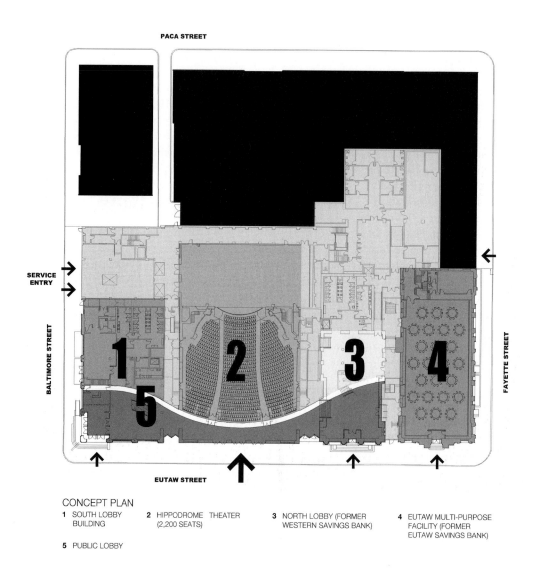

PACA STREET

SERVICE
ENTRY

BALTIMORE STREET

FAYETTE STREET

EUTAW STREET

1 **2** **3** **4**

5

CONCEPT PLAN

1 SOUTH LOBBY
  BUILDING

2 HIPPODROME THEATER
  (2,200 SEATS)

3 NORTH LOBBY (FORMER
  WESTERN SAVINGS BANK)

4 EUTAW MULTI-PURPOSE
  FACILITY (FORMER
  EUTAW SAVINGS BANK)

5 PUBLIC LOBBY

▲ *France-Merrick
Performing Arts Center
(formerly the Hippodrome),
Baltimore, Maryland,
expanded stage. Thomas
Lamb, 1914, architect; HHPA.*

sands in elaborately decorated auditoriums. However, because scenic needs were minimal beyond illuminated backdrops, the actual stage space is surprisingly small, with short fly lofts appropriate for vaudeville. Unless these stages are expanded, they cannot house contemporary touring productions. No matter how dazzling the auditorium's plasterwork, these

buildings can be converted for contemporary performance only if adjacent land is available for stage expansion. This was accomplished at the Ohio Theater (1928), Columbus, Ohio, by adding 2,000 sq ft of stage space and an expanded fly loft. At the France-Merrick Performing Arts Center (once the Hippodrome Theater, 1914) in Baltimore, Maryland, 3,700 sq

ft were added to the original 1,800 sq ft stage. The 4,500-seat Uptown Theater in Chicago, however, is landlocked because the stage is parallel to a major street.

PUBLIC SPACE

Lobby

The great fun of attending live performance is seeing other people in the audience. Staircases, level changes, overlooks, and transparent walls in public spaces all contribute to audience enjoyment by

making people-watching possible. Existing buildings often have no such facilities, so that intermission is a cramped and inhospitable experience. The cost of constructing additional lobby space can be offset by the income it produces in concession sales and rentals for community functions. Independent of performance, parties, receptions, and weddings are often held in these lobby spaces. Baltimore's 2,100-seat Hippodrome Theater (now the France-Merrick), built for vaudeville, had virtually no public space.

▲ Uptown Theater, Chicago, Illinois. Rapp + Rapp, architect. Photo courtesy of the Theatre Historical Society of America.

Buildings were therefore added to either side of the auditorium for circulation, toilets, concessions, VIP lounge, ticketing, and a gift shop. Designed so that new seamlessly meets old, the expanded public space and its circulation patterns offer ample opportunity for audiences to discover each other.

Box Office

The box office was once a place that handled large amounts of cash, requiring physical security appropriate to its function. However, in the era of credit cards, the Internet, and telephone reservations, cash box offices are all but obsolete. Theater ticketing can now be as electronically sophisticated as ordering an airplane ticket. Box offices therefore use a limited amount of cash and need no longer be equivalent to the teller's window in a bank. In fact, an open counter equipped with the ubiquitous computer can now provide the welcoming ease of a hotel reception desk. The results are far more pleasant for theatergoers to experience. In existing theaters, the original box office may be restored for historical accuracy, but an additional, more commodious, up-to-date ticketing space should also be contemplated. The 1999 renovation of Orchestra Hall in Minneapolis, Minnesota, achieved a far more inviting, open reception area for box-office use.

Restrooms

In the nineteenth century, women were conditioned not to use public restrooms, because they were unable to remove their elaborate costumes unaided. Men were provided smoking lounges in which to relax and discuss business during intermission, but neither sex had access to more than a handful of plumbing fixtures.

These days, no matter what the cause—increased bottled-water sales or a shift in cultural mores—there is no doubt that Americans have changed their habits, requiring more fixtures. It is now all but impossible to provide enough toilets to prevent intermission lines for restroom facilities. Therefore, according to the Inter-

◄ *France-Merrick Performing Arts Center (formerly the Hippodrome), Baltimore, Maryland. Thomas Lamb, architect; HHPA. Photo courtesy of Alain Jaramillo.*

▼ *Minnesota Orchestra Hall, Minneapolis, box office. HHPA. Photo courtesy of Baker Associates, Inc.*

▶ *Vivian Beaumont Theater, Lincoln Center, New York City, restroom. Eero Saarinen, architect; HHPA. Photo by Elliott Kaufman.*

national Building Code, restrooms in older theaters must be expanded to provide at least 1 fixture per 125 males and at least 1 fixture per 65 females, and the plan locations for these fixtures must meet standards of accessibility. Men spend less time than women in restrooms, so it is appropriate to plan for twice the number of fixtures for women.

SUPPORT SPACES

In older theaters, administrative operations were simple and did not require elaborate marketing, publicity, or fundraising. Today, much more administrative

space is required, as are other support areas, namely rehearsal rooms, shops, expanded dressing rooms, locker rooms for musicians, and active storage spaces immediately adjacent to the stage. Commercial theaters require dressing rooms for a minimum of 90 people, at a total of 6,000 sq ft; community theaters might need dressing rooms for 34 and require only 2,000 sq ft.

STRUCTURE

Many theater buildings from the early 1900s were constructed of wood and plaster within a masonry shell. Although

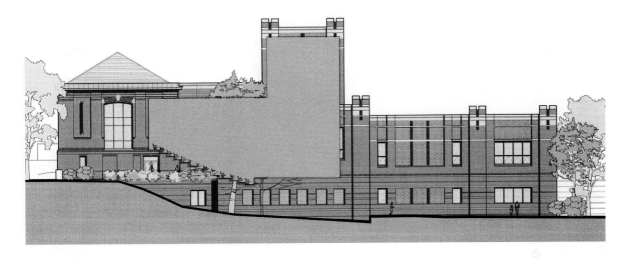

▲ Royden B. Davis, S.J., Center, and MBNA Performing Arts Center, Georgetown University, old-and-new hybrid, Washington, D.C. HHPA and H³ Hardy Collaboration Architecture, architect.

they appear to be solid, they are in fact built like scenery, with decorative surfaces supported by little more than wooden slats. New theaters, however, are made of steel and concrete. Sometimes construction of a new theater requires adaptation of an existing building so that both old and new structures form the auditorium. The resulting hybrid can be successful, though contemporary structural modifications, such as reinforcing roof trusses, often have to be made to the older buildings. At Georgetown University, Washington, D.C., the architects are restoring and extending an existing gymnasium with a new structure to make a 350-seat theater housed in both old and new construction.

Fire Prevention

Building-code issues are addressed in Chapter 6, but it should be noted here that an existing building's fire rating can be improved with the installation of sprinkler systems. Routing piping through old buildings requires great care, however. To comply with contemporary building codes, these systems must be installed in attic space above the auditorium, in passageways surrounding it, or within the room itself. Full sprinkler coverage is difficult to achieve in some areas, and the process can be costly. Improved fire separations, such as metal closures and smoke dampers in air ducts and fire doors between the auditorium and the lobby, may also be required.

Buildings made of steel and concrete are less vulnerable to fire, but they, too, must meet contemporary codes that call for fire separation between the auditorium, lobby, and stage areas, together with smoke dampers in ductwork to prevent the spread of toxic air in a conflagration. The integration of piping and sprinkler heads, even if they are concealed, requires great care to ensure they do not interfere with the decorative character of the existing auditorium.

Air-Conditioning

The addition of air-conditioning equipment may require structural modifications to the roof. These modifications may call for an acoustic enclosure to prevent noise from disturbing neighbors as

▲ Mahaiwe Theater, Great Barrington, Massachusetts, air-conditioning. H³.

▶ Lyceum Theater, New York City, overbuild. Herts + Tallant, architect; HHPA.

BUILDING EXTERIOR

Air Rights

Air space over a landmark property can be a valuable asset, because it represents a large volume that could contain more floor area if the landmark were not there. Those who believe preservation of landmark buildings has value for the larger community have enacted legislation that permits this unused space to be sold to owners of contiguous properties, thereby allowing bigger buildings on adjacent lots. Although these transfers change the architectural context by increasing the size of neighboring buildings, they often ensure the survival of the landmark property. Theaters are logical candidates for such negotiations. They usually occupy dense urban areas where land costs are at a premium. In some instances theaters are landlocked between tall buildings and cannot sell their air rights to adjacent properties. In those cases, a zoning analysis is required to determine whether air-rights transfers are possible through a common ownership or other zoning device.

Marquees

Everyone associates live-performance theaters with marquees that blaze with blinking light bulbs and illuminated titles. These embellishments date from the 1920s era of movie palaces. In an effort to compete with the energy and salesmanship of movie-house marquees, even legitimate theaters in the 1920s added light-bulb adornments to attract audiences to New York's side streets. Their effectiveness is based on appealing to pedestrians or passengers in slow-moving vehicles passing slowly through crowded city streets. Marquees cannot be read

well as theater patrons. At the Joyce Theater, New York, a 10-ft metal panel enclosure was placed around rooftop units to reduce airborne noise (Color plate 15). At the Mahaiwe, in Great Barrington, Massachusetts, new fan units have been placed in steel and concrete enclosures above the auditorium ceiling, under the roof, in new space separated structurally and acoustically from the auditorium enclosure. Placing these units on isolators and enclosing them with specially constructed walls provides the required sound isolation. All ductwork contains sound traps isolating fan noise from the auditorium.

▶ Pentagram's LED sign for the Brooklyn Academy of Music (BAM), New York. Herts + Tallant, architect. Photo by James Shanks.

from speeding cars or the large distances of shopping-center parking lots.

Therefore, marquee restoration must be considered in relation to the theater building's present context. The original marquee displays may need amplification to compete with nearby buildings. LED (light-emitting diode) signage displays are becoming commonplace, and may overwhelm the original marquee illumination. Although not consistent with the idea of restoration, perhaps they can be included to agreeably complement the original neon and incandescent light-bulb presentations of traditional marquees. Freestanding pylons, such as the

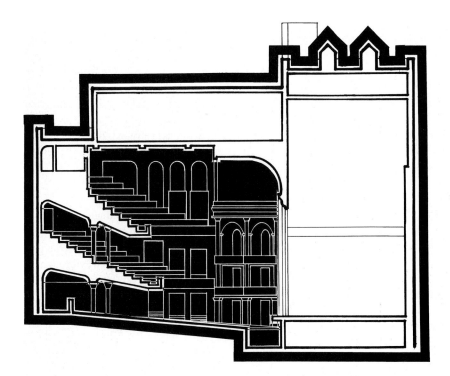

◀ Brooklyn Academy of Music, section before. HHPA.

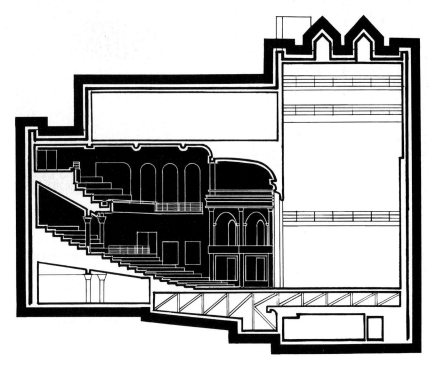

◀ Brooklyn Academy of Music, section after. HHPA.

one on Flatbush Avenue announcing the Brooklyn Academy of Music (BAM), with LED signage and motion can be provided to signify the activities within the building without disfigurement of the historic structure.

RADICAL CHANGE

Sometimes a radical transformation of the audience-performer relationship is desirable. This accomplishment can mean a wholly new interior configuration. The Harvey Theater, at the Brooklyn Academy of Music, New York, was transformed to accommodate Peter Brook's production *Mahabharata*. The audience-performer relationship was changed when the two-balcony theater became an amphitheater set beneath a single, shortened balcony. Although this altered architectural section brought new design elements into the theater, its surfaces remained rough, without restoration, scarred by water, disintegrated from disuse and the passage of time. The result is a new theater steeped in history, a contemporary performance place that resonates with the past (Color plate 16).

A CONVERSATION

Whatever a theater's configuration, the key to its restoration lies in balancing contemporary cultural values and design ideas with those that originally brought it into being. As you can see from the accompanying illustrations, this approach opens a conversation across generations that can yield wonders.

CHAPTER 11

ORGANIZATION: PROCESS AND TEAM

HUGH HARDY *H³ Hardy Collaboration Architecture*

Theater design has become increasingly specialized, calling for input from many different disciplines. Like performance itself, which is dependent upon interaction among varied talents, theater design requires that a group of professionals work together as a team to produce the construction documents. But the architect must be responsible for orchestrating these experts' contributions and for creating a successful whole.

PLANNING TEAM

Total membership of the team includes:

Architect

Theater consultant

Acoustical consultant

Structural engineer

Mechanical engineer

Graphic designer

Lighting designer

Theater management consultant

Cost consultant

PHASES OF WORK

Upon completion of a feasibility study developed in consultation with the architect and appropriate team members, each project passes through six phases.

1. Preschematic program study
2. Schematic design
3. Design development
4. Construction documents
5. Bid and negotiation
6. Construction administration

1. Preschematic Program Study

Chapter 1 discusses the planning of a theater and the value of having a theater consultant participate in this phase of work. In the preschematic programming phase the team must address a number of crucial issues.

Auditorium use

The team must consider all possible uses of the auditorium and prioritize them. Its members must discuss with the client what types of performance will take place, their frequency, maximum number of performers involved, support services they will need, and the time required to change over from one activity to another. The auditorium's character also needs to be addressed. Should it be a formal, polished interior intended to impress or a rough-and-ready work space? Will it be used for nontheatrical events? Lectures? Movies? Music? If so, in what order of importance?

Auditorium mechanical systems

Because the acoustics of the audience chamber are so intimately tied to the design and operation of mechanical systems, it is important to include a mechanical engineer in the early phases of planning a theater. To insure quiet, large amounts of air must be moved slowly, requiring large ductwork and fans. (Chapter 4 discusses how a supply-air system under orchestra seating can offer cost savings.) These distribution systems take up considerable space and must be positioned so they do not interfere with activities on the stage or in public areas. In addition, air movement must be carefully considered so that it does not cause drafts in the auditorium or make scenery and curtains move or flutter. Smoke-purge systems may be required in large atrium spaces, and this equipment, together with a large-scale fan unit must also find space.

Proscenium stage

In the nineteenth century the stage was separate from the auditorium and had its own changing lighting and scenery. Similarly, the auditorium was an independent chamber with permanent décor, lighting, and circulation. One room containing the audience looked into the other containing the performers, and they were separated by a house curtain.

Having fallen out of fashion in the 1960s, the formal proscenium stage has again become the dominant form for live performance. Criticized as inflexible and old-fashioned, this frontal relationship has reasserted its primacy but with a looser definition of where performances take place. Now the auditorium and the stage are often joined, and performers are free to roam through the entire volume, even though the audience has a fixed frontal view of the stage. The opening sequence of *The Lion King* includes a procession of characters down the aisles in the orchestra seating, and the second act begins with musicians playing from box seating on either side of the proscenium. Broadway productions frequently do not use a house curtain, presenting an unpeopled set as a visual prelude to performance.

Thrust stage

In a thrust stage, originated on this continent by Sir Tyrone Guthrie in a theater at Stratford, Ontario, Canada, the performers are surrounded on three sides by steeply raked banks of seats so that movement becomes an especially important aspect of directing—and performing—a play. The Arena Stage, in Washington, D.C. (1961), designed by Harry Weese, was America's first new building for theater-in-the-round, where performers are completely surrounded by the audience, making static positioning of actors undesirable. Great professional skill is required to make productions seem natural and accomplished in these configurations. Variations on the frontal stage formation are far easier for amateur performers to use. Three alternative seating configurations (cinema, courtyard, and surround) are discussed in Chapter 3.

Seating capacity

Capacity is the most crucial factor in planning and has the greatest impact on the auditorium's character and intimacy. Commercial theaters are driven to house the highest possible number of seats to generate income. A capacity of more than 2,000 people is not uncommon. Community theaters need to create places that enhance amateur performances and therefore do not often accommodate more than 500 people. Experimental groups need only a few hundred audience members with whom they can try their ideas. Whatever the decision, a balance must be struck among configuration, income, and audience experience.

Balcony

It is not possible to see human expression on actors' faces from farther away than 65 ft. The addition of balconies results in a larger capacity, but for acoustical reasons, a balcony's overhang of orchestra seating can be no more than the vertical dimension from orchestra floor to the underside of the balcony fascia. Addition of a second or third balcony is also possible for even greater capacity, but sight lines will be steep, and code-mandated riser heights will determine the total height limit. Planning a thrust or arena stage yields different results, but the 65-ft limit still applies, and sight lines dictate how best to position the audience for maximum stage and performer visibility.

Public amenities

Theaters have traditionally been designed, like churches, as places for specific activities set apart from everyday experience. Their lobbies, auditoriums, and restrooms are self-contained, separate halls used at only specific times of day. Now, however, the most efficient theaters have public spaces that are used for a variety of activities and can be populated throughout the day. At the Brooklyn Academy of Music, a theater complex built in 1905 has been transformed from a traditional, formal place, alive only during evening performance, to a complex containing a large performance hall (1,200 seats) and four movie theaters of (111, 156, 216, and 300 seats). An addition to an entrance lobby, a combination cafe, lounge, lecture hall, and video parlor, has been constructed in a former ballroom.

Theater lobby spaces can also become public gathering places for dinners, social events, lecture-demonstrations, weddings, festivals, and retail activities. Properly designed, at a minimum of 10 sq ft per person, public spaces generate income and provide amenities their audiences can enjoy as part of the theater-going experience.

Support facilites

Chapter 5 provides insight about planning of backstage facilities for a theater housing touring productions. Although it was written specifically to consider that type of building, its basic principles can be applied to all support spaces. Theater people work long and unusual hours, all the more reason to be attentive to the introduction of natural light, even in rehearsal areas. Offices, meeting rooms, and corridors also benefit from views to the outside world.

Resident technical director

Each resident technical crew has its own methods of storing equipment, ordering supplies, and organizing shop areas. To gain insight about these facilities while planning backstage areas, the architect and theater consultant must talk with resident technical personnel who will operate the new building. There is no right or wrong in many of the configurations except in relation to how the technical crew is organized and prefers to operate. Even a totally new theater organization will benefit from including a designated technical director in the planning phase who can speak for the future building's backstage operation.

Stage access

Loading access to the stage is a crucial factor in site selection and architectural design. Even theaters built with scene shops directly adjacent to the stage need a load-in dock for materials. Although the large semitrailers used for touring shows may not be needed, vans and other trucks must make deliveries. To ensure ease of movement, the truck-bed level must be the same as the stage level. If this cannot be achieved and an elevator at the loading door is required, it has to be at least 10×25 ft. Sloping the access drive to make the truck bed level with the stage creates awkward unloading and creates hazardous conditions when snow and ice are present.

Site selection

Suburban sites often have the advantage of greater nighttime visibility of the building from a distance, but unless they are designed to include illuminated walkways, their ubiquitous parking lots create an unfortunate, lonely landscape for pedestrians. Urban areas demand ingenuity in organizing all the program elements to fit constricted sites, and their dimensions may preclude the inclusion of rehearsal rooms and shops, requiring a program change, off-site components, or land acquisition. Preliminary layouts can determine whether or not the site accommodates the program. If not, it may be possible to adjust the program, or it may be that because service access is inadequate another site has to be chosen.

Budgeting costs

Cost should be calculated at each step of the design process, most particularly at the beginning, when the program and site are defined. Because theaters are such individual and complex building types, their costs should be evaluated in ways that accurately represent their configuration. An overall budget based on square-foot costs can be established for areas in the building other than the auditorium. However, square-foot cost, when applied to the large volumes of a theater, are notoriously inaccurate, and it is best to separate the auditorium and stage from other areas and use separate figures for them based upon local precedent. Furnishings

and equipment, fees, and permits must be added to determine the toal project cost. Once the site layout is complete and the program, plan, and square-foot cost are in balance, it is possible to advance to Schematic Design.

2. Schematic Design

This phase of work establishes the basic systems and organization of the project. Whether the theater is to be a storefront conversion or a new multistage performing arts center, the basic design challenges are the same. These issues are as follows:

1. How the audience enters the building
2. How performers enter the building
3. How scenery enters the building
4. How support spaces get access to the stage
5. How to get from dressing rooms to the stage
6. How public amenities are placed in the public space
7. How circulation for the public, performers, and crew is best organized
8. How the resulting volumes relate to the site
9. Where the mechanical equipment and ductwork should be located
10. What type of acoustic separations are required

Because mechanical and electrical costs are 35–40 percent of the total building construction cost, a design approach to these elements must also be conceptually defined. For instance, acoustical requirements must be noted for the auditorium, for the separation between mechanical systems and the audience, and for the separation between the auditorium and other spaces. Rehearsal rooms must be isolated; roof drains, plumbing, and elevator machinery all generate noise and must be planned as acoustically separate. With all this information in place the planning team is advised to measure cost a second time, to make certain the project is on course.

Building configuration

After the core team has made the decisions discussed above and a budget has been accepted, design can begin on both the building's outside and its inside. Requisite volumes are combined in a configuration the site can easily sustain. Several configurations are considered before an acceptable design is defined. From these, one or two schemes are chosen for further development, and at this stage the program may require adjustment to meet budget limits.

3. Design Development

This is the phase that determines materials and finishes, together with the specific definition of room character and system coordination. The various systems compete with one another for space, and priorities must be established that recognize and resolve architectural and operational conflicts. In this phase, models of the auditorium are made, built at as large a scale as practical. It is difficult to judge relationships in the auditorium with a model smaller than a quarter-inch equaling one foot. Large-scale models aid in accurate coordination of the different disciplines, helping the team members to apply their particular expertise to the project. This phase of design also advances development of structural and mechanical systems (particularly duct placement) as well as a general concept for lighting design and stage technology. Based upon

documentation from each consultant, a coordinated set of drawings is prepared, and the project is again reviewed for aesthetics and function. Cost must again be measured at the end of this phase, only now the team can use the building's actual components to figure expense instead of relying on square-foot measurements.

Mechanical and electrical systems

The mechanical and electrical systems of a theater grow more complex each day. With code requirements and the need for creature comforts constantly expanding, more than half the construction budget often goes to the provision of technology no one can see. Illumination, smoke alarms, strobe-light warning, CO_2 detection, temperature and humidity readings, and security systems are all dependent upon electricity. Distribution of these systems requires careful study. To meet acoustic criteria, mechanical systems must move large amounts of air slowly. This requires big, sometimes gigantic, ductwork that must be routed through the architecture and most likely placed out of sight. Alternative equipment locations and ductwork routing must be studied to find the best solution; the structural systems have their own requirements.

4. Construction Documents

Even more challenging than control of the theater's complex geometries of sloping, curving, non-Euclidean surfaces is coordination of fully developed systems within the auditorium envelope. Detached structural elements, ductwork, mechanical units, and electrical services all compete for accommodation in the same space and must be properly integrated with the overall design. This integration of systems coordinates the trades, combines the systems, and defines how the project comes together. The most difficult task is coordination, which involves intense deliberation among team members.

Interior finishes

Final finishes call for paint and materials mock-ups for the architect's review. Even in a small theater, mock-ups are essential to determine finishes in spaces whose surfaces will be seen both up close and at great distance. It is particularly important that these be seen in lighting that approximates that of the finished auditorium. Construction work-lights seldom match the color and intensity of completed house lighting, and viewing colors without the proper illumination is a waste of time.

5. Bid and Negotiation

Often the best way to select contractors and to evaluate the cost of construction is to observe conventional bidding practices, in which documents are released to a list of contractors for competitive pricing. However, it may be that a construction manager should be hired at the beginning of the design process to offer guidance about systems, materials, and construction methods and to be responsible for maintaining the budget and schedule. In some cases, the construction manager who assumes the role of general contractor is paid a fee and then manages the bidding process to select subcontractors. Large projects require expertise in the control of scope and cost, both likely to spiral upward without the continuity of construction-manager involvement. Small projects can be worked backward from a fixed budget and scheduled with a willing and reliable general contractor. A

careful evaluation of alternative strategies by the architect and the owner during the planning phase will determine the best route to be taken.

6. Construction Administration

Shop drawings provide another aspect of coordination and are of extreme importance in the construction process. Although difficult to determine, a schedule for their submission is essential so that the architect can allocate appropriate staff. It is also necessary to submit the drawings in a sequence that permits proper coordination. For instance, confirming duct dimensions before the basic structure has been located can lead to insurmountable problems.

THE THEATER OPENING

All new theaters require a shake-down period so that the stage crew can adjust to new systems, become familiar with new equipment, and learn the response of the building's various elements. It is therefore essential to have time to "break in" a new theater, anywhere from one to three months, depending upon the scope of the project. Management must not make the mistake of opening a new theater with a major stage production. Audiences will be sufficiently curious about the place to enjoy a tour, congratulatory speeches, perhaps readings or short musical presentations—something diverse to show off the hall's acoustics and technology—but by no means can the theater open with the serious presentation of a major work. The first audience has come to celebrate and have a good time, to see the architectural accomplishment, and to admire itself. Once this festive night is over, theater staff can settle in and present more serious fare.

A SEAMLESS WHOLE

Theater is a collaborative art. The team that plans, designs, and constructs for the stage must similarly work with a free exchange of ideas, understanding the importance of each discipline that contributes to the whole. Brilliant architecture can be rendered useless by faulty technology, or a structural system designed without knowledge of requirements for acoustic isolation can cause basic problems. It is essential that the architect coordinate the disciplines in a clearly articulated process that leads from abstract, large-scale design ideas to specific details. Aside from housing performance, theater architecture's most important goal is to heighten both the anticipation of the performance and the performance itself. The building should make theatergoing an event sustained by the informed contribution of each discipline.

THE BUSINESS AND ART OF THEATER MANAGEMENT

DUNCAN M. WEBB *Webb Management Services, Inc.*

This book is about the design of theaters, so the influence of design decisions on the operation and maintenance of performing arts facilities is well worth considering. The management of performing arts facilities is as complicated as their design. There are many facets to the job, and no simple way to approach it. This chapter considers models for the operation and management of performing arts facilities and reviews how they are activated, staffed, and sustained. It also brings an operating perspective to a series of design issues and reviews trends in the field.

OPERATING MODELS

Different entities operate performing arts facilities, including government, the private sector, educational institutions, professional management companies, and arts organizations. Commercial entities also own and operate performing arts facilities to generate a profit, but this model works well only when the facility supports commercially oriented, profit-generating activity. For example, a small group of real-estate interests owns almost all of the Broadway theaters in New York, and a few commercial producers then use those venues to produce live drama and musical theater. Similarly managed theaters exist around the country, such as the venues in Branson, Missouri, or the large historic theaters in downtown Chicago.

More recently, several larger facilities (with 3,000-plus seats) have emerged to accommodate the largest touring musicals and popular entertainment. Examples of this new kind of facility include the 4,600-seat Oakdale Theater in Wallingford, Connecticut (owned and operated by Clear Channel Entertainment), and the 3,600-seat Kodak Theater in Los Angeles, owned by the developer Trizec-Hahn and operated by Anschutz Entertainment. There are also several management companies that operate smaller, more culturally oriented venues, but their income is fee-based and comes from the public-sector owners of the facility.

Commercial facilities succeed when revenues exceed costs, enabling the operator to repay invested capital with positive returns. What this means is that less profitable activities, such as the presentation of a symphony orchestra, a ballet, or a play, require a different operating model. Local and touring groups that present performing arts programs have limited resources to pay rent, because production costs are high and the potential return is relatively low.

The economists William Baumol and William Bowen articulated this challenge in their groundbreaking book *Performing Arts: The Economic Dilemma,* published in 1966. Costs are escalating, and there is virtually no way to increase productivity. For instance, the same number of musicians is needed to perform Haydn's *The Creation* in 2004 as on its opening night in 1798. Presenting the fine arts requires increasing levels of subsidy and philanthropic support. That subsidy usually goes directly to the producing organizations themselves, and facilities must reduce rental rates and ticket prices for nonprofit events. Also, the audience for performing arts events is smaller than the audience for popular events, which further limits the revenue potential of these programs.

Single-User Facilities

The most basic issue in the operation of performing arts facilities is whether a particular building is to serve one organization or multiple users. A good example of a single-use venue is the Steppenwolf Theater, in Chicago, which controls and uses four performance spaces on an almost constant basis. Another is Symphony Hall, in Boston, which is owned and operated by the Boston Symphony for the express purpose of providing a home for the Symphony's annual performance season. Other examples of a single-use venue include Michigan Opera Theater's control of the Detroit Opera House and the Alvin Ailey American Dance Theater's new home under construction in New York City. Outside groups occasionally rent these halls, but management does not aggressively solicit these rentals.

Multiple-User Facilities

The more common (and more interesting) type of venue is the one used by multiple groups but run by a facility-based management organization. Unlike the single-use venue's exclusive focus on the resident company's work, the multi-use performing arts center is generally a mission-driven facility established to serve the community through programs that appeal to diverse audience groups. Think of the Joyce Theater in New York City, which accommodates dozens of dance companies each year. Or the Yerba Buena Center, in San Francisco, with its program of music, theater, and dance pre-

sented by local and touring groups. Or Florida's Tampa Bay Performing Arts Center, which has a large group of resident organizations that have access to its various halls. The key is that the local ballet, symphony, and opera company may use the performing arts center, but their interests are subservient to those of the facility, its funders, and the community in general.

Facility operators usually seek funding from the public or nonprofit sectors to support programming and operations. And, indeed, the funding sources for construction of a facility usually determine the nature of its operating entity. For example, if a facility's construction was funded by city-backed revenue bonds, then city government may well operate the building. But it is also the case that ownership and operating models can change. Some buildings that are developed and funded by the private sector can revert to local government when the building opens.

From this point on, this chapter considers facility management skills, challenges, and practices from the perspective of performing arts facility managers, whether they work for the government, a nonprofit, a college, or a professional management company.

RUNNING A THEATER

What does it take to run a theater and to do it well? Or, to put it another way, what is the job description of a successful theater manager? Here are a couple of typical job postings for facility managers:

Executive Director: An award-winning performing arts center seeks a highly qualified arts leader to continue its growth as a major regional arts institution. The executive director oversees, directs, and assures high quality in all operations and functions of the center in accordance with the by-laws and reports to the board of directors. The executive director will: direct a 60-person staff; develop and administer an annual budget of $1 million+; oversee financial and legal compliance and reporting; oversee events, resource development, marketing, and grant writing; provide local and statewide leadership and advocacy for the center; build relationships with artists, arts organizations, business, government, education, media, members, donors, and program users, and serve as chief spokesperson for the center.

General Manager: Arts center seeks an enthusiastic, self-motivated individual for senior staff position. Responsibilities include (but are not limited to) coordination of facility use with in-house and outside rentals of the theater, gallery, and meeting rooms; daily operation of facilities and personnel; budget creation and administration; artist contract negotiations, educational program development; strengthening and development of board and staff; building of local private, corporate, and business contributions and development of strategic plan for the next step in the center's growth.

Each ad goes on to list the qualifications and experience required for the positions, which generally include a postgraduate degree, experience in a similar position, communications and grant-writing skills, knowledge of computers, technical theater, production, and marketing, and the ability to present a positive public image of the facility.

The language in these job postings is rather aggressive—an effective way to discourage all but the most serious candidates. But it does suggest that the job has many different and demanding elements. Here are the tasks common to most facility managers.

Facility Management

The job starts with responsibility for a physical space, including the condition and maintenance of the structure and systems, liability, and neighborliness. The manager must oversee front-of-house operations, including the box office, food services, and ushers (with a strong emphasis on customer service). The job also requires an understanding of backstage operations, management of an industrial work space, and technologies that create the magic of performance. Finally, the facility manager must be heavily involved in capital planning, maintenance, budgeting, and managing a very expensive and heavily-trafficked building whose life span should be measured in centuries.

Activating the Facility

Next, the manager must activate the facility with some combination of the following:

Presented events

These are events purchased by the facility or an organization associated with the facility, promoted locally, and presented in the facility. There is a huge and sophisticated industry devoted to touring arts and entertainment programs made available to facility managers.

Arts-organization rentals

Theaters are often activated by local arts organizations that produce or present their own work. For this kind of use, the facility establishes rental arrangements, providing access to the facility and related services for a fee. These are important programs and are often the reason the facilities were developed in the first place.

Education programs

It is important to separate education programs from other kinds of events in a facility. Whether it is the touring Missoula Children's Theater in Montana, the local symphony adding a special school performance, or a teacher-training program, the building often plays a role in developing and promoting educational programs in the community. Facility managers recognize that educational programs attract funders in both the public and private sectors. And education is fundamental for nonprofit facilities, as their incorporation as 501(c)3 tax-exempt organizations depends on having an educational mission.

Produced events

Sometimes the facility itself creates a play, a dance performance, or an opera. In fact, more and more facilities are moving from renting and presenting toward a more active role in producing events. For example, the National Arts Centre in Ottawa, Ontario, manages and controls a symphony, a dance company, and both English- and French-language theater companies.

Other community uses

Finally, there are all of the other rental events that activate the facility and help pay the bills, from corporate meetings to wedding receptions. While these events tend not to be intrinsic to the building's mission, they can strengthen the relationship between the building and the community and improve financial performance.

The challenge for the theater manager is balancing the competing uses of a space. Starting in the 1980s this task became a major challenge for managers of larger performing arts centers, as communities became increasingly obsessed with the need to book *Cats, Phantom of the Opera,* and their offspring, often to the exclusion of local performing arts productions. The frenzy has subsided somewhat, but the facility manager still faces considerable pressure to give access to revenue-producing activities.

Managing Staff and Board

With a building and a program in place, the performing arts facility manager must maintain staff and volunteer organizations, which present significant challenges. The staff of a theater tends to be a committed and tight-knit group who work very hard for relatively little money. Running a theater requires diversity of skills and characters, from the disheveled, late-night technical director to the flashy breakfast-meeting development director. The manager must bring this group together to work as a team and to work long, hard hours for limited monetary rewards.

The second half of the challenge is working with a board of directors or trustees, a group of volunteers brought together as keepers of the mission, overseers of the operation, and fund-raisers. Facility managers are often surprised at how much time and effort goes into the care and feeding of the board.

Marketing and Fund-Raising

The two main sources of income are ticket sales as a result of successful marketing and contributions as a result of effective fund-raising. Both fund-raising and marketing depend on good information about customers and prospects. As information and communication technologies advance, managers will be able to obtain more and more information about their customers for the benefit of fund-raising and audience development.

Community Relations

Twenty years ago, no one would have thought that theater managers would have to become community-relations experts. The ability to understand, reach out to, and work with other segments of a community has become a critically important part of the job. Partly it is a matter of survival, as theater managers have come to understand that they must prove their facilities to be a fundamental part of the community, not just a place where the rich and famous dress up and mingle. This part of the job also reflects a growing awareness that a theater can have a profoundly positive impact on a community, whether it relates to downtown revitalization, improving the quality of life for all citizens, attracting companies and workers to a community, or building cultural tourism. The manager is responsible for reaching out to the community and making the theater responsive to and supportive of broad community goals.

General Management

Finally, the manager must fulfill the day-to-day responsibilities that come with being the boss, including budgeting, purchasing materials and supplies, developing relationships with suppliers and customers, and being an advocate for the building and the arts in general.

Note the contrast between the facility manager and the manager of a producing organization. In the producing organization, an artistic director usually deals with the creative output and an executive director serves as administrator. One generally reports to the other, or there is a fragile partnership reporting to the board. But for facility-based organizations there is only one leader, and that person is responsible for artistic as well as administrative decisions. In fact, the combination of these responsibilities may be what makes this such a challenging and rewarding job, at least for those who measure their rewards in more than monetary terms.

FINANCIAL OPERATIONS

Theaters that support cultural programming require fund-raising to balance the budget or even generate operating surpluses. Whether or not they are operated by the public or nonprofit sectors, costs are covered on an annual basis with a combination of earned and contributed income. This basic fact drives the two main principles of financing:

Start-Up

There are virtually no theaters that can generate sufficient operating profits and cash flow to service, let alone repay, a mortgage or any other kind of loan. Thus, the planning, design, and construction of theaters must be funded with grants, donations, and bequests from the private sector and allocations of various kinds from the public sector. Those allocations might be a lump-sum payment or an income stream that can support debt for construction. The sources of capital are different for each project, and there is no preferred method of financing the development of theaters. It is up to project backers to investigate the sources of funds in their community, develop a case for support, and then make the appropriate solicitations.

Fiscal Maintenance

Sustaining the financial operation of theaters depends on the ability of organizations to raise contributed income. The amount of fund-raising required depends on:

- the size of the facility and its managing organization
- the level of rental and presenting activity in the building
- commercial versus cultural orientation of the programming

As with capital fund-raising, there are no simple rules or guidelines as to the source of funds. They might come from the public or private sector through annual gifts and grants, deferred giving, or the employment of an endowment whose annual income supports operating needs on a perpetual basis.

THE IMPACTS OF DESIGN ON OPERATIONS

Capacity

The seating capacity of a new hall is the single most contentious issue at the beginning of facility-development projects. There is often significant pressure to increase capacity to attract touring programs to the facility. There is also pressure to keep the capacity down to support local groups seeking intimacy and affordability. The answer, different for every facility, usually comes from a discussion early in the process about the facility's fundamental goals and mission.

The most frustrating issue for many is that, all other things being equal, the annual funding requirement (operating expenses less earned income) for facilities that support cultural programming tends to increase as capacity rises. While a larger capacity often increases financial returns to those who produce and present work, it does not necessarily improve the financial performance of the hall itself. For example, a symphony renting a hall has the financial upside of selling additional tickets against the incremental cost of higher rent in the larger space. But the financial upside for the facility itself is that higher rent, which is generally eclipsed by the higher operating costs of the larger building. Facilities that also act as presenters have the ability to improve this equation, but the overall return is lower, as the facility cannot push rental rates beyond the financial capacity of nonprofit renters.

Flexibility

The second great debate is how flexible the hall must be to accommodate different sizes of audience and types of programs. In fact, the debate has been raging for centuries, moving from one extreme, "Let's do one thing very well," to the other, "Let's do everything the best we can." From an operating perspective, flexibility is good when it increases utilization and maximizes the facility's value to the community. But flexibility is bad when it increases the cost of labor and forces compromises in production quality for audiences and artists. These days, we encourage our clients to seek a level of flexibility that accommodates the main potential users of facilities without causing major aesthetic compromises or substantial additional operating costs.

Public Space

Large public spaces are increasingly important to performing arts facilities, because they generate significant amounts of revenue from meetings and receptions, enhance the preperformance experience, and provide a public space in which to recognize donors. At the same time, this is expensive real estate. Thus, facility designers and managers must weigh additional capital costs against the potential for additional operating revenues and make appropriate investment decisions. The answer is usually based on whether the greater fund-raising challenge is the one-time effort of raising capital funds or the ongoing effort of raising operating funds.

Backstage Space

Here, the issue is the size of the backstage area and its ability to accommodate increasingly larger shows. It is good to have lots of space backstage, but that space comes at a cost and, like the capacity argument, benefits the users more than the facility itself in terms of return on investment.

Backstage Technologies

Technologies such as lighting, sound, rigging, projections, and control systems are advancing rapidly, but not in a way that will fundamentally change the nature of performance. Rather, these innovations are about saving time and money in the production and operation of shows. Some are more dramatic than others, like mechanized rigging systems that reduce labor costs and improve safety, or wireless lighting controls that allow a lighting designer to set the design of a show in hours instead of days. From an operating perspective, decisions about investing in new technologies often address incremental improvements in efficiency and timing; when will a particular upgrade be cost-efficient as costs come down and productivity increases?

Theater managers, like all others wrestling with these issues, are vulnerable to the "clean-cab" theory. Imagine you are at the airport waiting for a cab to take you home. One approaches, but as you are about to climb in you notice that the back seat is filthy, and you wave it off. Along comes another cab in five minutes, but this one has loud music blaring from the front seat. Another ten minutes pass, and along comes another cab. But as you are about to climb in you notice a much bigger cab coming up from behind. And so on...The point is made. No new technology is ever perfect, and there are always reasons to wait a bit longer. But unless you bite the bullet and choose something, you will be left, at least figuratively, standing at the airport.

Quality

Finally, there is the debate about the level of quality as it is represented in the design, room acoustics, furnishings and finishes, and those other elements that affect the experience of the audience and the performing artist. These high standards are expensive to achieve and maintain, but they are important as facilities compete with each other for programs, with the other worthy causes in a community for funding, and with the myriad sources of entertainment for audiences. It is difficult to quantify the impact of good workmanship on the operation of performing arts facilities, but they are there—in the renewal rate for subscriptions, in the return of presenters and promoters to the facility, and in the continuing support of funders.

PREPARING FOR OPERATIONS

As with other complex building types, preparations for the operation of performing arts facilities must begin years before the doors open. The most important steps and their timing include the following.

The Business Plan

Performing arts facilities need a business plan early in the development process. In fact, most funders of these projects require that a business plan be in place before they commit capital funds or provide seed funding to begin the project. The business plan addresses how facilities will be owned, operated, staffed, managed, scheduled, and sustained. Many of the business plans we complete also include an economic-impact analysis that demonstrates the effects of the project on the local economy. These parts of the plan are critical to show that new facilities can succeed financially and that there is significant positive return to the community (financial and otherwise) for the capital invested to build them.

Hiring Staff

The personnel needed to run facilities must be in place well before operations begin. The key is the hiring of the executive director, who is often brought on three to four years before opening, to play the dual role of project manager, driving the planning, design, and construction effort, and visionary, building the organization so it operates smoothly as soon as the doors open. It is an immensely challenging job, with huge pressures to manage the complex building project, raise

money to complete construction and support operations, sell the project to local politicians and community leaders, book artists and events, and balance the needs of the local arts community and their limited resources.

Booking

Seasons must be planned and booked well in advance of opening. The local symphony might need to book dates up to twenty-four months before the event to contract with soloists. The local opera might need eighteen months to set up a coproduction deal with an opera company in another city. And the Broadway presenter needs at least a year in which to book tours coming through the region. The great challenge is often balancing the demands of local groups with the presenting to be done by the facility itself. These challenges are best addressed two years before opening so that precedents and patterns of use have been set by the time the building opens.

Preopening Budgets

With staff coming on board so far in advance, theaters incur personnel and other operating costs well before there are any offsetting revenues. Some of these costs can be capitalized into the construction budget, but most facilities must also start to raise operating support up to two years before receiving box-office revenue or rental income. Because this money is difficult to raise and there is little to show for it, a top-notch fund-raiser and a fund-raising board must be engaged well in advance of opening.

Training and Commissioning

As the opening date approaches, management shifts its focus to training staff and commissioning the building, which means the physical start-up and testing of all elements of the operation, including performance equipment systems. Management must also introduce training for safety and emergency procedures and begin the endless effort of building a customer-service orientation in all areas of the building.

Soft Openings

More and more often, performing arts facilities do not open with one big event, opting instead to stage a series of opening events for each component of the facility. This allows management to introduce the facility into the community in a manageable way, all the while testing and tweaking the building and its operating systems.

Opening Events

With these soft openings, there is also the opportunity for a whole series of opening events. This allows the building to bring many different groups in for all sorts of reasons. There can be a black-tie event for funders, an opening event for local politicians and city staff, and an open house for citizens. The facility risks appearing elitist with the separation of groups, but multiple opening events can generate positive press and community goodwill.

Public Relations

Finally, there is always some controversy as new buildings are completed, with the local media drawn inexorably to stories about cost overruns, acoustic challenges, high rental rates for local users, inadequate parking, and so on. Thus, management is well advised to develop a public-relations plan to anticipate these issues and respond appropriately.

TRENDS IN FACILITY MANAGEMENT

Management of performing arts facilities is different from what it was thirty years ago, and it continues to change. Trends we are observing in the world of facility management follow.

Complexity

Thirty years ago, running a performing arts center was much simpler. Facilities usually survived with a small operations staff and a manager principally concerned with booking rentals. What has happened?

- Local arts audiences want to see the best shows and artists in the world, which requires that facility managers become much more adept at picking and promoting touring entertainment.

- There is much greater diversity of audiences, which requires that facility managers direct their programs at specific market targets.

- Performing arts facilities face intense competition from other entities competing for limited leisure time and leisure dollars.

- Performing arts facilities are much more expensive to build and operate, which raises the enterprise's economic risks.

- Public-sector support has been largely replaced by private-sector philanthropy, which causes intense competition among facilities.

- Communities that support performing arts facilities do so with the expectation that these facilities will contribute to the life and prospects of the community.

We are describing a job that did not exist thirty years ago. In those days, a facility manager was mostly engaged in taking care of a building. Now they are doing whatever they can to animate a facility, sustain its operation, and connect it to the community. And if that means launching targeted marketing campaigns, speaking at Rotary Club meetings, and delivering artists to schools, so be it.

From Rentals to Producing

Also over the past thirty years facility managers have become more and more involved with what is on the stage. The relatively passive act of booking rentals has given way to the risky step of becoming a presenter, choosing shows that fit the facility's mission and contribute to its financial performance. And now facility managers are making the next move, into the world of producing, by investing directly in touring shows or deploying their financial and human resources to commission opera, theater, music, and dance.

This trend is likely to continue. Many facility managers want more control of product for the benefit of the organization and the community. They also understand that gaps in a community's cultural offerings can be filled by the facility. And their mission is often to serve the community by offering more than simply what the people want.

Looking Outward

Performing arts facilities must have an increasingly outward perspective. Facility managers are spending more of their days outside the building and more time thinking about the role of the facility in the community. Thus they are obliged to pay much more attention to customer service, both inside and outside the building.

Extending Their Reach

More facility managers and management organizations these days are extending their skills and resources to run multiple facilities and programs, seeking economies of scale and greater operating efficiency. The skills and resources within facility-management firms can greatly benefit smaller producing and presenting organizations, so these multivenue management arrangements are likely to proliferate.

The Economics of the Arts

Because of the economic challenge of building productivity in the performing arts and the cost squeeze cited by Baumol and Bowen, every decade is financially harder than the one before. The number of seats in a facility and the number of performances that can be given are the same. Twenty years from now, economic viability will be even harder to achieve, which means managers and administrators will have to run their facilities in an even more entrepreneurial fashion, finding revenues and resources wherever possible and spending them wisely.

The High and the Low

One of the most important changes is the breakdown of the traditional separation of "high" arts and the "lower" forms of entertainment, the rarified versus the popular. Nowhere is this blurring more apparent than in the world of music, where adjectives such as classical, modern, world, serious, and popular are becoming less meaningful. Successful managers of performing arts facilities make programming choices that transcend these distinctions, focusing on their mission as well as their sense of the market.

The Role of the Arts

In the final chapter of *The Performing Arts in a New Era,* the authors picture the future of the performing arts. They identify three critical functions of the performing arts in society:[1]

1. The arts act as a source of entertainment, enrichment, and fulfillment for individuals.

2. The arts serve as a vehicle for the preservation and transmission of culture.

3. The arts provide a variety of benefits to society at the individual, community, and national levels.

Benefits of the third category are substantial. For individuals, the arts promote openness to new ideas as well as creativity and competency at school and work. For communities, the arts increase economic activity, create a more livable environment, and promote community pride. Major events like the Spoleto Festival in Charleston, South Carolina, and the Brooklyn Academy of Music's Next Wave Festival attract visitors from all over the world. And at the national level, the arts promote an understanding of diversity and pluralism, reinforce national identity, and help export the most positive aspects of that cultural identity abroad.

Performing arts facilities are the means by which these benefits are delivered. Managers and their staffs offer works from different cultures. Education and outreach programs touch the lives of thousands of people in diverse communities. Active facilities attract economic activity and commercial development. Facility-based festivals build cultural tourism. And all of these successes become a point of pride and identity for the community and the country.

Thus the support sought by facilities from the public and private sectors is more than justified by the entertainment, enrichment, and fulfillment from artist to audience at individual, community, and societal levels.

---

[1] Kevin McCarthy, Arthur Brooks, Julia Lowell, Laura Zakaras, *The Performing Arts in a New Era.* (Washington, D.C.: Rand Corporation, 2001), p. 115.

GLOSSARY

absorption. Interception of radiant energy or sound waves.

adaptation. The process taking place as the eye becomes accustomed to the luminance or the color of the field in view or to its darkness.

air pallet (air castor). A device the principle of which is used in the Hovercraft, a vehicle that can travel over land and water supported by a cushion of air that it creates by blowing air downward. Developed by Boeing, the technology was used theatrically at the Derngate Center in the United Kingdom, where multiple air castors moved three-level seating towers (8–10 tons each) to reconfigure the theater and auditorium.

attenuator. A device for reducing the amplitude of an electrical signal without appreciable distortion.

batt. A square piece of batting.

batting. Layers or sheets of raw cotton or wool or of synthetic fibrous material used for lining quilts or for stuffing or packaging; also, a blanket of thermal insulation (as fiberglass).

bed height. The level of a loading-dock floor that meets the bed (floor) of a truck

catchment area. The seats in an area of a theater auditorium that "drain" directly into an aisleway. The catchment area is bordered by a network of main aisleways, side aisles, and cross aisles that form the primary pedestrian pathways to exits that are evenly and remotely distributed in the auditorium.

clean power. An electrical power supply to sensitive electrical equipment, fed via a conditioner to eliminate irregularities in phase and voltage.

decibel (dB). A scale unit used in the comparison of powers, mainly in electronics and acoustics.

degree day. A unit of temperature used to estimate the total heating and cooling requirements for a building based on climatic data.

design temperature. Typical average winter and summer outdoor design temperature for conditions that reflect local climate.

end stage. A stage at one end of a rectangular room.

exit discharge code. The portion of the means of egress between the exit (such as an exterior door, interior fire stairs, or exterior fire stairs) and a public way (such as a street, alley, or open land that leads to the safe destination).

initial time-delay gap. Acoustics: a measure of early reflections received by audience members.

rated. Code: fire-rated by building code, on a scale of flammable to inflammable.

GFI (Ground Fault Interrupt) outlet. An electrical power receptacle with built-in ground-fault protection, required by the National Electric Code, to be used in wet applications, such as outdoor and sink areas, to eliminate dangerous shock hazards. The device detects differences in the current flowing in the hot and neutral wiring of a circuit, indicating a ground fault or leak in the current, and tripping or interrupting the power.

gobo. 1. A dark strip (as of wallboard) to shield a motion-picture or television camera from light; 2. a device to shield a microphone from sound; 3. a lighting accessory.

MEP. A building's mechanical, electrical, and plumbing systems.

noise criteria (NC). Acoustics: a numerical rating system, or family of curves used to specify background sound levels over a given frequency range.

nosing. The ususally rounded edge of a stair tread that projects over the riser, or a similar rounded projection.

plenum. An air-filled space in a structure, especially one that receives air from a blower for distribution (as in a ventilation system). Plural is **plena.**

plosive. Acoustics: K, P, or T sounds.

road box. A large work box, often on casters, in which tools and other equipment used by the crew department of a traveling production is both stored and transported

reverberation time. Acoustics: the persistence of sound within a space after the sound source has stopped.

standpipe. Code: a high vertical pipe or reservoir that is used to secure a uniform pressure in a water-supply system.

three-dimensional. In theatrical terms, a three-dimensional relationship between performer and audience, i.e., the audience are disposed on multiple levels around the performer.

vomitorium or **vomitory.** An entrance piercing the banks of seats of a theater, amphitheater, or stadium — origin: Latin *vomere,* to disgorge (the spectators).

walking cable net. A grid of cables over a stage platform or seating area that is erected in place of catwalks.

world music. Popular music originating from or influenced by non-Western musical traditions and often having a danceable rhythm.

BIBLIOGRAPHY

STANDARDS AND CODES

Accessible and Useable Buildings and Facilities. Falls Church, Va. American National Standards Institute (ANSI) A1171.1, International Code Council (ICC), 1998.

ADAAG Manual: A Guide to the Americans with Disabilities Act Accessibility Guidelines. Washington, D.C.: U.S. Architectural and Transportation Barriers Compliance Board, 1998.

Americans with Disabilities and Fair Housing Amendments Act. Hauppauge, NY: Manual of Acts and Relevant Regulations, Construction Book Express, 1999.

Code of Federal Regulations. Washington, D.C.: 28 CFR Part 36, Revised July 1, 1994.

Cote, P. E., Ron, ed. *Life Safety Code Handbook,* NFPA 101, 8th Ed. Quincy, Mass.: National Fire Protection Association, Inc., 2000.

International Building Code 2000. Falls Church, VA: International Code Council (IBC, ICC), 2000.

International Building Code 2000. Falls Church, VA: International Code Council (IBC, ICC), Commentary, Volume I, 2000.

International Energy Conservation Code 2000. Country Club Hills, IL: International Code Council (IECC), 2000.

Introduction to Building Codes and Guide to Effective and Efficient Codes Administration. Herndon, VA: National Council of States on Building Codes and Standards, Inc., 2004.

Lawrence, Harry J., Jr. *The Architects Handbook of Professional Practice, Building Codes and Regulations 3.72.* Washington, D.C.: AIA Press, American Institute of Architects, 1994.

Life Safety Code, NFPA 101. Quincy, Mass.: National Fire Protection Association, Inc., 2003.

GENERAL

Appia, Adolphe. 1969. *Music and the Art of the Theatre.* Ed. Barnard Hewitt. Coral Gables, Fla: University of Miami Press.

Appleton, Ian. 1996. *Buildings for the Performing Arts.* Oxford: Butterworth Architecture.

Armstrong, L., and R. Morgan. 1984. *Space for Dance: An Architectural Design Guide.* Washington, D.C.: National Endowment for the Arts.

Around the Fire Service, 1900–1909, The Iroquois Theater Fire, December 30, 1903. Tulsa, Okla.: Fire Engineering and Fire EMS, Fire Engineering.com

Barbe, E., and N. Savarese. 1991. *The Secret Art of the Performer.* New York: Routledge.

Barron, Michael. 1993. *Auditorium Acoustics and Architectural Design.* New York: E & FN Spon.

Bentham, F. 1970. *New Theatres in Britain.* London: Rank Strand.

Beranek, Leo L. 1996. *Concert and Opera Halls; How They Sound.* Woodbury, NY: Acoustical Society of America.

Beranek, Leo L. 1962. *Music, Acoustics and Architecture.* New York: John Wiley & Sons.

Bergman, R. 1987. *The Great Theatres of London.* London: Admiral Books.

Boulet, M-L, C. Moissinac, and F. Soulignac. 1990. *Sale da Concerto.* Milan: Techniche Nouve.

Breton, Gaelle. 1989. *Theatres.* Paris: Editions du Moniteur.

Brett, Richard. 2004. *Theatre Engineering and Architecture.* London: ABTT Theatrical Events, Ltd.

Brockett, Oscar. 1987. *History of the Theatre.* London: Allyn & Bacon, Inc.

Brook, Peter. 1968. *The Empty Space.* New York: Touchstone, 1995 reprint.

Brown, C. R., W. B. Fleissig, and W. R. Morrish. 1984. *Building for the Arts: A Guidebook for the Planning and Design of Cultural Facilities.* Denver, CO: Western States Arts Federation.

Burdick, Jacques. 1974. *Theater (World of Culture).* New York: Newsweek Books.

Burnett, Kate, and Peter Ruthven Hall. 1994. *Make Space!: Design for Theatre and Alternative Spaces.* London: Theatre Design Umbrella.

Burris-Meyer, H. 1975. *Theatres and Auditoriums.* New York: Kriefer, R. E., Huntingdon.

Cartaz Editorial Ltd. 1995. *Theatros do Brasil.* Brasil: Mercedes-Benz.

Contant, C., and J. deFilippi. 1968. *Parallele des Principaux Theatres Modernes de l'Europe.* Manchester, NH: Benjamin Bloom, Inc.

Cowan, Henry J., and Peter R. Smith. 2004. *Dictionary of Architectural and Building Technology.* London: Spon Press.

Davis, Don, and Carolyn Davis. 1987. *Sound System Engineering.* Indianapolis, Ind.: Howard W. Sams & Co.

Diderot, D., and J. d'Alembert. 1972. *Theatre Architecture and Machines.* New York: Arno Press, New York Times.

Doelle, Leslie. 1972. *Environmental Acoustics.* New York: McGraw-Hill Book Company.

Edström, Per. 1990. *Why Not Theatres Made for People?* Värmdo, Sweden: Arena Theatre Institute.

Egan, M. David. 1972. *Concepts in Architectural Acoustics.* New York: McGraw-Hill Book Company.

———. 1988. *Architectural Acoustics.* New York: McGraw-Hill Book Company.

Elder, Eldon. 1993. *Will It Make a Theatre?: A Guide to Finding, Renovating, Financing, Bringing Up-to-Code, the Nontraditional Performance Space.* Washington, D.C.: Americans for the Arts.

Forsyth, Michael. 1985. *Buildings for Music: The Architect, the Musician, and the Listener from the Seventeenth Century to the Present Day.* Cambridge, Mass: The MIT Press.

Gishford, Anthony, ed. 1972. *Grand Opera; The Story of the World's Leading Opera Houses and Personalities.* New York: The Viking Press.

Goodwin, John. 1989. *British Theatre Design: The Modern Age.* London: Weidenfeld & Nicholson.

Graham, Rob. 1999. *Theater: A Crash Course.* New York: Watson-Guptill Publications.

Ham, R. 1987. *Theaters: Planning Guidance for Design and Adaptation.* Oxford: Butterworth Architecture.

Hardy Holzman Pfeiffer Associates. 1999. *Buildings and Projects 1992–1998.* New York: Rizzoli International Publications, Inc.

Hardy Holzman Pfeiffer Associates. 2000. *Theaters.* Australia: The Images Publishing Group Pty., Ltd.

Harris, Cyril M. 1994. *Noise Control in Buildings.* New York: McGraw-Hill, Inc.

Henderson, Mary C. 1986. *Theater in America: 250 Years of Plays, Players, and Productions.* New York: Harry N. Abrams, Inc.

Henderson, Mary C. 1973. *The City and the Theatre.* Clifton, N.J.: James T. White and Company.

Izenour, George C. 1977. *Theatre Design.* New York: McGraw-Hill Book Company.

———. 1977. *Theater Technology.* New York: McGraw-Hill Book Company.

Leacroft, R. 1973. *The Development of the English Playhouse.* London and New York: Methuen.

Leacroft, R., and H. Leacroft. 1984. *Theatre and Playhouse: An Illustrated Survey of Theater Buildings from Ancient Greece to the Present Day.* London and New York: Methuen.

Macgowan, Kenneth. 1921. *Theatre of Tomorrow.* New York: Boni and Liveright Publishers.

Mackintosh, I., and V. Glasstone. 1982. *Curtains!!! or a New Life for Old Theatres.* London: John Offord.

McNamara, B., J. Rojo, and R. Schechner. 1975. *Theatres, Spaces, Environments: Eighteen Projects.* New York: Drama Book Specialists.

Meyer, Jurgen. 1988. *Acoustics and Performance of Music.* Westport, Conn.: Bold Strummer, Ltd.

Mielziner, Jo. 1970. *The Shape of Our Theatre.* New York: Clarkson N. Potter, Inc.

Mullin, D. C. 1970. *The Development of the Playhouse: A Survey of Theater Architecture from the Renaissance to the Present.* Berkeley and Los Angeles: University of California Press.

Naylor, David, and Joan Dillon. 1997. *American Theaters: Performance Halls of the Nineteenth Century.* New York: Preservation Press, John Wiley & Sons, Inc.

Nicoll, Allardyce. 1946. *The Development of the Theatre: A Study of Theatrical Art from the Beginnings to the Present Day.* 3rd ed. New York and London: Harcourt Brace and Company; Harrap.

Report on the Adoption of a Model Building Code, New York City Buildings. 2002. New York: The Mayor's Advisory Commission.

Sachs, Edwin O. 1968. *Modern Opera Houses and Theatres.* Manchester, N.H.: Benjamin Bloom, Inc.

Saunders, George. 1968. *A Treatise on Theatres.* New York: B. Blom.

Schubert, H. 1971. *The Modern Theatre.* London: Pall Mall Press.

Silverman, Maxwell, and Ned Bowman. 1965. *Contemporary Theatre Architecture: An Illustrated Survey: A Checklist of Publications 1946–1964.* New York: The New York Public Library.

Southern, Richard. 1964. *The Seven Ages of Theatre.* London: Faber & Faber.

Steele, James. 1996. *Theatre Builders.* London: Academy Editions.

Taylor, William R., ed. 1991. *Inventing Times Square.* New York: Russell Sage Foundation.

Todd, Andrew, and Jean-Guy Lecat. 2003. *The Open Circle.* London: Faber & Faber.

van Hoogstraten, Nicholas. 1991. *Lost Broadway Theatres.* New York: Princeton Architectural Press.

Whelchel, Harriet, ed. 2001. *The Shuberts Present 100 Years of American Theater.* New York: Harry N. Abrams, Inc.

Wickham, Glynne, and Gladstone Wickham. 1985. *A History of the Theatre.* Oxford: Phaidon.

Wilkes, Joseph, ed. *Encyclopedia of Architecture Design, Engineering and Construction,* Volume 5, Zoning and Building Codes. New York: American Institute of Architects, John Wiley & Sons. Pp. 514–523.

Yanagisawa, Takahiko, and Tak Associated Architects, Inc. 1995. *Theaters and Halls: New Concepts in Architecture and Design.* Tokyo, Japan: Meisei Publications.

INDEX

Aaron, Judith, 45
absorption, acoustic design, 97, 121
accessibility, egress system, 77–80
acoustic abnormality control, acoustic design
  principles, 95–97
acoustic banners, acoustic design principles,
  94
acoustic curtains, acoustic design principles,
  95
acoustic design flexibility, 115–128. *See also*
  flexibility
  amplification, 121–124
  bid conference, 116
  Broadway theaters, 124–126
  construction, 116
  construction drawings, 116
  criteria, 117–127
  design development, 116
  feasibility study, 115
  found spaces, 121
  future theaters, 127–128
  multipurpose road houses, 126–127
  new theaters, 120–121
  postconstruction, 117
  program study, 115
  schematic design, 115–116
  small unamplified theaters, 118–120
acoustic design principles, 87–113
  audio systems, 44
  auditorium/stage design, 39
  balance, 101–102
  balconies, 95, 96
  case study, 98–100
  checklist for, 112–113
  direct sound, 87
  echo and abnormality control, 95–97
  materials, 100–101
  modernization, 141
  orchestra-pit design, 103–104
  orchestra-shell design, 104–105
  performance types, 110–112

  performer's hearing, 102
  reflected sound, 87–89
  reverberation time and volume,
    93–94
  room height, 90–93
  room shape, 101–102, 106
  room width, 89
  sidewall boxes and galleries, 89–90
  sound isolation, 106–110
  variable elements, 94
acoustic reflectors, acoustic design principles,
  91–93
acoustic volume, acoustic design principles,
  93–94
adjacencies, backstage design/planning,
  62–63
Aeschylus, 36
air rights, modernization, 150
aisles, egress system, 71–73
Altoon + Porter Architects, 51, 52
Alvin Ailey American Dance Theater (New
  York City), 164
American Institute of Architects (AIA),
  building codes, 66–67
American National Standards Institute
  (ANSI), 77
American Society of Heating, Refrigerating,
  and Air-Conditioning Engineers
  (ASHRAE), 82
Americans with Disabilities Act (ADA), 3, 7,
  42, 43, 77–80. *See also* egress system
amplification. *See also* technology
  acoustic design flexibility, 121–124
  modernization, 141
Anchorage Performing-Arts Center, Atwood
  Concert Hall (Anchorage, Alaska),
  128
Anschutz Entertainment, 163
Anspacher Theater, Public Theater (New York
  City), 121
Appia, Adolphe, 41, 128

arena stage
  courtyard theater, 22
  described, 23, 24, 25
Arena Stage (Washington, D.C.), 10, 120, 156
Argos Stage, South Coast Repertory-Julianne Argyrus Stage for the South Coast Repertory Theater (Costa Mesa, California), 27, 28
Arnoff Center for the Performing Arts (Cincinnati, Ohio), 91
Artec, 14
arts-organization rentals, theater management, 165–166
Atwood Concert Hall, Anchorage Performing-Arts Center (Anchorage, Alaska), 128
audience, auditorium/stage design, 19–21
audience seating, 35–38. See also seating capacity
  balconies and boxes, 38
  capacity, 36
  costs, 35–36
  egress system, 73–76
  modernization, 140–141
  orchestra (stalls) seating, 38
  seat design, 36
  sidewalls, 38
  sightlines, 36–38
  stage design, 43
  theater design, 16
audio systems, stage design, 44
auditorium/stage design, 19–40. See also audience seating; backstage design/planning; stage design; theater design; theater planning
  acoustics, 39
  arena stage, 23, 24, 25
  audience seating, 35–38
  concert halls, 31–35
  configuration, 19–21
  courtyard theater, 24–25
  diversity in, 21, 23
  flexibility, 39
  future trends, 39–40
  interior architecture and design, 38–39
  intimacy, 19
  live events, 19

mechanical, electrical, and plumbing (MEP) systems, 155–156
  multiform theater, 30–31
  multipurpose hall, 30
  process team, 155
  proscenium theater, 25–30
  surround stage, 23
  technology, 39
  thrust stage, 23–24
  types of, 21, 23
  unconventional theater, 31
Auerbach Pollock Friedlander, theater consultants, 45–47, 48, 49, 51, 52

background noise, acoustic design principles, 106–107
back-of-house requirements
  building codes, 80–81
  load-in requirements, 56–58
backstage design/planning, 53–63. See also auditorium/stage design; load-in requirements (backstage design/planning); stage design; theater design; theater planning
  adjacencies, 62–63
  break rooms, 62
  building codes, 80–81
  design parity, 63
  design-team review, 53–54
  dressing rooms, 61–62
  hair-and-makeup and props rooms, 61
  load-in requirements, 54–59
  offices, 59–60
  overview, 53
  process team, 157–158
  rehearsal spaces, 62
  storage (temporary), 59
  theater management, 169
  wardrobe, 60–61
backstage equipment rooms
  lighting, 60, 61
balance, acoustic design principles, 101–102
balconies
  acoustic design principles, 95, 96, 99
  described, 38
  egress system, 71

modernization, 140–141
process team, 156–157
ballet, acoustic design principles, 111
Barnes, Edward Larrabee, 15
Barranger, Milly S., 128n1
Barton Myers Associates, 14
bathrooms. *See* restrooms
Baumol, William, 163, 172
Bayreuth Festspielhaus (Bayreuth, Germany), 41
beacons, lighting, 137
Beatlemania (show), 7
Beckley/Meyers Architects, Inc., 126
Bellagio Hotel Casino (Las Vegas, Nevada), 48
Bellie, Brian, 87–97, 103–104, 107
Benjamin and Marian Schuster Performing Arts Center (Dayton, Ohio), 122, 123
Benjamin and Marian Schuster Performing Arts Center, Mead Theatre (Dayton, Ohio), 32
Berke, Deborah, 11, 13
Berlind Theater, Princeton University (Princeton, New Jersey), 11
bid conference, acoustic design flexibility, 116
bidding, process team, 160
Bing Thom Architects, 10, 120
black-box theater, theater design, 12
board of directors, theater management, 166
bookings, theater management, 165, 166, 170
Bowen, William, 163, 172
boxes, described, 38
box-in-box sound isolation, 106–109
box office, modernization, 147
break rooms, backstage design/planning, 62
Broadway theaters
    acoustic design flexibility, 124–126
    acoustic design principles, 110–111
    modernization, 141
Brook, Peter, 154
Brooklyn Academy of Music (BAM, New York City), 2, 152, 153, 154, 157, 173
Brooks, Arthur, 173n1
budgets. *See* costs; financial operations
building codes, 65–85. *See also* Americans

with Disabilities Act (ADA); egress system
    American Institute of Architects (AIA), 66–67
    building types, 67–68
    code analysis, 66
    documentation plan approval, 66
    egress system, 69–80
    environmental requirements, 81
    existing buildings, 84–85
    exterior envelope, 81–82
    fire-suppression system, 69
    importance of, 65, 85
    jurisdiction, 65–66
    lighting, 135–136
    marquees, 83
    occupancy and construction types, 80–81
    occupancy establishment, 67
    program requirements, 66
    site factors, 68–69
    structural factors, 82–83
    toilets, 83
building types, building codes, 67–68
business plan, theater management, 170

California Nanosystems Institute, University of California, Santa Barbara (UCSB) case study, 50–52
capacity. *See* seating capacity
Carnegie, Andrew, 45
Carnegie Hall, Judy and Arthur Zankel Hall (New York City), 45–47
Casa Mañana (Fort Worth, Texas), 122
ceilings, acoustic design principles, 90–93, 100–101
Cesar Pelli Associates, 27, 30, 31, 32, 107, 123
Chicago Shakespeare Theater, Navy Pier (Chicago, Illinois), 25
choral music, acoustic design principles, 111–112
circulation
    backstage design/planning, 63
    lighting, 132–133
    restrooms, building codes, 83
    theater planning, 3, 4
Cirque du Soleil, 9, 42, 48–50

Clear Channel Entertainment, 163
codes. *See* building codes
collaboration, theater planning, 5
commercial rental houses, theater design, 7–8
commissioning, theater management, 170–171
community relations
    future trends, 173
    theater management, 166, 167
community theaters, theater design, 12
concert halls, described, 31–35
Concord Pavilion (Concord, California), 128
conferences, acoustic design principles, 112
construction
    acoustic design flexibility, 116
    process team, 159
construction administration, process team, 160
construction documents, process team, 159–160
construction drawings, acoustic design flexibility, 116
construction materials, acoustic design principles, 100–101
construction types, building codes, 67–68
consultants. *See also* process team
    planning team members, 155
    theater planning, 4
context, theater planning, 4
Corrao, Marnell, 48, 49
corridors, backstage design/planning, 62–63
costs. *See also* financial operations
    audience seating, 35–36
    process team, 158
    stage design, 43
    theater management, 163–164, 170, 172
    theater planning, 4
Cottesloe Theater, Royal National Theatre of Great Britain (London, England), 26
courtyard theater, described, 22, 24–25
crossover corridors, backstage design/planning, 62–63

dance, acoustic design principles, 111
Deborah Berke & Partners, 11, 13

decorative painting, modernization, 143
dedicated commercial venues, theater design, 8–9
Derngate Theatre (Northampton, England), 32, 33
design development/process
    acoustic design flexibility, 115–117, 116
    process team, 159
design-team review, backstage design/planning, 53–54
Detroit Opera House (Detroit, Michigan), 164
diffusion, acoustic design principles, 96, 99
direct sound, 87. *See also* acoustic design principles
doors, sound isolation, 108
Dorothy Schmidt Center, Florida Atlantic University (Boca Raton, Fla.), 15
dramatic works, acoustic design principles, 110
dressing rooms, backstage design/planning, 61–62
dry-cleaning facilities, backstage design/planning, 61
Durante, Jimmy, 128

earthquake, building codes, 82–83
echo control, acoustic design principles, 95–97
education programs, theater management, 166
Egan, David, 119
egress system, 69–80. *See also* Americans with Disabilities Act (ADA); building codes
    accessibility, 77–80
    aisles, 71–73
    back-of-house requirements, 80–81
    exits (capacity, number, and location), 70–71
    exits (travel distance), 71
    guards, 76–77
    handrails, 76, 77
    occupant load calculation, 69–70
    seating capacity, 73–76
    steps, ramps, and sightlines, 76
electrical power requirements. *See also*

heating, ventilation, and air-conditioning (HVAC) systems; mechanical, electrical, and plumbing (MEP) systems
backstage design/planning, 60, 62
stage design, 44
Elizabethan theater, 19
employees, theater management, 164–165, 166
end-stage, courtyard theater, 22
endurance, theater design, 16
energy conservation, building codes, 81–82. See also environmental requirements
environmental requirements, building codes, 81. See also energy conservation
equipment, theatrical, sound isolation, 109–110
equipment rooms, lighting, 60, 61
equipment storage, process team, 157
escalators, egress system, 71
executive director, job description, 164–165
existing buildings, building codes, 84–85
exits. See also egress system
capacity, number, and location, 70–71
travel distance, 71
exterior
building codes, 81–82
lighting, 131, 137
modernization, 150–154
exterior sound, sound isolation, 106–110

feasibility study, acoustic design flexibility, 115
financial operations, theater management, 167–168, 170. See also costs
finishes
acoustic design principles, 101
building codes, 81
construction documents, 160
load-in requirements, 58, 59
fire hazards. See also egress system
egress system, 69–80
occupancy and construction types, 80–81
site factors, 68–69
fire-suppression system
back-of-house requirements, 81

building codes, 69
design development, 159
egress system, 71
modernization, 149
Fisher Dachs Associates, 10, 13, 14, 15
flexibility. See also acoustic design flexibility
auditorium/stage design, 39
lighting, 136
stage design, 43
theater design, 12
theater management, 168
flexible enclosure, stage design, 42
Florida Atlantic University, Studio Theater (Boca Raton, Florida), 15
Florida Community College, Wilson Center (Jacksonville, Florida), 90
fluorescent lamps, 136–137
flutter, acoustic design principles, 95, 96
focus, acoustic design principles, 95, 97
food and beverage, theater planning, 2
Ford Theater (New York City), 124
form, theater design, 12
France-Merrick Performing Arts Center (formerly the Hippodrome, Baltimore, Maryland), 144, 145–147
Frangetto, Polyanna, 107
Frank O. Gehry Associates, 35
freight elevator. See load-in requirements (backstage design/planning)
front-of-house requirements, load-in requirements, 58–59
fund-raising, theater management, 166–167

galleries, acoustic design principles, 89–90
Gehry, Frank O., 35
general manager, job description, 165
geometry, theater design, 16
Georgetown University (Washington, D. C.), 149
gift shop, theater planning, 2
glass, theater planning, transparency, 2–3
Glimmerglass Opera (Cooperstown, New York), 1
Globe Theater (England), 19
Glyndebourne Opera House (Sussex, England), 29

Greece (ancient), 19
green rooms, backstage design/planning, 62
guards, egress system, 76–77
Gund, Graham, 91
Guthrie, Tyrone, 156
Guthrie Theater (Minneapolis, Minnesota), 10

hair-and-makeup rooms, backstage design/planning, 61
handicapped access, theater planning, circulation, 3
handrails, egress system, 76, 77
Harris Theater for Music and Dance (Chicago, Illinois), 118
Harvey Theater (Brooklyn, New York), 154
heating, ventilation, and air-conditioning (HVAC) systems. See also electrical power requirements; mechanical, electrical, and plumbing (MEP) systems
    building codes, 81
    modernization, 141, 149–150
    noise control, 110
    stage design, 43
Herts, Henry B., 8, 9
Herts + Tallant, architect, 150, 151, 152
Hippodrome Theater (France-Merrick Performing Arts Center, formerly the Hippodrome, Baltimore, Maryland), 144, 145–147
historic restoration, building codes, 84
Hobby Center for the Performing Arts, Sarofim Hall (Houston, Texas), 127
Holcombe T. Green, Jr., Theater and the School of Art, Yale University (New Haven, Connecticut), 11, 13
Hopkins, Michael, 29
Horne, Marilyn, 45
H³ Hardy Collaboration Architecture, 129, 134, 135, 143, 144, 149, 150, 151, 153
Hult Performing Arts Center, Silva Hall (Eugene, Oregon), 128, 129, 133–135
human hearing, reflected sound, 89

Hummingbird Centre for the Performing Arts (Toronto, Ontario, Canada), 20

Illuminating Engineering Society (IES), 82
Illuminating Engineering Society of North America (IESNA), 135
incandescent lamps, 136–137
innovation, theater design, 17
interactive environments, stage design, 44
interior architecture and design, auditorium/stage design, 38–39
interior finishes. See finishes
International Building Code (IBC), 66, 67–83, 85, 147–148
International Energy Conservation Code (IECC), 82
International Existing Building Code (IEBC), 84–85
intimacy
    acoustic design principles, 89
    auditorium/stage design, 19, 21
    sightlines, 38
Iroquois Theater fire (Chicago, Illinois, 1903), 65
isolation. See sound isolation
Izenour, George, 42

Jaffe Holden Acoustics, 13, 15
Joyce Theater (New York City), 150, 164
Judy and Arthur Zankel Hall, Carnegie Hall (New York City), 45–47

Kahn, Louis, 13
Kai Orion, Brian Bellie, Kirkegaard Associates, 87–97
Kaiser, Henry, 122
Kamper, Laurie, 106
KA™ (show), 50
Kimmel Center for the Performing Arts, Verizon Hall (Philadelphia, Pennsylvania), 34
Kirkegaard Associates, 87–97, 101–109
Kodak Theater (Los Angeles, California), 163

Ladd + Kelsey Architects, 14, 15
Laliberté, Guy, 48
Lamb, Thomas, 144
Lasdun, Denys, 26
laundry facilities, backstage design/planning, 60–61
Leadership in Energy Efficient Design (LEED), 43
lectures, acoustic design principles, 112
Lee, John M. Y., 15
Lee, Ming Cho, 13
Levitt Bernstein Associates, 23, 24
light emitting diode (LED) displays, 152, 154
lighting, 129–137. See also electrical power requirements; heating, ventilation, and air-conditioning (HVAC) systems
   backstage equipment rooms, 60, 61
   beacons, 137
   exterior, 131, 137
   flexibility, 136
   importance of, 129
   lobby, 131–133
   maintenance, 137
   modernization, 142–143, 150, 152
   natural light, theater planning, 3
   performance space, 133–135
   sources, 136–137
   stage design, 43–44
   standards, codes and safety, 135–136
   theater planning, 1
Lincoln Center (New York City), 1, 4
Lincoln Center, Vivian Beaumont Theater (New York City), 30–31, 122, 148
live events. See also auditorium/stage design; intimacy
   auditorium/stage design, 19–21
   stage design, 44
   theater design, 15
loading dock, backstage design/planning, 54
load-in requirements (backstage design/planning), 54–59
   back-of-house requirements, 56–58
   front-of-house requirements, 58–59
   loading dock, 54
   personnel, 54
   pit equipment, 59

   sets, 59
   stage equipment, 54–56
lobbies. See also support space
   lighting, 131–133
   modernization, 145–147
   theater planning, 2
Long Wharf Theatre (New Haven, Connecticut), 117
Lowell, Julia, 173n1
Lyceum Theater (New York City), 150, 151

Mahaiwe Theater (Great Barrington, Massachusetts), 142, 150
maintenance, lighting, 137
management. See theater management
marketing, theater management, 166–167
Marnell Corrao Architects, 48, 49
marquees
   building codes, 83
   modernization, 150–154
Marriot Marquis Theater (New York City), 125, 127
materials, acoustic design principles, 100–101
MBNA Performing Arts Center and Royden B. Davis, S. J., Center, Georgetown University (Washington, D. C.), 149
McCarter Theater, Princeton University (Princeton, New Jersey), 11
McCarthy, Kevin, 173n1
Mead Theatre, Benjamin and Marian Schuster Performing Arts Center (Dayton, Ohio), 32
mechanical, electrical, and plumbing (MEP) systems. See also electrical power requirements; heating, ventilation, and air-conditioning (HVAC) systems
   auditorium, 155–156
   design development, 159
   noise control, 105, 107, 110, 155
Media Users Space for Education (MUSE), California Nanosystems Institute, University of California, Santa Barbara (UCSB) case study, 50–52
MGM Grand Hotel and Casino (Las Vegas, Nevada), 50

Michigan Opera Theater (Detroit, Michigan), 164
Middlebury College Center for the Arts (Middlebury, Connecticut), 134
Minskoff Theater (New York City), 124–125
mirrors, rehearsal spaces, 62
Mobilia, Joe, 12–13
modernization, 139–154. *See also* preservation
  acoustics, 141
  balance in, 154
  box office, 147
  building codes, 84
  decorative painting, 143
  exteriors, 150–154
  heating, ventilation, and air-conditioning (HVAC) systems, 141
  historical research for, 140
  lighting, 142–143
  lobbies, 145–147
  radical change, 154
  restoration, 139–140
  restrooms, 147–148
  seating, 140–141
  selective restoration, 143
  social change, 139
  stage design, 143–145
  structural factors, 148–150
  support spaces, 148
  technology, 139
Modular Theater, California Institute of the Arts (CalArts, Santa Calita, California), 14, 15
Morris, James, 28
multiform theater, auditorium/stage design, 30–31
multiple theaters, theater planning, 3
multipurpose theaters
  acoustic design flexibility, 126–127
  described, 30
  stage design, 42
  theater management, 164
MUSE (Media Users Space for Education), California Nanosystems Institute, University of California, Santa Barbara (UCSB) case study, 50–52
musical theater, acoustic design principles, 110–111. *See also* Broadway theaters

nanotechnology, California Nanosystems Institute, University of California, Santa Barbara (UCSB) case study, 50–52
National Arts Centre (Ottawa, Ontario, Canada), 166
National Fire Protection Association (NFPA), 71–72
natural light, theater planning, 3. *See also* lighting
New Amsterdam Theater (New York City), 124, 140, 141, 142
New Jersey Performing Arts Center (Newark, New Jersey), 14
New Victory Theater (New York City), 124, 141
New York, New York Hotel and Casino (Las Vegas, Nevada), 48–49
Next Wave Festival (New York City), 173
noise control, mechanical, electrical, and plumbing (MEP) systems, 105, 107, 110, 155–156
North Shore Center for the Performing Arts (Skokie, Illinois), 91

Oakdale Theater (Wallingford, Connecticut), 163
occupancy, building codes, 67, 80–81. *See also* seating capacity
occupant load calculation, egress system, 69–70
offices, backstage design/planning, 59–60
Ohio Theater (Columbus, Ohio), 143, 144
Olivier, Laurence, 36n1
opening events, theater management, 171
opera, acoustic design principles, 111
operational preparations, theater management, 170–171
Orchestra Hall (Minneapolis, Minnesota), 147
orchestral pops, acoustic design principles, 112
orchestra-pit design, acoustic design principles, 103–104
orchestra (stalls) seating, described, 38
orchestra-shell design, acoustic design principles, 104–105

Orion, Kai, 87–97
O (show), 48
outdoor theaters, acoustic design, 87, 122
Overture Center for the Arts (Madison, Wisconsin), 30, 31, 98–102, 107

painting, decorative, modernization, 143
parking, theater planning, 1. *See also* site factors
Parsifal (opera), 41
Pelli, Cesar, 27, 30, 31, 32, 107, 123
performer's hearing, acoustic design principles, 102
performing arts centers, theater design, 9–10
Phantom of the Opera (show), 42
pit equipment, load-in requirements, 59
planning. *See* theater planning
plays, acoustic design principles, 110
Polshek Partnership Architects, 45–47
popular music, acoustic design principles, 112
postconstruction, acoustic design flexibility, 117
preschematic program study, process team, 155–158
preservation, building codes, 84. *See also* modernization; restoration
Princeton University, McCarter Theater (Princeton, New Jersey), 11
process team, 155–161. *See also* consultants; program
    bid and negotiation, 160
    construction administration, 160
    construction documents, 159–160
    cooperation among, 161
    design development, 159
    opening shake-down period, 160
    planning team members, 155
    preschematic program study, 155–158
    schematic design, 158–159
professional producing theaters, theater design, 10–11
program. *See also* process team; theater planning
    acoustic design flexibility, 115–117
    building code requirements, 66
    preschematic study, 155–158

project process. *See* process team
prop rooms, backstage design/planning, 61
proscenium theater
    described, 25–30
    historical perspective, 23
    process team, 156
    sightlines, 38
    stage design, 42–43
public relations, theater management, 171
public space. *See also* lobbies; support space
    process team, 157
    theater management, 169
    theater planning, 2, 4
Public Theater, Anspacher Theater (New York City), 121
pylons, marquees, 152, 154

quality control, theater management, 169–170

Radio City Music Hall (New York City), 130, 131, 132, 140
Rafael Vinoly Architects, 34
ramps, egress system, 76
Rapp + Rapp, architect, 145
reflected sound, 87–89. *See also* acoustic design principles
reflection, glass, theater planning, 3
reflectors, acoustic design principles, 91–93
rehearsal spaces, backstage design/planning, 62
Renton Howard Wood Levin Partnership, 32, 33
restoration. *See also* modernization
    modernization, 139–140
    selective, 143
restrooms
    backstage design/planning, 63
    building codes, 83
    modernization, 147–148
reverberation time, acoustic design principles, 93–94
road houses, acoustic design flexibility, 126–127
Rockefeller Center (New York City), 140
Rome (ancient), 19

room height, acoustic design principles,
    90–93
room shape, acoustic design principles,
    101–102, 106
room width, acoustic design principles, 89
Royal Center, Theatre Royal (Nottingham,
    England), 21
Royal Exchange Theatre (Manchester,
    England), 23, 24
Royal National Theatre of Great Britain,
    Cottesloe Theater (London,
    England), 26
Royden B. Davis, S. J., Center, and MBNA
    Performing Arts Center,
    Georgetown University
    (Washington, D.C.), 149

safety, lighting, 135–136
Sarofim Hall, Hobby Center for the
    Performing Arts (Houston, Texas),
    127
scale
    audience seating, 36
    theater design, 12
scenery moving, stage design, 42
scenography, historical perspective, stage
    design, 41
schematic design
    acoustic design flexibility, 115–116
    process team, 158–159
school auditoriums, theater design, 12
Schuette, Dawn, 101, 103–104, 106–107
Schwab, Twitty & Hanser Architects, 15
seat design, audience seating, 36
seating. See audience seating
seating capacity. See also audience seating;
        occupancy
    audience seating, 36
    egress system, 73–76
    process team, 156
    theater management, 168
seismic factors, building codes, 82–83
selective restoration, modernization, 143
sets, load-in requirements, 59
Shakespeare, William, 12
Shou, Anthony, 101–103, 105, 108
Shubert Theater (New York City), 8, 9

sidewall seating
    acoustic design principles, 89–90
    described, 38
sightlines
    audience seating, 36–38
    egress system, 76
    stage design, 41–42
    theater design, 16
signage, theater planning, 1
Silva Hall, Hult Center (Eugene, Oregon),
    128
Sir Michael Hopkins & Partners, 29
site factors
    building codes, 68–69
    process team, 158
social change, modernization, 139
sound. See also acoustic design flexibility;
        acoustic design principles
    direct, acoustic design principles, 87
    reflected, acoustic design principles,
        87–89
sound-absorptive panels, acoustic design
    principles, 94
sound isolation
    acoustic design principles, 106–110
    modernization, 150
South Coast Repertory-Julianne Argyrus
    Stage for the South Coast Repertory
    Theater (Costa Mesa, California),
    27, 28
special events, theater planning, 2
Spoleto Festival (Charleston, South Carolina),
    173
staff
    hiring of, 170
    theater management, 166
    training of, 170–171
stage access, process team, 157–158
stage design, 41–52. See also auditorium/stage
        design; theater design; theater
        planning
    audience seating, 43
    audio systems, 44
    building codes, 80–81
    California Nanosystems Institute,
        University of California, Santa
        Barbara (UCSB) case study,
        50–52

Cirque du Soleil case studies, 48–50
costs, 43
electrical power requirements, 44
flexibility, 43
flexible enclosure, 42
historical perspective, 41
HVAC, 43
interactive environments, 44
Judy and Arthur Zankel Hall, Carnegie
        Hall (New York City) case study,
        45–47
lighting, 43–44
modernization, 143–145
proscenium area, 42–43
sightlines, 41–42
technology, 42
stage equipment, load-in requirements,
        54–56
stalls (orchestra) seating, described, 38
Standard Building Code (SBC), 66
standards, lighting, 135–136
Steppenwolf Theater (Chicago, Illinois), 28,
        164
steps, egress system, 76
Stern, Isaac, 45
Stern, Robert, 127
Stone, Edward Durell, 130, 131
storage
        backstage design/planning, 59
        process team, 157
structural factors, building codes, 82–83
Studio Theater, Florida Atlantic University
        (Boca Raton, Florida), 15
studio theater, theater design, 12
suburban location, theater planning, 4
Sunga, Louise, 109
support space. *See also* lobbies; public space
        adjacencies, backstage design/planning,
                62–63
        backstage equipment rooms, lighting, 60,
                61
        box office modernization, 147
        break rooms, backstage design/planning,
                62
        dressing rooms, backstage
                design/planning, 61–62
        dry-cleaning facilities, backstage
                design/planning, 61

gift shop, theater planning, 2
green rooms, backstage design/planning,
        62
hair-and-makeup rooms, backstage
        design/planning, 61
laundry facilities, backstage
        design/planning, 60–61
modernization, 148
process team, 157
prop rooms, backstage design/planning,
        61
rehearsal spaces, backstage
        design/planning, 62
surrounding spaces, sound isolation, 106–110
surround stage, described, 23
symphonic music, acoustic design principles,
        111–112
Symphony Hall (Boston, Massachusetts), 164

Talaske Group, 10
Tampa Bay Performing Arts Center (Tampa,
        Florida), 164
technology. *See also* amplification; stage
        design
        auditorium/stage design, 39
        historical perspective, stage design, 41
        modernization, 139
        stage design, 41, 42
        theater design, 12–15
        theater management, 169
temporary storage, backstage design/planning,
        59
theater design, 7–17. *See also*
        auditorium/stage design; backstage
        design/planning; stage design;
        theater planning
        cautions in, 16–17
        commercial rental houses, 7–8
        community theaters, 12
        dedicated commercial venues, 8–9
        diversity in, 7
        endurance, 16
        factors in, 7
        flexibility, 12
        form, 12
        geometry, 16
        live events, 15

performing arts centers, 9–10
professional producing theaters, 10–11
scale, 12
seating and sightlines, 16
technology, 12–15
theater management and, 168–170
university theaters, 11
theater management, 163–173
community relations, 167
employees, 164–165, 166
facility activation, 165–166
facility management, 165
financial operations, 167–168
future trends, 171–173
general management, 167
marketing and fund-raising, 166–167
models for, 163–164
operational preparations, 170–171
staff and board of directors, 166
theater design impacts on, 168–170
theater planning, 1–5. *See also*
auditorium/stage design; backstage
design/planning; stage design;
theater design
circulation, 3
collaboration, 5
consultants, 4
context, 4
costs, 4
diversity in, 1
flaws in, 4
food and beverage, 2
multiple theaters, 3
natural light, 3
parking, 1
public space, 2
signage, 1
special events, 2
transparency, 2–3
wayfinding, 1–2
wheelchair access, 3
Theater Projects Consultants, Inc., 23, 24,
27, 28, 29, 32, 33, 34, 35, 37
Theatre Royal, Royal Center (Nottingham,
England), 21
theatrical equipment, sound isolation, 109–110
Thompson, Ventulett, Stainback + Associates,
90

thrust stage
courtyard theater, 22
described, 23–24
process team, 156
toilets. *See* restrooms
touring shows
technology, 13
theater management, 165, 166, 170
transparency, theater planning, 2–3
traverse stage, courtyard theater, 22
Trizec-Hahn (developer), 163

unconventional theater, described, 31
Uniform Building Code (UBC), 66
United States Constitution, 65–66
University of California, Santa Barbara
(UCSB), California Nanosystems
Institute case study, 50–52
university theaters. *See also* specific
universities
acoustic design flexibility, 126–127
theater design, 11
Uptown Theater (Chicago, Illinois), 145
urban renewal, theater planning, 4
Uris Theater (New York City), 124–125

Vance, J. Mc A., 142
Venturi Scott Brown + Associates, 51, 52
Verizon Hall, Kimmel Center for the
Performing Arts (Philadelphia,
Pennsylvania), 34
vestibules. *See also* lobbies
lighting, 132–133
sound isolation, 108
Victorian Royal Cotton Exchange
(Manchester, England), 23, 24
Vinoly, Rafael, 34
Viola, Bill, 7
Vivian Beaumont Theater, Lincoln Center
(New York City), 30–31, 122, 148
VOA Associates, 25
volume, acoustic design principles, 93–94

Wagner, Richard, 41
walls, acoustic design principles, 100–101

Walt Disney Concert Hall (Los Angeles, California), 35
wardrobe, backstage design/planning, 60–61
wayfinding
    lighting, 132
    theater planning, 1–2
Weese, Harry, 10, 120, 156
Weidner Center for the Performing Arts (Green Bay, Wisconsin), 126
wheelchair access, theater planning, 3
Wilson Center, Florida Community College (Jacksonville, Florida), 90

Yale University , Holcombe T. Green, Jr., Theater and the School of Art (New Haven, Connecticut), 11, 13
Yerba Buena Center (San Francisco, California), 164

Zakaras, Laura, 173n1
Zankel Hall, Carnegie Hall (New York City), 45–47
Zumanity, New York, New York Hotel and Casino (Las Vegas, Nevada), 48–49

BUILDING TYPE BASICS FOR PERFORMING ARTS FACILITIES:

1. Program (predesign)
What are the principal programming requirements (space types and areas)?
Any special regulatory or jurisdictional concerns?
7–17, 19–21, 135–36

2. Project process and management
What are the key components of the design and construction process?
Who is to be included on the project team?
115–17, 155–62, 170

3. Unique design concerns
What distinctive design determinants must be met?
Any special circulation requirements?
2–3, 7–17, 21–40, 45, 48–64, 89–91, 110–12, 131

4. Site planning/parking/landscaping
What considerations determine external access and parking?
Landscaping?
1–2, 4, 150, 158

5. Codes/ADA
Which building codes and regulations apply, and what are the main applicable provisions?
(Examples: egress; electrical; plumbing; ADA; seismic; asbestos; terrorism and other hazards)
3, 65–85, 77–85, 135–36, 149, 157

6. Energy/environmental challenges
What techniques in service of energy conservation and environmental sustainability
can be employed?

7. Structure system
What classes of structural systems are appropriate?
148–49

8. Mechanical systems
What are appropriate systems for heating, ventilating, and air-conditioning (HVAC) and plumbing?
Vertical transportation? Fire and smoke protection? What factors affect preliminary selection?
43, 110, 141, 147, 149, 159

9. Electrical/communications
What are appropriate systems for electrical service and voice and data communications?
What factors affect preliminary selection?
44, 110, 123–24, 159